Step by Step

CHICKEN COOKING

Step by Step

CHICKEN COOKING

KERENZA HARRIES & JO CRAIG

PHOTOGRAPHED BY

JON STEWART

GREENWICH EDITIONS

This edition published 1999 by Greenwich Editions,
10 Blenheim Court, Brewery Road, London N7 9NT

© Salamander Books Ltd., 1993

ISBN 0 86288 256 7

Managing Editor: Felicity Jackson
Art Director: Roger Daniels
Editor: Louise Steele
Photographer: Jon Stewart, assisted by Nicole Mai
Home Economists: Kerenza Harries and Jo Craig
Typeset by: BMD Graphics, Hemel Hempstead
Colour separation by: Scantrans Pte. Ltd. Singapore
Printed in Spain

ACKNOWLEDGEMENTS
The Publishers would like to thank the following for their help and advice:
Barbara Stewart at Prop Exchange, Unit F,
51 Calthorpe Street, London WC1.

Notes:
All spoon measurements are equal.
1 teaspoon = 5 ml spoon
1 tablespoon = 15 ml spoon

CONTENTS

INTRODUCTION

Chicken, as well as being a healthy alternative to red meat, is incredibly versatile – it can be cooked in dozens of interesting ways, and combines well with a whole host of other ingredients.

Step-by-Step Chicken Cooking is an exciting collection of over 100 recipes, some new and exotic, others classic, traditional and everyday, all equally delicious and easy to prepare. Each recipe is illustrated in full colour with step-by-step instructions. Many of the recipes call for chicken pieces and, although they are readily available you may like to joint a chicken yourself so you have the carcass for making stock: the book starts with step-by-

step directions showing how to do this.

Recipes reflect the distinctive flavours of Far Eastern, Mexican-American and European cooking, starting with Soups & Starters and followed by Canapés & Finger Food, Salads, Snacks, Classical dishes, Tex-Mex & Far Eastern dishes, Casseroles & Pies and European dishes. There are quick and simple low-fat recipes for everyday eating, and when you want to entertain, chicken is perfect combined with wine and cream or fruit, herbs or spices for a delicious dinner party dish

JOINTING A CHICKEN

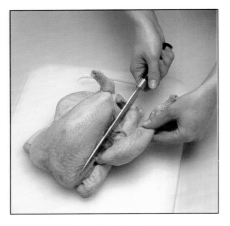

Pull the legs away from the chicken carcass and cut through the skin.

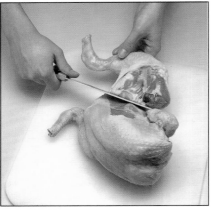

Bend the leg back to break the bone and cut through the socket. Repeat on the other side.

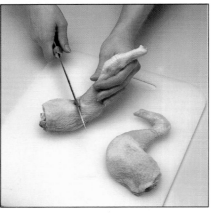

Hold the drumstick and cut through the socket to separate it from the thigh, cut the knuckle off the drumsticks.

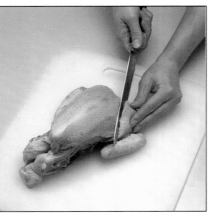

Pinch the lump of breast meat nearest to the wing, slice down and remove the wing completely.

Cut off the wing tip and fold the breast meat over the joint. Repeat with the other side.

Cut along the rib cage to separate the breast from the base of the carcass. You can use poultry shears to do this if you have them.

Cut the breast in half either lengthways or diagonally to give 2 breast portions.

The chicken is now in 8 portions. Recipes in this book which specify skinned and boned chicken breasts are using breast portions weighing about 115 g (4 oz) unless specified otherwise.

CONSOMMÉ

1.2 litres (40 fl oz/5 cups) homemade chicken stock
  (see Note)
115 g (4 oz) raw chicken breast
2 large eggs
4 tablespoons finely chopped fresh parsley
salt and pepper
1 teaspoon vegetable oil

Put the stock in a large pan and bring to the boil. In a blender or food processor, finely chop chicken. Separate 1 of the eggs and beat the white with a fork. Crush the shell. Mix together chicken, egg white, shell and 3 tablespoons parsley. Add to the stock.

Bring stock to just below boiling point, stirring. Lower heat and simmer very gently for 25 minutes. Beat remaining egg with remaining yolk and parsley and season with salt and pepper. In a small omelette pan, heat the oil, pour in the egg mixture and cook until set. Turn out and roll up like a Swiss roll, then cut into thin strips. Strain soup through a sieve lined with muslin or cheese-cloth, pour into bowls and add strips of omelette.

Serves 4.

Note: To make your own stock, put a raw or cooked chicken carcass, 1 quartered large onion, 2 halved carrots, 2 halved leeks, 2 sliced celery sticks, 1 bay leaf, some parsley stalks, 1 bunch of thyme and 6 peppercorns in a large pan with enough cold water to cover. Bring to the boil, then reduce heat and simmer for 2-3 hours. Skim off any scum. Strain into a large bowl and cool as quickly as possible. Chill in the refrigerator, then remove any fat that has set on the surface. Use within 2-3 days or freeze in convenient amounts.

HOT & SOUR SOUP

25 g (1 oz) dried Chinese mushrooms
850 ml (30 fl oz/3¾ cups) chicken stock
25 g (1 oz) egg thread noodles, roughly crushed
115 g (4 oz) cooked chicken, shredded
1 stick celery, thinly sliced
2 small red chillies, deseeded and sliced
2 teaspoons sugar
2 tablespoons cider vinegar
pinch of white pepper
3 tablespoons dark soy sauce
1 tablespoon cornflour
1 egg
3 teaspoons sesame oil
2 spring onions, finely chopped
1 tablespoon finely chopped coriander

Soak the mushrooms in 300 ml (10 fl oz/1¼ cups) of the stock for 20 minutes, then drain, reserving any soaking liquor. Squeeze out any excess liquid and finely shred the mush-rooms. Soak the noodles in the mushroom liquor for 5 minutes. Bring all the stock and the reserved soaking liquor to the boil and add the chicken, mushrooms, noodles, celery, chillies, sugar, vinegar, pepper and 2 tablespoons of the soy sauce and simmer to-gether for 2 minutes.

Blend the cornflour with the remaining soy sauce and pour into the soup, stirring well, and continue to simmer for a further 2 minutes. Beat the egg with the sesame oil and pour into the simmering soup in a fine stream, whisking with a fork as you pour. Stir in the onions and coriander and serve at once.

Serves 4.

—CREAM OF CHICKEN SOUP—

25 g (1 oz/6 teaspoons) butter
1 small leek, washed and diced
45 g (1½ oz/¼ cup, plus 6 teaspoons) plain flour
850 ml (30 fl oz/3¾ cups) chicken stock
150 ml (5 fl oz/⅔ cup) dry white wine
115 g (4 oz) cooked chicken, finely chopped
pinch of ground nutmeg
150 ml (5 fl oz/⅔ cup) single (light) cream
2 teaspoons chopped fresh chives
150 ml (5 fl oz/⅔ cup) thick sour cream and croûtons,
    to serve

In a saucepan, melt the butter and gently sauté the leek until soft. Stir in the flour and cook over a low heat for 1-2 minutes.

Remove the pan from the heat and slowly add the stock, a little at a time, stirring well. Return to the heat and bring to the boil, stirring until thickened.

Add the wine, cover and simmer gently for 15 minutes; add the chicken and nutmeg and simmer for a further 5 minutes. Pour in the cream and heat gently without boiling, then stir in the chopped chives. Serve in warmed bowls with spoonfuls of thick sour cream and croûtons.

Serves 4.

—CORN & PRAWN CHOWDER—

425 ml (15 fl oz/2 cups) milk
425 ml (15 fl oz/2 cups) chicken stock
350 g (12 oz) sweetcorn kernels
25 g (1 oz/6 teaspoons) butter
1 small onion, finely chopped
2 teaspoons plain flour
225 g (8 oz) raw potatoes, cubed
175 g (6 oz) cooked chicken, diced
175 g (6 oz) cooked peeled prawns
2 tablespoons chopped fresh parsley
salt and pepper
55 g (2 oz/¼ cup) grated Cheddar cheese

Mix together the milk and the chicken stock in a jug.

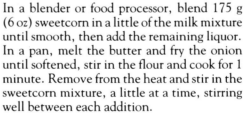

In a blender or food processor, blend 175 g (6 oz) sweetcorn in a little of the milk mixture until smooth, then add the remaining liquor. In a pan, melt the butter and fry the onion until softened, stir in the flour and cook for 1 minute. Remove from the heat and stir in the sweetcorn mixture, a little at a time, stirring well between each addition.

Return to the heat and bring to the boil, stirring continuously. Add the potatoes and simmer gently for 15 minutes. Stir in the remaining sweetcorn, chicken, prawns and parsley and season to taste. Sprinkle with the grated cheese and serve with warm crusty bread.

Serves 4.

COCK-A-LEEKIE SOUP

6 skinned chicken thighs
1 litre (35 fl oz/4½ cups) chicken stock
3 leeks

Place the chicken thighs in a large pan with the chicken stock and simmer gently for 35-40 minutes.

Meanwhile, trim the leeks and slice into rings. Remove the cooked chicken from the stock with a slotted spoon. Remove the meat from the bones and cut into bite-sized pieces. Put to one side.

Increase the heat and bring the stock to a fast simmer. Add the prepared leeks and cook for 3-4 minutes until the leeks are just tender. Add the chicken to the pan and simmer for 2-3 minutes. Serve hot with warm rolls.

Serves 4.

Variation: Add 12 ready-to-eat stoned and quartered prunes with the chicken at the final stage.

CHICKEN SOUP WITH KREPLACH

225 g (8 oz/2 cups) plain flour
salt and pepper
3 eggs, beaten
2 tablespoons chopped fresh parsley
2 tablespoons chopped fresh oregano
1 tablespoon oil
1 small onion, finely chopped
175 g (6 oz) skinned and boned chicken, minced
finely grated rind of 1 lemon
2 tablespoons Greek yogurt
550 ml (20 fl oz/2½ cups) Consommé

Sift the flour and a pinch of salt into a bowl and make a well in the centre. Add the eggs and 1 tablespoon each of parsley and oregano.

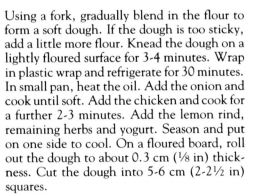

Using a fork, gradually blend in the flour to form a soft dough. If the dough is too sticky, add a little more flour. Knead the dough on a lightly floured surface for 3-4 minutes. Wrap in plastic wrap and refrigerate for 30 minutes. In small pan, heat the oil. Add the onion and cook until soft. Add the chicken and cook for a further 2-3 minutes. Add the lemon rind, remaining herbs and yogurt. Season and put on one side to cool. On a floured board, roll out the dough to about 0.3 cm (⅛ in) thickness. Cut the dough into 5-6 cm (2-2½ in) squares.

Place a spoonful of the filling on each square, brush the edges with a little water and fold the dough in half over the filling to make a triangle. Pinch the edges together to seal, then pull 2 corners together and pinch them to make them stick. Repeat with the remaining dough and filling. Bring a pan of salted water to the boil and cook the kreplach for 5-7 minutes or until the dough is cooked. Heat the consommé, add the kreplach, heat through and serve.

Serves 4.

CHICKEN & PRAWN QUENELLES

350 g (12 oz) skinned and boned chicken breasts
salt and pepper
2 egg whites
150 ml (5 fl oz/⅔ cup) double (thick) cream
115 g (4 oz) cooked peeled prawns, chopped
55 g (2 oz) smoked salmon, chopped
300 ml (10 fl oz/1¼ cups) chicken stock
4 tablespoons crème fraîche
1 teaspoon cornflour mixed with 1 tablespoon chicken stock
finely grated rind and juice of ½ lemon
3 teaspoons chopped fresh dill

Put the chicken in a blender or food processor and mince finely.

With the motor running, add the salt and pepper, egg whites and cream. Process again for a few seconds (making sure you do not overbeat the mousse). Transfer to a bowl and gently fold in the prawns and smoked salmon. Leave to chill for 30 minutes. Bring the stock to a simmer. Using 2 dessertspoons, shape the mixture into neat quenelles and slide into the stock. Poach for 1-2 minutes until firm to touch. Carefully remove with a slotted spoon. Transfer to a dish, cover with buttered foil and keep warm while cooking the remaining mixture.

Increase the heat under the stock and boil rapidly until the stock is reduced by half. Add the crème fraîche and the cornflour mixed with the stock and, stirring all the time, simmer the sauce until it thickens. Add the lemon rind and juice and season with a little salt and pepper. Add the chopped dill. Pour the sauce over the quenelles and serve hot.

Serves 4.

RICOTTA-STUFFED MUSHROOMS

3 tablespoons olive oil
2 shallots, finely chopped
175 g (6 oz) skinned and boned chicken breast
115 g (4 oz) ricotta cheese
4 tablespoons grated Parmesan cheese
8 black olives, chopped
55 g (2 oz/½ cup) chopped pine nuts
2 tablespoons chopped fresh basil
¼ teaspoon freshly grated nutmeg
salt and pepper
8 open cup mushrooms

In a pan, heat 1 tablespoon oil and fry the shallots gently until soft and transparent. Remove from the heat and set aside.

Preheat oven to 230C (450F/Gas 8). In a food processor, finely process the chicken breast and transfer to a bowl. Add the ricotta cheese, 3 tablespoons Parmesan, olives, pine nuts, basil, shallots and nutmeg and season with a little salt and pepper.

Put the mushrooms, stalk-ends up, in an ovenproof dish and fill each one with the chicken mixture. Sprinkle over the remaining oil and Parmesan cheese and bake for 10-12 minutes or until golden. Serve hot.

Serves 4.

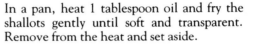

CHICKEN MOUSSELINES

350 g (12 oz) skinned and boned chicken breasts
25 g (1 oz/6 teaspoons) butter, softened
1 large egg, beaten
150 ml (5 fl oz/²⁄₃ cup) double (thick) cream
1 tablespoon chopped fresh chives
1 teaspoon finely grated lemon rind
salt and pepper
FILLING:
78 g (2¾ oz) pepper full fat soft cheese
2 teaspoons lemon juice
SAUCE:
2 red peppers (capsicums), deseeded and halved
25 g (1 oz) sun-dried tomatoes in oil, drained
3 tablespoons Greek yogurt
1 teaspoon red wine vinegar

Place the chicken and butter into a blender or food processor and process until smooth. With the blades running, pour in the egg and 85 ml (3 fl oz) of the cream. Stir in the chives, lemon rind and seasoning and spoon into six 115 ml (4 fl oz/½ cup) capacity moulds, tapping them well on the worktop to level the surface. For the filling, cream together the soft cheese, the remaining 55 ml (2 fl oz) cream and the lemon juice and put into a large piping bag fitted with a large plain nozzle.

Plunge the piping nozzle deep into the centre of the filled moulds and pipe one-quarter of the filling into each; use a wet finger to smooth the chicken back over the filling where the nozzle has been. Cover each with a small round of baking parchment and place in a shallow pan half-filled with boiling water. Cover and simmer for 15 minutes.

Preheat grill. For the sauce, place the pepper (capsicum) halves under a very hot grill and cook until the skins are blackened, allow to cool and peel.

In a blender or food processor, process the peppers (capsicums), tomatoes, yogurt and vinegar until smooth, then pour into a pan and heat gently. Pour some sauce into 6 individual side plates, remove the chicken mousselines from the pan and drain off any excess liquid which has collected in the moulds.

Peel off the baking parchment and tip the mousselines on top of the sauce. Serve at once, garnished with herbs. Serve any extra sauce separately.

Serves 6.

CHICKEN & HAM MOUSSE

175 g (6 oz) cooked chicken, finely minced
115 g (4 oz) cooked ham, finely minced
1 tablespoon lemon juice
1 tablespoon chopped fresh parsley
1 tablespoon chopped fresh chives
150 ml (5 fl oz/²⁄₃ cup) mayonnaise
2 teaspoons powdered gelatine
3 tablespoons chicken stock
150 ml (5 fl oz/²⁄₃ cup) double (thick) cream

In a bowl, mix the chicken with the ham, lemon juice, chopped herbs and mayonnaise.

In a small pan, sprinkle the gelatine over the chicken stock and leave for 5 minutes to soften. Melt very gently over a low heat until gelatine dissolves, then cool and fold into the ham and chicken mixture.

Lightly beat the cream to form soft peaks and then carefully fold into the chicken and ham mixture. Pour the mixture into a 1 litre (35 fl oz/4½ cups) mould and leave to set in the refrigerator for 2-3 hours. Unmould carefully and garnish with fresh herbs. Serve with hot crusty rolls.

Serves 4.

HOT CHICKEN LIVER MOUSSES

225 g (8 oz) chicken livers
2 eggs
300 ml (10 fl oz/1¼ cups) single (light) cream
salt and pepper
1 tablespoon oil
2 shallots, finely chopped
½ clove garlic, crushed
200 g (7 oz) can chopped tomatoes
6 tablespoons port
3 tablespoons Madeira
2 teaspoons tomato purée (paste)
1 teaspoon sugar
150 ml (5 fl oz/²⁄₃ cup) chicken stock
25 g (1 oz/6 teaspoons) butter

Preheat oven to 160C (325F/Gas 3). Remove the cores from the chicken livers. Chop the livers coarsely and put into a blender or food processor with the eggs, cream and salt and pepper and purée until smooth. Pour into a jug and refrigerate for 30 minutes. Half-fill a roasting tin with boiling water. Lightly grease four 150 ml (5 fl oz/²⁄₃ cup) capacity ramekins, pour the mousse mixture into the ramekins and place in the roasting tin. Cover with greased foil and bake for 20-25 minutes until mousses are firm.

In a pan, heat the oil, add shallots and garlic and cook for 1-2 minutes. Add tomatoes and cook for a further 3-4 minutes. Add the port and Madeira and boil rapidly for 1 minute. Add the tomato purée (paste), sugar and chicken stock, season, and simmer for 10-12 minutes. Purée in a a blender or food processor, return to pan and whisk in the butter. Run a knife around the edge of each ramekin and turn onto a plate. Spoon the sauce around the mousses and serve.

Serves 4.

CHICKEN LIVER PÂTÉ

450 g (1 lb) chicken livers
225 g (8 oz/1 cup) unsalted butter
1 clove garlic, crushed
2 tablespoons brandy
2 tablespoons port
salt and pepper
2 tablespoons redcurrant jelly

Soak the livers in cold water for 1 hour, drain and remove the cores. In a frying pan, heat 25 g (1 oz/6 teaspoons) butter, add the livers and fry for 2 minutes, then add the garlic and cook for a further 2-3 minutes until the livers are cooked through, but still pink.

Cut the remaining butter into cubes and add to the pan. Remove the pan from the heat and allow the butter to melt over the livers. Meanwhile, put the brandy and port into a small pan and boil rapidly for about 1½ minutes until the liquid is reduced to a syrup; make sure you do not over reduce the liquid as it could burn and ruin the flavour of the pâté.

Add this mixture to the pan of livers, season with salt and pepper and leave the mixture to cool for 15 minutes. Put the liver mixture into a blender or food processor and blend until you have a smooth pâté. Pour into 8 individual ramekins or 1 large serving dish. Melt the redcurrant jelly and pour over the pâté. Chill for at least 3-4 hours before serving.

Serves 8.

LAYERED COUNTRY TERRINE

8 rashers rindless, smoked streaky bacon
115 g (4 oz) chicken livers
115 g (4 oz) minced pork
115 g (4 oz) herby sausagemeat
1 clove garlic
1 onion, finely chopped
3 tablespoons chopped fresh parsley
25 g (1 oz/½ cup) fresh white breadcrumbs
55 ml (2 fl oz/¼ cup) brandy
1 small egg, beaten
¼ teaspoon freshly grated nutmeg
1 teaspoon finely grated lemon rind
salt and pepper
2 skinned and boned chicken breasts
1 bay leaf

Preheat oven to 180C (350F/Gas 4). Place the bacon on a board and stretch with the back of a knife. Use 4 rashers to line a 1.2 litre (40 fl oz/5 cup) loaf tin, reserving 4 rashers for the top. Roughly chop the chicken livers, mix them together with the pork, sausage-meat, garlic, onion and parsley. Soak the breadcrumbs in the brandy, then add to the meat mixture with the egg, nutmeg, lemon rind and seasonings.

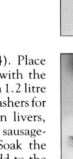

Spread one third of the meat mixture over the bacon in the tin. Cut the chicken into very thin slices and layer half over the meat mix-ture. Cover with half the remaining meat mixture, then cover with the remaining chicken and the rest of the meat mixture. Lay the reserved bacon on top and add the bay leaf. Cover with foil. Stand the terrine in a baking tin three-quarters full of boiling water. Bake for 1½ hours. Allow to cool. Serve with crusty bread, salad and spiced chutney.

Serves 4-6.

WRAPPED TERRINE

115 g (4 oz) large spinach leaves, stalks removed
115 g (4 oz) carrots, peeled
115 g (4 oz) French beans, topped and tailed
450 g (1 lb) skinned and boned chicken meat
55 g (2 oz/1 cup) fresh white breadcrumbs
85 ml (3 fl oz/⅓ cup) double (thick) cream
4 teaspoons creamed horseradish sauce
2 teaspoons lemon juice
2 tablespoons dry sherry
¼ teaspoon ground nutmeg
salt and pepper
2 eggs, separated

Preheat oven to 180C (350F/Gas 4). Blanch spinach for 30 seconds, refresh and drain well.

Cut the carrots into even-sized sticks, about the same length as the beans. Blanch the carrots and beans for 3-4 minutes in separate pans of boiling, salted water, then plunge into cold water to refresh and drain thoroughly. Put the chicken, breadcrumbs, cream, horseradish, lemon juice, sherry, nutmeg and seasoning into a blender or food processor and blend until smooth, then stir in the egg yolks and mix well.

Stiffly whisk the egg whites and fold them into the chicken mixture. Lightly oil a 1.2 litre (40 fl oz/5 cup) capacity loaf tin and line with the spinach leaves, slightly overlapping them each time and leaving enough to overhang the top rim of tin to cover the top. Spread one-third of the chicken mixture over the base of tin and level the surface.

Cover with a neat layer of carrots, top with half the remaining chicken mixture and cover with a layer of beans.

Top with the final layer of chicken mixture and fold the overhanging spinach leaves over the mixture to neaten. Cover with a piece of baking parchment and a layer of foil, then stand in a deep baking tin. Add enough boiling water to three-quarters fill the tin.

Cook in oven for 50 minutes until firm, then leave to cool. Pour off any excess juices from the tin, turn out terrine onto a serving platter and garnish with lemon twists. Serve cold with a garlic and lemon mayonnaise.

Serves 6.

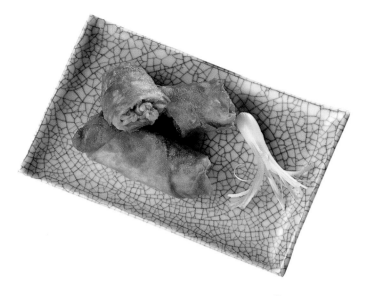

ORIENTAL CHICKEN PARCELS

2 tablespoons dry sherry
2 tablespoons soy sauce
2 tablespoons sesame oil
350 g (12 oz) skinned and boned chicken breasts
2.5 cm (1 in) piece fresh root ginger, finely chopped
8 spring onions, finely sliced
1 stick celery, finely sliced
oil for brushing

Cut the chicken into 16 equal-sized pieces and put into a shallow dish. Mix together the sherry, soy sauce and sesame oil, pour over the chicken and leave to marinate for 45 minutes.

Cut 16 squares of kitchen foil, each large enough to wrap around a piece of chicken and brush each square of foil with a little oil. Put a piece of chicken on each piece of foil and top with a little of the ginger, spring onion and celery. Spoon over any remaining marinade and fold the foil over to make parcels, making sure the edges are well sealed.

Place the parcels in a bamboo or metal steamer and cook for 10 minutes or until the chicken is cooked through. Serve in the foil.

Serves 4.

SPRING ROLLS

2 tablespoons vegetable oil
1 clove garlic, finely chopped
2.5 cm (1 in) piece fresh root ginger, finely chopped
115 g (4 oz) chicken breast, shredded
55 g (2 oz) mange tout (snow peas), finely sliced
175 g (6 oz) shiitake mushrooms, sliced
8 spring onions, finely chopped
55 g (2 oz) cooked peeled prawns, chopped
1 tablespoon soy sauce
1 teaspoon sesame oil
300 g (10 oz) filo pastry
1 egg white, for brushing
oil for deep frying
bottled chilli and hoisin sauces, to serve

In wok or large frying pan, heat the oil, add the garlic and ginger and stir-fry for 15 seconds, then add the chicken breast and continue cooking for 2-3 minutes. Add the mange tout (snow peas), mushrooms, spring onions and prawns, followed by the soy sauce and sesame oil. Mix well and transfer to a bowl to cool. Cut the filo pastry into sixteen 17.5 cm (7 in) squares. On a board, place one square of pastry diagonally towards you and cover with another square of pastry to give 2 layers.

Place a large tablespoon of mixture just below the centre of the pastry. Fold the bottom corner over and then the 2 side flaps to give an elongated open envelope. Brush with egg white and roll up, pressing gently. Repeat with the remaining filo pastry and filling. Half-fill a deep fat pan or fryer with oil and heat to 190C (375F). Fry the rolls, in 2 batches, for about 4 minutes or until golden Leave to drain on absorbent kitchen paper. Serve with chilli and hoisin sauces.

Serves 4.

CHICKEN APRICOT FILOS

½ tablespoon oil for frying, plus extra for brushing
½ onion, finely chopped
55 g (2 oz/½ cup) dried apricots, finely chopped
100 g (4 oz) cooked chicken, finely diced
4 tablespoons Greek yogurt
2 tablespoons chopped fresh coriander
salt and pepper
3 sheets filo pastry

Preheat oven to 190C (375F/Gas 5). In a small pan, heat the oil, add the onion and cook gently for 3-4 minutes without browning. Add the dried apricots and cook for a further 2 minutes.

Put the onion mixture into a bowl, add the chicken, yogurt, coriander and salt and pepper and mix well. Cut each sheet of filo pastry in half, then cut each half into 4 to form sixteen 10 cm (4 in) squares.

Brush each square with a little oil and place a spoonful of the chicken mixture in the centre. Gather up the corners of the filo pastry and pinch together to form a loose bag. Place the filo bags on 2 greased baking sheets and bake for 10-12 minutes or until the pastry is crisp and golden. Serve warm.

Makes 16.

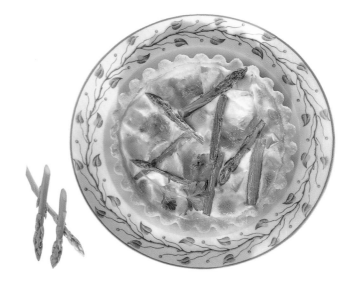

CHICKEN & BRIE TARTS

85 g (3 oz/¾ cup) plain flour
45 g (1½ oz/6 teaspoons) rice flour
4 teaspoons grated Parmesan cheese
1 teaspoon dry mustard powder
85 g (3 oz/⅓ cup) butter, diced
1 egg yolk
FOR THE FILLING:
115 g (4 oz) cooked chicken, diced
115 g (4 oz) blue brie, diced
16 asparagus sprue
1 large egg
115 ml (4 fl oz/½ cup) single (light) cream
salt and pepper

Preheat oven to 200C (400F/Gas 6). To make the pastry, place the flour, rice flour, Parmesan, mustard and butter in a food processor and blend for 45 seconds. Add the egg yolk and 2 teaspoons cold water and blend until the pastry binds together, adding a little more water, if necessary. Wrap in a polythene bag and set aside to relax in the refrigerator for 15-20 minutes. Divide the pastry into 4, roll out on a floured surface and use to line four 11 cm (4½ in) diameter, individual, loose-based flan tins.

Arrange the chicken and brie over the base of each flan. Blanch the asparagus in boiling, salted water for 2 minutes, drain and refresh under cold running water and pat dry on absorbent kitchen paper. Cut the asparagus in half and arrange over the chicken mixture. Beat together the egg, cream and seasoning and divide equally among the tarts. Bake in the oven for 25 minutes until firm and set.

Serves 4.

NUTTY GOUJONS

350 g (12 oz) skinned and boned chicken breasts
55 g (2 oz/½ cup) ground almonds
115 g (4 oz/2 cups) fresh white breadcrumbs
2 teaspoons finely chopped fresh parsley
25 g (1 oz/¼ cup) plain flour
salt and pepper
1 large egg, beaten
oil for deep frying
2 tablespoons spiced plum chutney
1 tablespoon mayonnaise
1 teaspoon finely grated orange rind
3 teaspoons orange juice

Cut chicken into thin strips. Mix together the almonds, breadcrumbs and parsley.

Put the flour, salt and pepper and chicken into a large polythene bag and shake well. Dip the chicken strips into the beaten egg, then roll in the breadcrumb mixture to coat completely. Chill in the freezer for 15-20 minutes. Half-fill a deep fat pan or fryer with oil and heat to 190C (375F) or until a cube of day-old bread browns in 40 seconds. Fry the chicken strips, a few at a time, for 3-4 minutes until golden. Drain on absorbent kitchen paper and keep warm while cooking the remaining goujons.

Mix together the spiced plum chutney, mayonnaise, orange rind and juice and spoon into a small dish. Serve the goujons with the sauce for dipping.

Serves 4.

DEVILLED CHICKEN WINGS

1 tablespoon vegetable oil
1 onion, chopped
1 clove garlic, crushed
2.5 cm (1 in) fresh root ginger, peeled and chopped
½ teaspoon cayenne pepper
½ teaspoon paprika
3 tablespoons red wine vinegar
85 ml (3 fl oz/⅓ cup) tomato ketchup (sauce)
2 tablespoons brown sugar
2 tablespoons hot pepper or chilli sauce
2 teaspoons Dijon mustard
16 chicken wings

Heat the oil, cook onion, garlic and ginger until soft. Add the cayenne and paprika.

Cook for 1 minute, stirring. Add the vinegar, tomato ketchup (sauce), brown sugar, chilli sauce and the mustard and simmer for 4-5 minutes. Preheat grill.

Arrange the chicken wings in a shallow oven-proof dish or roasting tin – do not pack them too tightly. Pour over the sauce and cook the chicken wings under the hot grill for 12-15 minutes, turning and basting frequently with the sauce until crisp, brown and sticky.

Serves 4.

ORIENTAL BACON ROLLS

225 g (8 oz) chicken livers
2 teaspoons soy sauce
1 teaspoon finely chopped fresh root ginger
6 teaspoons clear honey
4 teaspoons dry sherry
8 rashers streaky bacon
8 canned water chestnuts, drained

Soak the chicken livers in cold water for 1 hour, drain and remove the cores. Cut the livers into 16 pieces.

Mix together the soy sauce, ginger, 2 teaspoons honey and sherry. Add the prepared chicken livers and leave to marinate for 25 minutes. Preheat grill. Remove the rinds from the bacon. Using the back of a knife, stretch each rasher of bacon and cut in half.

Cut the water chestnuts in half, place at the end of a rasher of bacon, top with a piece of liver and roll up in the bacon. Secure with a wooden cocktail stick. Continue until all the ingredients are used. Place the bacon rolls in a frying pan or roasting tin, pour over the remaining marinade and drizzle with the remaining honey. Place under the hot grill and cook until the bacon is crisp and brown and the honey has caramelised.

Makes 16.

SPINACH ROULADE

15 g (½ oz/3 teaspoons) garlic and herb-flavoured butter
225 g (8 oz) frozen spinach, thawed and drained
salt and pepper
freshly grated nutmeg
2 large eggs, separated
2 tablespoons grated Parmesan cheese
FOR THE FILLING:
4 tablespoons mayonnaise
1 tablespoon creamed horseradish sauce
175 g (6 oz) smoked chicken, finely shredded
1 teaspoon finely grated lemon rind
1 large red pepper (capsicum), deseeded, skinned and chopped

Preheat oven to 200C (400F/Gas 6). Grease a 30 x 23 cm (12 x 9 in) Swiss roll tin and line with greased greaseproof paper. In a saucepan, melt the butter, add the spinach and cook for 1 minute, then season with salt and pepper and freshly grated nutmeg. Purée the mixture in a blender or food processor. Beat in the egg yolks. Stiffly whisk the egg whites and gently fold into the spinach mixture. Spoon into the prepared tin and level the surface. Bake in the oven for 7-10 minutes until well risen and springy to the touch.

Sprinkle the Parmesan over a large piece of baking parchment. Turn the roulade out onto the baking parchment, remove the lining paper, trim the edges and roll up loosely. Allow to cool. Mix together the mayonnaise, horseradish, chicken, lemon rind and chopped pepper (capsicum). Unroll the roulade, spread with the chicken filling and re-roll. Serve cut into slices.

Serves 4.

CHICKEN & MANGO YAKITORI

3 large skinned and boned chicken breasts, weighing
    about 175 g (6 oz) each
1 large ripe mango
70 ml (2½ fl oz/⅓ cup) chicken stock
70 ml (2½ fl oz/⅓ cup) sake or sweet white wine
85 ml (3 fl oz/⅓ cup) dark soy sauce
1½ tablespoons brown sugar
30 ml (1 fl oz/6 teaspoons) sweet sherry
1 clove garlic, crushed

Cut the chicken into long, thin strips about
0.5 cm (¼ in) wide. Peel and stone the
mango and cut the flesh into 2 cm (¾ in)
pieces. Thread a strip of chicken onto a
skewer, followed by a piece of mango.

Wrap the chicken over the mango, then
thread another piece of mango onto the
skewer and continue threading the ingredients in this way so that the chicken weaves
over and under the mango. Place all the
remaining ingredients in a small pan and heat
gently until the sugar has dissolved, then
bring to the boil for 1 minute. Set aside to
cool. Preheat grill.

Put a small amount of the sauce aside to use as
a dip. Brush a little of the remaining sauce
over the kebabs. Place under the hot grill for
30 seconds, then brush with a little more
sauce and return to the grill and cook for a
further 30 seconds. Repeat this process for 2-
3 minutes or until the kebabs are cooked.
Serve hot.

Makes 16-20.

CHICKEN SATAY

1 tablespoon grated fresh root ginger
1 teaspoon ground coriander
1 teaspoon turmeric
½ teaspoon chilli powder
1 teaspoon brown sugar
2 tablespoons light soy sauce
2 tablespoons seasame oil
2 cloves garlic, crushed
juice of 1 lime
350 g (12 oz) skinned and boned chicken breasts, cut
    into long, thin strips
85 g (3 oz) onion, chopped
55 g (2 oz) creamed coconut
1 teaspoon chilli powder
150 ml (5 fl oz/⅔ cup) boiling water
55 g (2 oz/3 tablespoons) crunchy peanut butter

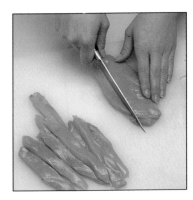

In a blender or food processor, blend together
the ginger, coriander, turmeric, chilli, sugar,
soy sauce, 1 tablespoon sesame oil, garlic and
the lime juice; pour over the chicken strips
and leave to marinate for 3-4 hours. To make
the sauce, sauté half the onion in the remaining sesame oil until soft.

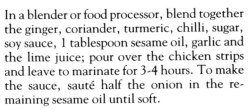

In a blender or food processor, blend the
remaining half of the onion, creamed coconut and chilli powder with the boiling water.
Add this paste to the sautéed onion, stir in
the peanut butter and 2 tablespoons of the
marinade, bring to the boil and simmer for
5 minutes until thickened. Preheat grill.
Thread the chicken onto skewers and cook
under the hot grill for 15-20 minutes turning
frequently. Serve with the peanut sauce for
dipping.

Serves 4.

CLUB SANDWICH

12 slices white or brown bread
a little butter or margarine, for spreading
12 rashers streaky bacon, rinds removed
350 g (12 oz) cooked chicken breasts, thinly sliced
6 tablespoons mayonnaise
freshly ground black pepper
3 tomatoes, sliced
½ iceburg lettuce, shredded

Toast the bread on both sides and spread one side with a little butter or margarine; keep warm. Grill the bacon until crispy and leave to drain on kitchen paper; keep warm. Mix together the chicken and mayonnaise.

To assemble the sandwich, place 4 slices of toast, buttered-sides up, on a board. Spoon on the chicken and spread evenly. Season with a little black pepper and top each with another slice of toast, buttered sides up.

To make the second layer, cover each sandwich with 3 slices of bacon, some sliced tomato and a little shredded lettuce. Season again with black pepper and top with the 4 remaining slices of toast, buttered-sides down. Insert 2 cocktail sticks into each sandwich, at opposite corners to help hold the sandwich together. Carefully slice between the cocktail sticks to cut the sandwich neatly into quarters.

Serves 4.

SESAME CHICKEN TOASTS

2 large spring onions
2 cloves garlic, crushed
2.5 cm (1 in) piece fresh root ginger, finely chopped
225 g (8 oz) skinned and boned chicken
2 tablespoons cornflour
2 teaspoons light soy sauce
2 teaspoons oyster sauce
10 slices day-old white bread
55 g (2 oz/⅓ cup) sesame seeds
vegetable oil for frying

In a blender or food processor, process the onions, garlic, ginger, chicken, cornflour and the soy and oyster sauces until smooth.

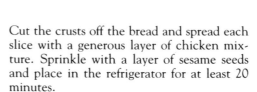

Cut the crusts off the bread and spread each slice with a generous layer of chicken mixture. Sprinkle with a layer of sesame seeds and place in the refrigerator for at least 20 minutes.

Half-fill a deep fat pan or fryer with oil and heat to 190C (375F) or until a cube of day-old bread browns in 40 seconds. Cut each slice of bread into 3 and fry, a few at a time, until golden. Drain on absorbent kitchen paper and serve hot.

Makes 30.

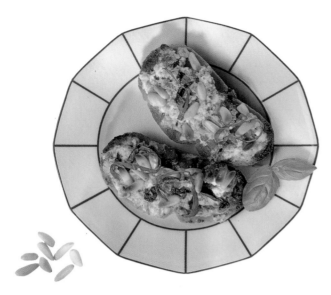

ITALIAN LIVER TOASTS

4 tablespoons oil from a jar of sun-dried tomatoes
1 clove garlic, crushed
1-2 small ciabatta or other Italian bread
115 g (4 oz) chicken livers, cores removed and livers
  sliced
3 tablespoons ready-made red pesto sauce
115 g (4 oz) ricotta cheese
4 teaspoons shredded basil leaves
4 teaspoons pine nuts

Place the tomato oil and garlic in a bowl and
set aside to infuse for 2-3 hours.

Preheat grill. Slice the ciabatta or other bread
into 1 cm (½ in) thick slices and brush with
the oil. Toast under the hot grill until golden.
Heat remaining oil and garlic in a frying pan
and quickly fry the livers until lightly
browned, then stir in the pesto and remove
from the heat.

In a bowl, break up the ricotta and fold in the
pesto mixture. Pile each slice of toast with
the ricotta mixture, sprinkle with a few basil
shreds and some pine nuts and return to the
grill for a further 1 minute until bubbly. Serve
at once, garnished with basil leaves.

*Makes about 20 slices, depending on the size of
the bread.*

WALDORF SALAD

4 tablespoons mayonnaise
2 tablespoons crème fraîche
1 tablespoons honey
a few drops of lemon juice
salt and pepper
2 teaspoons chopped fresh chives
450 g (1 lb) cooked chicken
175 g (6 oz) seedless muscat grapes
2 eating apples
2 sticks celery
175 g (6 oz/1¾ cups) walnut halves
mixed salad leaves
FOR THE VINAIGRETTE:
4 tablespoons olive oil
1 tablespoon lemon juice

In a bowl, mix together the mayonnaise,
crème fraîche and honey. Add the lemon
juice, season with salt and pepper and stir in
the chopped chives. Remove the skin from
the cooked chicken and cut into thin strips.
Halve the grapes; core and slice the apples
and chop the celery. Add these ingredients to
the mayonnaise with the walnuts, then mix
gently.

Make the vinaigrette. In a jug, whisk together the oil, lemon juice and salt and pepper; pour over the salad leaves and toss until
coated in the dressing. Arrange the salad
leaves on a plate and spoon over the chicken
mixture.

Serves 4.

MARINATED CHICKEN SALAD

150 ml (5 fl oz/²/₃ cup) olive oil
4 tablespoons balsamic vinegar
2 tablespoons chopped fresh basil
2 tablespoons chopped fresh rosemary
2 cloves garlic, crushed
4 skinned and boned chicken breasts
1 red pepper (capsicum), deseeded and quartered
1 yellow pepper (capsicum), deseeded and quartered
2 courgettes (zucchini), cut into 1 cm (½ in) thick
    slices
2 large open cup mushrooms
55 g (2 oz/¼ cup) toasted pine nuts
8 sun-dried tomatoes
½ teaspoon sugar
salt and pepper

Mix together 4 tablespoons olive oil, 2 table-spoons vinegar, 1 tablespoon basil, 1 table-spoon rosemary and the garlic. Put the chicken into a shallow, flameproof dish and pour over the mixture. Leave for 30 minutes. Preheat grill. Place dish of chicken under the hot grill and cook for 10-14 minutes, turning halfway through cooking until the chicken is brown and crispy; cool. Lay the peppers (capsicums), courgettes (zucchini) and mushrooms in the grill pan, brush with 2 tablespoons oil and grill for about 10 minutes, turning them once: cool.

Peel the skins from the peppers, using a sharp knife, and cut the mushrooms into quarters. Slice the chicken breasts into 2.5 cm (1 in) thick slices and arrange with the grilled vegetables in a dish. Sprinkle over the pine nuts and sun-dried tomatoes. In a small jug, mix the remaining herbs with the oil and vinegar. Add the sugar and season with a little salt and pepper. Pour over the chicken and marinate for 1 hour, stirring occasionally.

Serves 4.

TROPICAL CHICKEN SALAD

2 cooked smoked chicken breasts, weighing about
    150 g (5 oz) each
2 ripe avocados
2 large ripe mangoes
1 head each of red and white chicory, trimmed
55 g (2 oz) rocket, cleaned
8 teaspoons bottled dill sauce
1 teaspoon crushed pink peppercorns
2 teaspoons white wine vinegar
2 tablespoons olive oil

Cut the chicken crossways into thin slices. Remove the skin and stone from the avocados and cut each half lengthways into slices.

Cut each mango in half by cutting either side of the fibrous stone, peel and thinly slice. Separate the chicory into leaves and arrange with the rocket on 4 plates. Place alternate slices of avocado and mango on top of the leaves and arrange a quarter of the chicken slices on each serving.

Whisk together the dill sauce, peppercorns, vinegar and oil and drizzle over each salad. Serve with warm poppy seed rolls.

Serves 4.

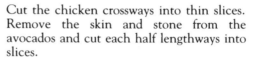

CHICKEN SATAY SALAD

2 tablespoons dry sherry
4 tablespoons crunchy peanut butter
2.5 cm (1 in) piece fresh root ginger, finely chopped
2 tablespoons hoisin sauce
3 teaspoons lemon juice
2 tablespoons dark soy sauce
150 ml (5 fl oz/⅔) cup chicken stock or water
4 tablespoons sunflower seeds
2 teaspoons sesame oil
2 tablespoons vegetable oil
salt and pepper
1 Cos lettuce, washed and broken into leaves
115 g (4 oz) beansprouts
115 g (4 oz) cooked green beans
4 skinned and boned chicken breasts

Mix together the sherry, peanut butter, ginger, hoisin sauce, 2 teaspoons of the lemon juice and 1 tablespoon of the soy sauce. Mix well, then beat in the stock or water. Put the sunflower seeds in a pan over a high heat. Stir constantly and after about 1 minute the seeds should start to turn golden. Still stirring, add the remaining soy sauce; it will instantly evaporate and coat the seeds. Tip the seeds onto a saucer and leave to cool. Mix together the sesame oil, 1 tablespoon vegetable oil, the remaining lemon juice and salt and pepper.

Put the lettuce leaves and beansprouts into a bowl, pour over the salad dressing and toss gently. Arrange the leaves and beans on 4 serving plates. Slice chicken into thin strips. In a frying pan, heat the remaining 1 tablespoon vegetable oil and add the chicken. Stir-fry over a high heat until the chicken starts to brown. Lower the heat and pour over the peanut butter mixture; stir until the sauce is simmering and thick. Spoon over the salad leaves and sprinkle with the sunflower seeds.

Serves 4.

YELLOW SALAD

1 clove garlic, crushed
2 teaspoons wholegrain mustard
1 teaspoon clear honey
3 tablespoons white wine vinegar
8 tablespoons olive oil
2 tablespoons chopped fresh chives, plus extra to serve
150 ml (5 fl oz/⅔ cup) natural yogurt
a large pinch of saffron strands
850 ml (30 fl oz/3¾ cups) chicken stock
2 skinned and boned chicken breasts
175 g (6 oz/1¼ cups) pasta shapes
3 yellow peppers (capsicums), halved and deseeded
55 g (2 oz) sun-dried tomatoes
6 spring onions
1 celery heart, with leaves
salt and pepper

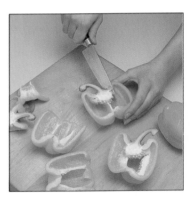

In a bowl, whisk together the garlic, mustard, honey, vinegar, oil, chives and yogurt and reserve. Soak the saffron strands in the chicken stock in a pan, bring to the boil, then reduce to a simmer. Add the chicken breasts and poach gently for 15 minutes. Drain and set aside to cool slightly. Add the pasta to the poaching liquor and cook for 8-10 minutes until the pasta is *al dente* (cooked but firm to the bite). Drain well and pour over the reserved dressing. Preheat grill.

Place the peppers cut-sides down under the hot grill until the skins blacken and blister. Remove and allow to cool, then peel off the blackened skins, cut into thick strips and stir into the pasta. Cut the chicken into strips, slice the tomatoes, spring onions and celery heart and stir into the pasta. Season to taste with salt and plenty of ground black pepper, sprinkle with remaining chives and serve warm or cold with chunks of garlic bread.

Serves 4.

WARM CHICKEN LIVER SALAD

175 g (6 oz) young spinach leaves, cleaned
1 small radicchio, cleaned
2 oranges, peeled and cut into segments
1 red onion, sliced into rings
25 g (1 oz/6 teaspoons) butter
3 teaspoons hazelnut oil
450 g (1 lb) chicken livers, cores removed and livers
   halved
1 clove garlic, crushed
1 tablespoon sherry vinegar
1 heaped teaspoon wholegrain mustard
3 tablespoons dry sherry
1 teaspoon clear honey
salt and pepper
15 g (½ oz/3 teaspoons) roughly chopped toasted
   hazelnuts, to garnish

Arrange the spinach and radicchio leaves on
4 plates and scatter over the orange segments
and onion rings.

In a heavy-based frying pan, heat the butter
and oil, add the chicken livers and cook,
stirring, over a high heat until well browned.
Push the livers to the side of the pan, then
add the garlic, vinegar, mustard, sherry,
honey and seasonings, bring to the boil and
reduce slightly. Add the livers to the sauce
and coat well, then spoon onto the salad.
Sprinkle with the chopped toasted hazelnuts.

Serves 4.

SPICY THAI SALAD

2 teaspoons sesame oil
2 red chillies, deseeded and chopped
1 clove garlic, crushed
juice of 1 lime
2 teaspoons brown sugar
1 tablespoon fish sauce
1 stem lemon grass, chopped
2 tablespoons shredded fresh basil
225 g (8 oz) cooked chicken, shredded
55 g (2 oz) rice noodles
4 spring onions, sliced into matchstick strips
1 large carrot, cut into matchstick strips
1 yellow pepper (capsicum), cut into matchstick strips
3 Chinese leaves, shredded
2 tablespoons dry roasted peanuts, chopped

In a small pan, heat the oil and quickly fry the
chillies and garlic, then remove from the heat
and stir in the lime juice, sugar, fish sauce,
lemon grass and basil. Pour mixture over the
shredded chicken and allow to stand for 30
minutes.

Cook the rice noodles according to the
packet instructions, then drain, rinse well in
cold water and drain well again. Mix together
the noodles, onions, carrot, pepper
(capsicum) and Chinese leaves. Spoon over
the chicken and sauce and sprinkle with the
chopped peanuts.

Serves 4.

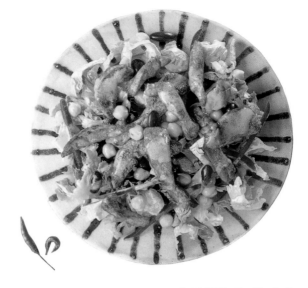

CORONATION CHICKEN

1 tablespoon olive oil
1 small onion, diced
2 teaspoons mild curry paste
200 g (7 oz) can chopped tomatoes
55 ml (2 fl oz/¼ cup) white wine
2 tablespoons hot mango chutney, chopped if
  necessary
2 teaspoons apricot jam
2 teaspoons lemon juice
150 ml (5 fl oz/⅔ cup) mayonnaise
150 ml (5 fl oz/⅔ cup) Greek yogurt
450 g (1 lb) cooked chicken
350 g (12 oz/2 cups) cooked, long-grain rice
1 red pepper (capsicum), diced
2 tablespoons chopped fresh mint
3 tablespoons prepared vinaigrette

In a small saucepan, heat the oil and fry the onion gently without browning until the onion is soft. Stir in the curry paste, tomatoes and wine, bring to the boil and simmer gently for 15 minutes. Add the chutney, jam and lemon juice and cook for a further 5 minutes until thick and syrupy.

Remove from the heat and strain into a small bowl; set aside to cool. When completely cold, stir in the mayonnaise and yogurt and mix well. Cut the chicken into large pieces and stir into the sauce. Combine the rice, pepper (capsicum), mint and vinaigrette and spoon onto a large serving dish and pile the chicken in the centre.

Serves 4.

MEXICAN CHICKEN SALAD

115 g (4 oz/⅔ cup) canned kidney beans, drained
115 g (4 oz/⅔ cup) canned chick peas, drained
1 red pepper (capsicum), sliced
3 Little Gem lettuces, shredded
3 teaspoons made English mustard
2 teaspoons sugar
2 tablespoons red wine vinegar
150 ml (5 fl oz/⅔ cup) olive oil
salt and pepper
4 teaspoons paprika
2 teaspoons cayenne pepper
1 teaspoon chilli powder
4 skinned and boned chicken breasts, cut into strips
2 tablespoons vegetable oil

Mix together the kidney beans, chick peas, red pepper (capsicum) and shredded lettuce and arrange on 4 serving plates. In a bowl, whisk together the mustard, sugar and vinegar and slowly drizzle in the olive oil, whisking well all the time to make a dressing the consistency of runny mayonnaise. Season with salt and pepper and set aside.

Mix the paprika, cayenne pepper and chilli powder together on a plate. Add the strips of chicken and toss until evenly coated in the mixture. Heat the vegetable oil in a frying pan and fry the coated chicken for 2-3 minutes or until cooked. Spoon the chicken over the salad and pour over the salad dressing. Serve immediately.

Serves 4.

CLUBHOUSE SALAD

2 thick slices white bread, crusts removed
oil for frying
350 g (12 oz) cooked chicken breasts
175 g (6 oz) cooked smoked ham
175 g (6 oz) Emmental cheese
1 ripe avocado
2 hard-boiled eggs, shelled
5 tablespoons mayonnaise
1 tablespoon chopped fresh parsley
4 tablespoons olive oil
1 tablespoon white wine vinegar
salt and pepper
1 teaspoon Dijon mustard
1 teaspoon granulated sugar
mixed salad leaves, washed and trimmed
16 cherry tomatoes, halved

Cut the bread into small cubes. Heat 5 cm (2 in) oil in a pan and fry the cubes of bread until golden brown. Remove with a slotted spoon and leave to drain on absorbent kitchen paper. Slice the chicken into strips; cut the ham into 2.5 cm (1 in) cubes; cut the Emmental into strips. Peel and core the avocado and cut into cubes. Cut each egg into quarters. Mix together the mayonnaise and chopped parsley, add the chicken, ham, Emmental, hard-boiled eggs and avocado and mix gently until all the ingredients are well coated in mayonnaise.

In a jug, whisk together the oil, vinegar, salt and pepper, mustard and sugar. Put the salad leaves, cherry tomatoes and croûtons in a bowl, pour over the dressing and toss the salad. Arrange the salad on a plate and spoon over the chicken and ham mixture.

Serves 4.

CHICKEN & SAFFRON SAUCE

45 g (1½ oz) fresh root ginger, peeled and chopped
1 clove garlic, crushed
2 teaspoons each ground cumin and coriander
4 cardamom pods, cracked and the seeds crushed
finely grated rind and juice of ½ lemon
½ teaspoon garam masala
150 ml (5 fl oz/⅔ cup) Greek yogurt
4 boned and skinned chicken breasts
pinch of saffron strands
1 tablespoon hot water
1 shallot, finely chopped
55 ml (2 fl oz/¼ cup) dry white wine
150 ml (5 fl oz/⅔ cup) chicken stock
85 ml (3 fl oz/⅓ cup) double (thick) cream
1 tablespoon chopped fresh coriander

In a blender or food processor, purée the ginger with the garlic, cumin, coriander, crushed cardamom seeds, lemon rind and garam masala. Add two-thirds of the yogurt, mix well and put to one side. Cut each chicken breast into 8 strips, put into shallow dish and spoon over the yogurt mixture. Cover and marinate for 1½-2 hours. Meanwhile, soak the saffron strands in the hot water. Put the shallot in a small pan with the wine and boil rapidly until reduced by half. Add the stock, saffron and water and boil until reduced to about 150 ml (5 fl oz/⅔ cup).

Add the cream and simmer for about 2 minutes until the sauce starts to thicken. Leave to cool, then add the remaining yogurt and season with a little lemon juice, salt and pepper. Remove the chicken strips from the marinade and place on a grill pan, leaving a slight gap between the strips to ensure even cooking. Grill for 5 minutes until browned, turning halfway through cooking. Arrange on a serving dish and cool. Drizzle over the sauce and sprinkle with the chopped coriander.

Serves 4.

-CHICKEN & HAM CROQUETTES-

55 g (2 oz/¼ cup) butter
1 onion, finely chopped
55 g (2 oz/½ cup) plain flour
300 ml (10 fl oz/1¼ cups) milk
300 g (10 oz) cooked chicken, finely chopped
55 g (2 oz) ham, finely chopped
2 tablespoons chopped fresh parsley
1 teaspoon Dijon mustard
salt and pepper
85 g (3 oz/1½ cups) fresh white breadcrumbs
vegetable oil for frying
lemon wedges and green salad, to serve

Melt the butter, add the onion and fry gently for 3-4 minutes until soft but not browned.

Add the flour and cook for 1 minute. Gradually blend in the milk and bring to the boil, stirring all the time. Reduce heat and simmer for 2 minutes until sauce forms a thick paste. Add the chopped chicken, ham, parsley, mustard and season with a little salt and pepper. Mix well and put to one side to cool. Place the breadcrumbs on a board and drop tablespoonsful of the mixture onto the breadcrumbs.

Roll mixture in crumbs to give an even coating. Chill for 30 minutes. Heat 5 cm (2 in) oil in a frying pan. Fry the croquettes until golden brown all over. Drain on kitchen paper. Serve with wedges of lemon and a salad.

Makes 12-14.

Note: To make a sauce to serve with the croquettes, mix 2 teaspoons chopped capers with 3 tablespoons crème fraîche and a squeeze of lemon.

-HONEY CHICKEN DRUMSTICKS-

8 chicken drumsticks
4 tablespoons clear honey
2 teaspoons Dijon mustard
2 teaspoons wholegrain mustard
1 teaspoon soy sauce
1 teaspoon dried rosemary

Cut 3 diagonal slashes in the flesh on both sides of the drumsticks and place in a shallow, ovenproof dish or roasting tin.

Mix together the honey, mustards and soy sauce and pour over the drumsticks. Cover and leave to marinate for 1 hour, turning from time to time.

Preheat the oven to 200C (400F/Gas 6). Sprinkle the rosemary over the drumsticks and cook on the top shelf of the oven for 25 minutes. Increase the heat to 230C (450F/Gas 8) and cook for a further 10 minutes, basting and turning the drumsticks several times. Any leftover marinade from the pan can be added to 4 tablespoons mayonnaise with a squeeze of lemon to serve with the drumsticks.

Serves 4.

—DOLCELATTE & PEAR GRILLS—

4 muffins
55 g (2 oz/¼ cup) garlic and herb-flavoured butter
2 small cooked chicken breasts
85 g (3 oz/⅔ cup) dolcelatte cheese
1 small dessert pear, cored and sliced
freshly ground black pepper
watercress sprigs, to garnish

Preheat grill. Split the muffins in half and toast on both sides until lightly browned.

Spread with a little flavoured butter. Cut the chicken and cheese into thin slices. Arrange alternate pieces of chicken, cheese and pear on top of each muffin half.

Sprinkle with black pepper and return to the grill until the cheese has melted. Serve at once, garnished with sprigs of watercress.

Serves 4.

—CHICKEN & SCRAMBLED EGG—

115 g (4 oz) cooked smoked chicken
55 g (2 oz/¼ cup) butter
6 large eggs
2 tablespoons double (thick) cream
juice of ½ lemon
salt and pepper
4 thick slices of brioche
1-2 tablespoons chopped fresh chives

Cut the chicken into matchstick strips. In a non-stick pan, melt the butter, add the chicken strips and cook for 1 minute.

Whisk the eggs with 1 tablespoon of the cream and half of the lemon juice. Season well with black pepper and pour onto the chicken. Cook over a very low heat, stirring continuously, until the egg thickens. Remove from the heat when eggs are almost fully cooked, but still creamy, stir in the remaining cream and lemon juice and season to taste.

Toast the brioche, and put onto 4 warmed serving plates. Top with generous spoonfuls of the scrambled egg mixture and sprinkle with chives and freshly ground black pepper.

Serves 4.

CHICKEN & HAM CRÊPES

1 small onion, quartered
550 ml (20 fl oz/2½ cups) milk
1 bay leaf
25 g (1 oz/6 teaspoons) butter
25 g (1 oz/¼ cup) plain flour
85 g (3 oz/¾ cup) grated mature Cheddar
225 g (8 oz) cooked chicken, diced
225 g (8 oz) broccoli flowerets, cooked al dente
8 thin slices ham
FOR THE PANCAKES:
115 g (4 oz/1 cup) plain flour
1 egg
225 ml (8 fl oz/1 cup) milk
55 ml (2 fl oz/¼ cup) beer
salt and pepper
oil for frying

Put the onion, milk and bay leaf into a small saucepan, bring to the boil and simmer gently for 10-15 minutes until the onion softens. Discard the bay leaf and purée the onion and milk in a blender or food processor. Melt the butter in a pan, stir in the flour and cook for 1 minute, then add the onion milk a little at a time, stirring well between each addition, and bring to the boil.

Remove from the heat, pour half the sauce into a bowl and stir in 55 g (2 oz/½ cup) of the cheese. Add the chicken and broccoli to the remaining sauce in the pan and return to the heat to warm through.

Meanwhile, make the pancakes. In a blender or food processor, blend together all the pancake ingredients, except the oil, to form a creamy batter. Heat a 15 cm (6 in) pancake pan, brush with a very little oil and pour in about 2-3 tablespoons of pancake batter, tilting the pan to cover the base of the pan with a thin layer. Cook until the top is opaque, then flip over and cook the other side. Place between 2 plates over a pan of simmering water to keep warm, while cooking the remaining batter in the same way to make 8 in total.

Preheat grill. Lay a slice of ham on each pancake and top with generous spoonful of chicken mixture. Roll each pancake to enclose the filling and place, fold-side down, in a buttered flameproof dish.

Spoon over the reserved cheese sauce and sprinkle the remaining cheese on top. Place under the hot grill until golden and bubbly.

Serves 4.

HERBY CHICKEN FRITTATA

2 tablespoons olive oil
2 large onions, thinly sliced
175 g (6 oz) waxy potatoes
5 large eggs
85 g (3 oz/¾ cup) grated mature Cheddar cheese
2 tablespoons finely chopped parsley
salt and pepper
25 g (1 oz/6 teaspoons) butter
175 g (6 oz) cooked chicken, cut into chunks
parsley sprigs, to garnish

Heat the oil and fry the onions for 20 minutes until golden brown; allow to cool slightly. Cook the potatoes in boiling, salted water until just tender. Cut into bite-sized chunks.

Beat together. the eggs, cooked onions, cheese and parsley and season with salt and pepper. Melt the butter in the frying pan and stir in the chicken, pour in the egg mixture, then stir in the potatoes and allow to cook over a very gentle heat until the base sets and the top is runny. Preheat grill.

Cook the frittata top under the hot grill until it is golden and bubbly. Serve at once, cut into wedges and garnished with sprigs of parsley.

Serves 4.

ORIENTAL FRIED RICE

175 g (6 oz/1¼ cups) long-grain rice
300 ml (10 fl oz/1¼ cups) chicken stock
2 tablespoons sesame oil
1 cm (½ in) cube fresh root ginger, grated
1 clove garlic, crushed
175 g (6 oz) raw chicken, thinly sliced
6 spring onions, sliced
1 small red pepper (capsicum), deseeded and sliced
115 g (4 oz) cooked peeled prawns
2 large eggs
2 tablespoons light soy sauce
1 tablespoon chopped fresh coriander
55 g (2 oz/⅓ cup) toasted cashew nuts

Put the rice and stock into a pan, bring to the boil, cover and simmer gently for 10 minutes. Remove from the heat and leave for a further 10 minutes. Drain off any excess liquid and allow to cool slightly. Heat the sesame oil in a large frying pan or wok and add the ginger, garlic and chicken and stir-fry for 4-5 minutes until the chicken is cooked.

Add the onions, pepper (capsicum) and prawns and stir-fry for a further 1 minute. In a bowl, beat together the eggs and the soy sauce and stir in the rice. Tip onto the chicken mixture and continue to cook over a high heat for 1 minute, stirring. Remove from the heat and stir in the coriander. Serve garnished with toasted cashew nuts.

Serves 4.

CHICKEN STIR-FRY

350 g (12 oz) skinned and boned chicken breasts
2 tablespoons soy sauce
3 tablespoons dry sherry
3 tablespoons vegetable oil
1 clove garlic, finely chopped
2.5 cm (1 in) piece fresh root ginger, chopped
1 small red pepper (capsicum), deseeded and sliced
4 spring onions, cut into 2.5 cm (1 in) lengths
55 g (2 oz) mange tout (snow peas), topped and tailed
8 baby corn, cut into halves lengthways
1 teaspoon cornflour
few drops sesame oil
few drops lemon juice

Cut the chicken breast into thin strips. Place in a bowl and add 1 teaspoon soy sauce and 1 tablespoon sherry and leave to marinate for 35 minutes. In a wok or large frying pan, heat the oil over a high heat, add the garlic and ginger and stir-fry for 15 seconds, then add the chicken and stir-fry for 2-3 minutes. Add the red pepper (capsicum), spring onions, mange tout (snow-peas) and baby corn and stir-fry for a further 1 minute.

Mix together the cornflour with the remaining soy sauce and sherry, pour the mixture into the wok and cook for 30 seconds until the sauce thickens and glazes the ingredients. Just before serving drizzle over the sesame oil and the lemon juice.

Serves 4.

COQ AU VIN

550 ml (20 fl oz/2½ cups) red wine
3 cloves garlic, sliced
1 small onion, chopped
2 tablespoons olive oil
1 teaspoon brown sugar
1 teaspoon mixed peppercorns, crushed
1 teaspoon coriander seeds, crushed
1 bouquet garni
1.5 kg (3¼-3½ lb) chicken, cut into 8 pieces
45 g (1½ oz/3 tablespoons) seasoned flour
115 g (4 oz) piece smoked bacon, derinded and diced
175 g (6 oz) button onions, peeled
175 g (6 oz) button mushrooms
425 ml (15 fl oz/2 cups) chicken stock
2 tablespoons chopped parsley
fried bread croûtons, to garnish

Mix together the wine, garlic, chopped onion, 1 tablespoon of the oil, sugar, peppercorns and coriander. Add the bouquet garni and the chicken pieces. Cover and marinate in the refrigerator for 2-3 hours, turning regularly. Remove chicken from marinade (reserving marinade) and pat dry on kitchen paper, then toss in the seasoned flour. Heat the remaining oil in a casserole and fry the bacon until browned, remove with a slotted spoon and set to one side. Add the chicken pieces to the casserole and fry until well browned, set aside with the bacon.

Add the button onions and cook until browned. Add mushrooms and any remaining flour. Cook for 1 minute. Add the stock and marinade, stirring until thick. Return chicken and bacon, cover and simmer for 40 minutes. Remove the chicken and vegetables to a serving dish using a slotted spoon; keep warm. Bring the sauce to the boil for 3-4 minutes until thick. Check the seasoning and stir in the parsley. Spoon the sauce over the chicken and garnish with bread croûtons.

Serves 4.

–CHICKEN VEGETABLE HOTPOT–

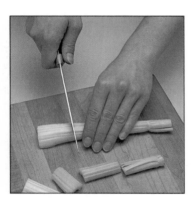

55 g (2 oz/¼ cup) butter
115 g (4 oz) smoked bacon, chopped
2 large chicken quarters, halved
2 carrots, peeled and sliced
1 onion, sliced
2 sticks celery, cut into 5 cm (2 in) lengths
2 leeks, trimmed and sliced
2 tablespoons plain flour
1 kg (2 lb) potatoes, peeled
2 tablespoons chopped fresh thyme
2 tablespoons chopped fresh parsley
salt and pepper
425 ml (15 fl oz/2 cups) chicken stock

Preheat oven to 150C (300F/Gas 2). Heat half the butter in a frying pan, add the bacon and chicken and fry until golden. Remove from the pan and drain on absorbent kitchen paper to remove excess fat. Add the carrots, onion, celery and leeks to the pan and fry for 2-3 minutes until the vegetables are turning golden. Sprinkle over the flour and mix well.

Slice the potatoes into 0.5 cm (¼ in) thick slices. Arrange half the slices in the bottom of a casserole, add the chicken and bacon, cover with the vegetables and chopped herbs and season well with salt and pepper. Cover with the remaining sliced potato, dot with the remaining butter and pour over the stock. Cover and bake for 1 hour, then uncover and continue cooking for a further 25-30 minutes until the chicken is tender and cooked and the potatoes are crisp and brown.

Serves 4.

—CHICKEN IN CAPER SAUCE—

1 onion, quartered
1 carrot, peeled and quartered
1 teaspoon finely grated orange rind
1 orange, peeled and sliced
bay leaves
55 ml (2 oz/¼ cup) dry white wine
225 ml (8 fl oz/1 cup) chicken stock
4 skinned and boned chicken breasts
25 g (1 oz/6 teaspoons) butter
25 g (1 oz/¼ cup) plain flour
150 ml (5 fl oz/⅔ cup) single (light) cream
1 tablespoon chopped fresh parsley
2 teaspoons capers, drained

Place the first 5 ingredients in a frying pan.

Add the wine and stock and bring to the boil. Add the chicken breasts, reduce the heat until barely simmering, then cover and poach for 20 minutes or until cooked. Remove the cooked breasts, drain well on absorbent kitchen paper and keep warm. Strain and reserve the poaching liquor.

In a pan, melt the butter, add the flour and cook for 1 minutes, remove from the heat and slowly add the poaching liquor, stirring well between each addition. Return to the heat and bring to the boil, stirring continuously, until thickened. Stir in the cream, parsley and capers and season to taste. Spoon over the chicken breasts and serve with cardamom-scented rice.

Serves 4.

LEMON CHICKEN

1 egg white
350 g (12 oz) chicken breast, sliced
3 teaspoons cornflour
finely grated rind and juice of 1 lemon
2 tablespoons dry sherry
1 teaspoon soy sauce
2 teaspoon clear honey
3 tablespoons vegetable oil
4 spring onions, sliced
55 g (2 oz) mange tout (snow peas), topped and tailed
½ red pepper (capsicum), finely sliced
55 g (2 oz) beansprouts

Whisk egg white until frothy. Stir in chicken, 2 teaspoons cornflour and lemon rind.

In another bowl, mix together the remaining cornflour, sherry, lemon juice, soy sauce and honey. Put to one side. Heat the oil in a wok or large frying pan, add the chicken pieces a few at a time to prevent them sticking together. Stir-fry for 2 minutes or until the chicken is cooked through.

Add the spring onions, mange tout (snow peas), red pepper (capsicum) and beansprouts and continue to stir-fry for a further 1 minute. Add the lemon juice and cornflour mixture and cook for 1-2 minutes, stirring until the sauce thickens and coats the chicken and vegetables.

Serves 4.

CHICKEN CORDON BLEU

4 skinned and boned chicken breasts
4 slices smoked ham
115 g (4 oz) Emmental cheese
2 eggs, beaten
175 g (6 oz/3 cups) fresh white breadcrumbs
oil for deep frying

Lay the chicken breasts between 2 sheets of greaseproof paper and beat out with a rolling pin to about 0.5 cm (¼ in) thick, taking care not to tear the flesh. Trim the slices of ham so they are smaller than the chicken breasts and lay a slice on top of each breast.

Cut the cheese into very thin slices and place on top of the ham. Fold the chicken breast in half to enclose the filling. Carefully dip each chicken breast first in the beaten egg, then in the breadcrumbs. Repeat this process so that the chicken is well coated and the filling completely enclosed.

Half-fill a deep fat pan or fryer with oil and heat to 190C (375F). Fry the chicken for 7 minutes, then decrease the heat and cook for a further 5 minutes to ensure that the coating doesn't burn before the chicken is cooked. Remove from the oil with a slotted spoon and drain on absorbent kitchen paper. Serve immediately.

Serves 4.

CHICKEN KIEV

115 g (4 oz/½ cup) unsalted butter, softened
3 cloves garlic, crushed
finely grated rind of ½ lemon
1 tablespoon chopped fresh parsley
salt and pepper
4 skinned and boned chicken breasts
2 eggs, beaten
175 g (6 oz/3 cups) fresh white breadcrumbs
oil for deep frying

Beat together the softened butter, crushed garlic, grated lemon rind, parsley and salt and pepper. Transfer to a piping bag fitted with a plain 0.5 cm (¼ in) nozzle.

Lay the chicken breasts on a board and insert a sharp knife into the breast to form a pocket. Take the piping bag and pipe the butter into the pocket (do not over-fill or the butter will burst through the flesh). Leave to refrigerate for 25 minutes.

Dip a filled chicken breast into the beaten eggs, then roll in the breadcrumbs. Repeat once more so chicken is well coated. Repeat with the remaining chicken. Half-fill a deep fat pan or fryer with oil and heat to 190C (375F). Lower in the chicken breasts, 2 at a time, and fry for 8-10 minutes or until cooked through and golden brown. Drain on absorbent kitchen paper and serve immediately with a squeeze of lemon.

Serves 4.

GRILLED CHICKEN & HERBS

4 chicken breasts, on the bone, weighing about 175 g (6 oz) each
2 cloves garlic, peeled and sliced
4 sprigs of fresh rosemary
6 tablespoons olive oil
grated rind and juice of ½ lemon
2 tablespoons dry white wine
salt and pepper
½ teaspoon Dijon mustard
2 tablespoons balsamic vinegar
1 teaspoon sugar

Make several incisions in the chicken breasts and insert pieces of garlic and rosemary. Place the chicken breasts in a flameproof dish.

Mix together 2 tablespoons olive oil with the rind and juice of ½ lemon, the white wine and salt and pepper and pour over the chicken breasts and leave to marinate for 45 minutes. Preheat grill.

Place the chicken breast, skin-sides down, in the dish and cook under the hot grill for 5 minutes. Turn over and spoon the marinade over the top and grill for a further 10 minutes until the skin is crisp and brown. Whisk together the mustard, vinegar, sugar, salt and pepper and remaining oil. Add any cooking juices or marinade from the pan and spoon over the chicken to serve.

Serves 4.

TANDOORI CHICKEN

4 chicken leg quarters, skinned
juice of 1 lemon
salt
2 teaspoons ground turmeric
2 teaspoons paprika
1 teaspoon garam masala
1 teaspoon ground cardamom
½ teaspoon chilli powder
pinch saffron powder
2 cloves garlic, crushed
2 teaspoons chopped fresh root ginger
1 tablespoon olive oil
200 ml (7 fl oz/¾ cup) natural yogurt

Cut deep diagonal cuts in the chicken flesh.

Sprinkle with lemon juice and a little salt. Mix together all the remaining ingredients and use to coat the chicken quarters, cover and leave in a cool place to marinate for 4 hours or overnight.

Preheat grill and cook chicken for 25 minutes, brushing with any excess marinade and turning frequently until the chicken is tender and juices run clear when chicken leg is pierced with a knife. A slight blackening of the chicken gives an authentic look. Serve with wedges of lemon, boiled rice and an onion salad.

Serves 4.

SPATCHCOCK POUSSIN

2 poussins
75 g (3 oz/⅓ cup) butter, softened
4 teaspoons chopped fresh rosemary
4 teaspoons chopped fresh basil
8 sun-dried tomatoes, chopped
finely grated rind and juice of 1 lime
salt and pepper

Prepare the poussins. Using kitchen scissors, cut along the backbone of each poussin. Turn the poussin over so the breast is facing up and flatten the chicken out by pressing down gently on the breast.

Gently loosen the skin on the breast (starting at the pointed end) by running a sharp knife under the skin, taking care not to tear the skin or cut the flesh. The skin should not be separate but loosened enough to form a pocket in which to put the butter. In a bowl, beat the butter with a fork until soft, add the rosemary, basil, sun-dried tomatoes, rind and juice of the lime, and a little salt and pepper to taste. Preheat grill.

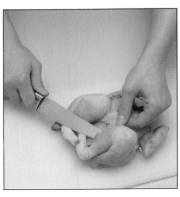

Using a table knife, spread the butter mixture onto the flesh under the skin, making sure the breast is well covered. Place the poussins, breast-sides down, in a grill pan and place under a very hot grill for 10 minutes until brown and crispy. Turn the poussins over and cook for a further 10 minutes until the skins turn crispy, spooning over any melted butter in pan. Serve with boiled new potatoes and a green salad and spoon over any melted butter left in the grill pan.

Serves 2.

HASH RISSOLES

350 g (12 oz) cooked chicken, minced
8 spring onions, chopped
450 g (1 lb) potatoes, boiled and mashed
2 tablespoons mayonnaise
2 tablespoons chopped fresh parsley
½ teaspoon finely grated lemon rind
¼ teaspoon freshly grated nutmeg
salt and pepper
2 large eggs
55 g (2 oz/1 cup) fresh white breadcrumbs
oil for frying

In a bowl, mix together the chicken, onions, potatoes, mayonnaise, parsley, lemon rind, nutmeg, seasonings and one of the eggs.

Form into 8 patties, dip into the remaining beaten egg, then coat in the breadcrumbs and set aside to chill for 20 minutes.

In a large frying pan, heat the oil and cook the patties on both sides for about 5-6 minutes until golden. Drain on absorbent kitchen paper. Serve at once with a crisp green salad and assorted relishes.

Serves 4.

MINTED MEATBALLS

1 small onion, quartered
400 g (14 oz) can chopped tomatoes
300 ml (10 fl oz/1¼ cups) chicken stock
grated rind and juice of ½ large orange
2 tablespoons tomato purée (paste)
4 tablespoons chopped fresh mint
1 teaspoon sugar
1 teaspoon red wine vinegar
450 g (1 lb) raw chicken, minced
8 spring onions, finely chopped
55 g (2 oz/1 cup) fresh white breadcrumbs
1 small egg, beaten
2 teaspoons ground cumin
salt and pepper
oil for frying

Place the onion, tomatoes, stock, orange rind and juice, tomato purée (paste), 2 tablespoons chopped mint, sugar and vinegar, in a blender or food processor. Blend until smooth, then pour into a saucepan and simmer for 10-15 minutes. In a large bowl, combine the chicken with the spring onions, breadcrumbs, egg, remaining 2 tablespoons chopped mint, cumin and seasonings. Using wet hands, form the chicken mixture into 40 small balls.

In a large non-stick pan, heat a little oil and fry the meatballs for about 6-8 minutes until slightly coloured all over. Remove from the pan and drain on absorbent kitchen paper. Wipe out the frying pan with absorbent kitchen paper and return the meatballs to the pan, spoon over the sauce and simmer, uncovered, for 15 minutes. Serve on a bed of freshly cooked spaghetti, sprinkle with Parmesan cheese and garnish with mint sprigs.

Serves 4.

PIQUANT MEATLOAF

25 g (1 oz/6 teaspoons) butter
1 onion, finely chopped
1 clove garlic, crushed
85 g (3 oz) mushrooms, coarsely chopped
25 g (1 oz/¼ cup) plain flour
300 ml (10 fl oz/1¼ cups) milk
55 g (2 oz) fresh white breadcrumbs
2 eggs, beaten
finely grated rind and juice of 1 lemon
450 g (1 lb) skinned and boned chicken breasts
55 g (2 oz) streaky bacon, rinds removed
55 g (2 oz) dried apricots, chopped
1 tablespoon chopped fresh thyme
2 tablespoons chopped fresh parsley
¼ teaspoon grated nutmeg
salt and pepper

Preheat the oven to 200C (400F/Gas 6). In a pan, gently melt the butter, add the onion and garlic and fry for 2-3 minutes until softened but not browned. Add the mushrooms and cook for a further 1 minute. Add the flour and cook until all the fat has been absorbed. Remove from the heat and gradually add the milk. Return the pan to the heat and simmer until the sauce has thickened, stirring contantly, then add the breadcrumbs. Transfer to a bowl and allow to cool, then beat in the eggs and lemon juice.

In a food processor, finely process the chicken breast and bacon. Transfer to a bowl and add the apricots, herbs, nutmeg, and lemon rind. Mix well. Add the cooled sauce to the chicken and bacon mixture and mix well. Season with salt and pepper and transfer to a 1 kg (2 lb) loaf tin. Cover the meat loaf with greased foil and put into a roasting pan half-filled with hot water. Bake in the oven for 55-60 minutes or until the loaf is firm to the touch. Serve hot or cold.
Serves 4.

CHICKEN BURGERS

85 g (3 oz) packet country stuffing mix
225 g (8 oz) raw chicken meat, minced
1 small egg, beaten
1 eating apple, peeled, cored and grated
salt and pepper
1-2 tablespoons oil
4 sesame seed baps
iceberg lettuce, shredded
2 tomatoes, sliced
4 squares processed Cheddar cheese slices
mayonnaise and relish, to serve

Make up the stuffing mix according to the packet instructions and set aside to cool.

In a bowl, mix together the chicken, stuffing, egg, apple and seasonings and shape into 4 burgers. In a frying pan, heat the oil and fry the burgers for 6-7 minutes on each side until cooked.

Split the buns in half and cover the bases with the shredded lettuce and tomato slices. Place the burgers over the lettuce and tomato, then cover each burger with a slice of cheese. Spoon on mayonnaise or relish and place the bap top in position.

Serves 4.

—FRIED SHREDDED CHICKEN—

1 egg white
1 tablespoon cornflour
salt and pepper
350 g (12 oz) chicken breast, cut into thin strips
oil for frying
2.5 cm (1 in) cube fresh root ginger, finely chopped
2 cloves garlic, sliced
115 g (4 oz) carrots, cut into matchstick strips
2 teaspoons sesame seeds
2 red chillies, deseeded and thinly sliced
FOR THE SAUCE:
2 teaspoons cornflour
55 ml (2 fl oz/¼ cup) chicken stock
1 teaspoon each chilli sauce, tomato purée (paste) and
    clear honey
1 tablespoon each dark soy sauce and dry sherry

Beat the egg white with the cornflour. Season the strips of chicken and coat in the egg white mixture. In a deep frying pan or wok, heat the oil and fry the chicken a few strips at a time for 2-3 minutes until golden and crisp. Drain on absorbent kitchen paper while cooking the remainder in the same way. Pour all but 1 tablespoon oil out of the pan. Stir fry the ginger, garlic, carrots, sesame seeds and chillies for 2-3 minutes without colouring.

Blend together all the sauce ingredients and pour onto the vegetables, then bring to the boil and cook, stirring, until thick and glossy. Add the chicken, stir well to coat in the sauce and cook for a further 1-2 minutes. Serve with egg fried rice and garnish with spring onions.

Serves 4.

—TOSTADAS WITH SALSA—

8 corn or wheat fried tortillas
200 g (7 oz) can refried beans
1 avocado, sliced
2 cooked chicken breasts, sliced
115 ml (4 fl oz/½ cup) thick sour cream
4 small tomatoes, sliced
1 red onion, sliced
115 g (4 oz/1 cup) grated Cheddar cheese
FOR THE SALSA:
4 spring onions
200 g (7 oz) can chopped tomatoes
½ teaspoon chilli sauce
1 teaspoon each tomato purée (paste), sugar and red
    wine vinegar
1 tablespoon chopped fresh coriander
pickled jalapeño peppers, to serve

Preheat grill. Arrange the tortillas on a grill pan. Warm the refried beans and divide equally between the tortillas. Top with the sliced avocado, chicken, thick sour cream, tomatoes and sliced onion and sprinkle with the cheese. Cook under the hot grill until the cheese begins to melt.

In a blender or food processor, blend together all the ingredients for the salsa for 15-20 seconds. Serve with the tortillas and garnish with pickled jalapeño peppers.

Serves 4.

JAMBALAYA

1 tablespoon olive oil
15 g (½ oz/3 teaspoons) butter
350 g (12 oz) skinned and boned chicken meat
175 g (6 oz) chorizo sausage
1 onion, thinly sliced
2 cloves garlic, sliced
1 red pepper (capsicum). sliced
1 yellow pepper (capsicum), sliced
1 green pepper (capsicum), sliced
115 g (4 oz) mushrooms, sliced
150 g (5 oz/1 cup) long-grain rice
½ teaspoon ground allspice
300 ml (10 fl oz/1¼ cups) chicken stock
150 ml (5 fl oz/⅔ cup) white wine
115 g (4 oz) large cooked peeled prawns
lime wedges and whole prawns, to garnish

In a large frying pan or paella pan, heat the oil and butter. Cut the chicken into thick strips and fry until well browned, then remove from the pan and set aside. Cut the chorizo into chunks and fry for 1 minute, stirring well, then using a slotted spoon, remove from the pan and add to the chicken. Fry the onion and garlic until slightly softened, add the peppers (capsicums), mushrooms, rice and allspice and cook for a further 1 minute.

Pour in the stock and wine and bring to the boil, return the chicken and chorizo to the pan and simmer, uncovered, for 15-20 minutes until the liquid is absorbed and the rice tender. Stir in the prawns, cook for a further 5 minutes, then season to taste. Serve garnished with wedges of lime and whole prawns.

Serves 4.

SOUTHERN-FRIED CHICKEN

4 chicken breasts
salt and pepper
3 tablespoons paprika
2 tablespoons ground coriander
1 tablespoon ground cumin
finely grated rind and juice of 1 lemon
3 tablespoons dark soy sauce
2 tablespoons chopped fresh coriander
1 teaspoon chopped fresh thyme
1 onion, finely choppd
2 cloves garlic, crushed
1 red chilli pepper, deseeded and chopped
vegetable oil for frying
85 g (3 oz/¾ cup) plain flour
lemon wedges and coriander sprigs, to garnish

Remove the skin from the chicken breasts. Place the chicken in a shallow dish. Make several incisions in the chicken portions and season well with salt and pepper. In a small bowl, mix together 2 tablespoons paprika, 1 tablespoon ground coriander and 2 teaspoons ground cumin and sprinkle over the chicken. Mix the rind and juice of the lemon with the soy sauce, then add the coriander, thyme, onion, garlic and chilli. Pour over the chicken – making sure it is well covered by the mixture. Cover the dish with cling film and leave to marinate for at least 3 hours or overnight.

Half-fill a deep fat pan or fryer with the oil and heat to 190C (375F). Put the flour on a plate and season with salt and pepper. Add the remaining paprika, cumin, coriander and mix well. Dip the chicken pieces in the flour to thoroughly coat. Deep fry the chicken, 4 pieces at a time, for approximately 15 minutes or until chicken is golden brown and cooked through. Serve garnished with lemon wedges and coriander sprigs.

Serves 4.

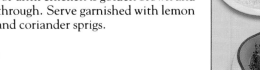

CHICKEN CHILLI TACOS

2 tablespoons oil
450 g (1 lb) skinned and boned chicken breasts, cubed
8 spring onions, chopped into 2.5 cm (1 in) pieces
1 green pepper (capsicum), chopped
1 clove garlic, crushed
2 fresh green chillies, deseeded and finely chopped
1 teaspoon each fresh basil and oregano
400 g (14 oz) can chopped tomatoes
2 teaspoons chilli sauce
2 teaspoons tomato purée (paste)
1 teaspoon sugar
200 g (7 oz) can red kidney beans, drained
salt and pepper
8 taco shells
1 iceburg lettuce, shredded
150 ml (5 fl oz/⅔ cup) thick sour cream

In a large frying pan, heat the oil and fry the chicken for 2-3 minutes. Add the spring onions, green pepper (capsicum), garlic, chillies and herbs and cook for a further 2 minutes. Add the chopped tomatoes, chilli sauce, tomato purée (paste), sugar, kidney beans and salt and pepper and simmer for 20-25 minutes or until the sauce starts to thicken.

Spoon some shredded lettuce into each taco shell, top with chilli chicken and spoon over a little thick sour cream.

Serves 4.

Note: Use a mixture of grated cheese, chopped sun-dried tomatoes and chopped olives as a topping for the tacos.

CHICKEN FAJITAS

55 ml (2 fl oz/¼ cup) dry white wine
finely grated rind and juice of 2 limes
1 tablespoon Worcestershire sauce
2 teaspoons brown sugar
½ teaspoon dried basil
½ teaspoon dried oregano
1 clove garlic, crushed
4 skinned and boned chicken breasts
6 teaspoons vegetable oil
8 spring onions, sliced
1 red pepper (capsicum), deseeded and sliced
1 green pepper (capsicum), deseeded and sliced
8 wheat flour tortillas, warmed gently
150 ml (5 fl oz/⅔ cup) thick sour cream
ripe avocado, peeled and chopped

Prepare the marinade for the chicken. In a bowl, mix together the wine, rind and juice of the limes, Worcestershire sauce, sugar, basil, oregano and garlic. Slice the chicken breast into thin strips and add to the marinade. Mix well and leave to marinate for 30-40 minutes, stirring from time to time. In a pan, heat 2 tablespoons oil and add the spring onions and peppers (capsicums) and fry until the onions are starting to colour, but the vegetables are still crisp. Remove from the pan and put to one side. Drain the chicken, reserving the marinade.

Heat the remaining oil, and when very hot, add the chicken and fry quickly until golden brown. Remove from the pan with a slotted spoon; set aside. Add the reserved marinade to the pan and boil until thickened and reduced. Return the chicken and peppers and mix well until all ingredients are coated in the marinade. Put tortillas on a plate, place the chicken mixture in the middle, spoon over some thick sour cream and chopped avocado. Roll up and serve.

Serves 4.

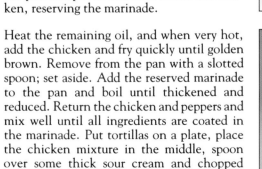

CHICKEN & CORN FRITTERS

1 banana
1 egg
85 g (3 oz) cooked chicken, finely chopped
200 g (7 oz) can sweetcorn kernels, drained
2 spring onions, finely chopped
½ teaspoon ground cumin
2 teaspoons chopped fresh coriander
salt and cayenne pepper
85 g (3 oz/¾ cup) self-raising flour
oil for frying

Mash the banana. Mix in the egg, chicken, sweetcorn, spring onions, cumin, coriander, salt and a pinch of cayenne pepper. Add the flour and form a soft batter.

Heat oil in a heavy frying pan or saucepan and add spoonfuls of the mixture, cooking for about 1 minute, turning halfway through cooking, until golden brown.

Remove from the pan with a slotted spoon and drain on absorbent kitchen paper. Serve the fritters warm with a chilli dip or relish.

Serves 4.

GUMBO

25 g (1 oz/6 teaspoons) butter
1 tablespoon oil
1.5 kg (3¼-3½ lb) chicken, cut into 8 pieces
25 g (1 oz/¼ cup) seasoned flour
1 large onion, sliced
2 cloves garlic, sliced
2 teaspoons chilli powder
400 g (14 oz) can chopped tomatoes
2 tablespoons tomato purée (paste)
300 ml (10 fl oz/1¼ cups) chicken stock
115 ml (4 fl oz/½ cup) red wine
1 red pepper (capsicum), deseeded and sliced
1 green pepper (capsicum), deseeded and sliced
350 g (12 oz) small okra, trimmed
2 teaspoons lemon juice
pinch of sugar

Preheat oven to 180C (350F/Gas 4). Heat the butter and oil in a flameproof casserole. Toss the chicken pieces in the seasoned flour, then fry in the hot fats until golden. Remove from the pan and set aside. Cook the onion and garlic in the casserole until slightly softened, stir in the chilli powder and any remaining flour, then add the tomatoes, tomato purée (paste), stock and wine and bring to the boil.

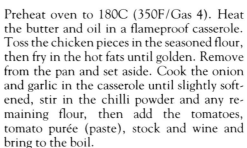

Stir in the vegetables, lemon juice and sugar and return the chicken to the casserole. Cover and cook in the oven for 50-60 minutes. Serve with rice, if wished.

Serves 4.

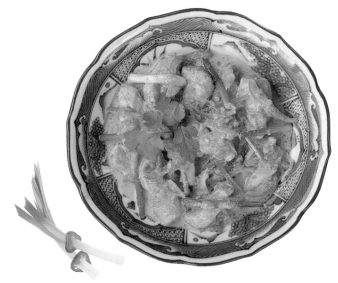

THAI CURRY

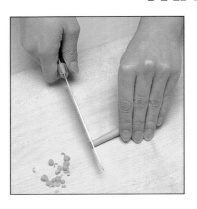

1 small onion, chopped
1 clove garlic, peeled
1 blade lemon grass, chopped
1 teaspoon ground coriander
½ teaspoon dried chilli flakes
1 teaspoon grated lime rind
1 teaspoon paprika
½ teaspoon ground cumin
2 teaspoons vegetable oil
450 g (1 lb) raw chicken meat, sliced
3 teaspoons light soy sauce
150 ml (5 fl oz/⅔ cup) coconut milk
2 lime leaves
55 ml (2 fl oz/¼ cup) chicken stock
2 red peppers (capsicums), deseeded and sliced
10 spring onions, sliced into matchstick strips

Blend or process the first 8 ingredients in a blender or food processor until smooth. Heat the oil in a large frying pan, stir in the paste and cook for 1-2 minutes. Add the chicken and stir gently, coating well in the curry paste.

Stir in the soy sauce, coconut milk, lime leaves, chicken stock, peppers (capsicums) and spring onions. Cover and cook for 20-25 minutes. Serve with plain boiled rice and garnish with sprigs of coriander.

Serves 4.

SWEET & SOUR CHICKEN

700 g (1½ lb) skinned and boned chicken breasts
salt
5 tablespoons cornflour
225 g (8 oz/2 cups) self-raising flour
3 large eggs, beaten
2.5 cm (1 in) piece fresh root ginger, finely chopped
1 tablespoon oil, plus extra for frying
100 ml (3½ fl oz/⅓ cup) white wine vinegar
55 ml (2 fl oz/¼ cup) dry sherry
100 ml (3½ fl oz/⅓ cup) orange juice
3 tablespoons soy sauce
4 tablespoons tomato purée (paste)
1 clove garlic, finely chopped
1 small onion, finely chopped
1 red pepper (capsicum), sliced
1 green pepper (capsicum), sliced

Cut the chicken into 2.5 cm (1 in) cubes. Sprinkle with salt and 2 tablespoons cornflour and mix thoroughly. Meanwhile, make the batter. Put the flour in a bowl, gradually add the eggs and 300 ml (10 fl oz/1¼ cups) water to make a smooth batter. Add half the ginger. Add the chicken and coat thoroughly. Half-fill a deep fat pan or fryer with oil and heat to 190C (375F). Add the chicken, in batches, and fry for 4-5 minutes until crispy. Remove with a slotted spoon, drain and transfer to a plate to keep warm.

In a jug, mix remaining 3 tablespoons cornflour with 150 ml (5 fl oz/⅔ cup) water, then add the wine vinegar, sherry, orange juice, soy sauce and tomato purée (paste). Heat 1 tablespoon oil in a wok or large frying pan, add the garlic and the rest of the ginger, stir-fry for 15 seconds. Add the onion and peppers (capsicums) and stir-fry for 1½-2 minutes, then pour over the sauce, stirring until it thickens. Put the chicken on a warm serving dish and pour over the sauce.

Serves 4-6.

CHICKEN CHOW MEIN

3 tablespoons dark soy sauce
2 tablespoons dry sherry
1 teaspoon soft brown sugar
1 teaspoon sweet chilli sauce
225 g (8 oz) skinned and boned chicken, shredded
225 g (8 oz) egg thread noodles
1 teaspoon cornflour
6 tablespoons chicken stock or water
3 tablespoons vegetable oil
2.5 cm (1 in) piece fresh root ginger, finely chopped
1 clove garlic, finely chopped
4 spring onions, sliced
85 g (3 oz) green beans, cut into 2.5 cm (1 in) lengths
1 small carrot, cut into matchstick strips
1 red pepper (capsicum), finely sliced
175 g (6 oz) beansprouts

In a bowl, mix together soy sauce, sherry, brown sugar and chilli sauce. Add the chicken and leave to marinate for 30 minutes. Drain the chicken, reserving the marinade. Cook the noodles following the packet instructions; drain and set aside. Mix the reserved marinade with the cornflour and chicken stock or water and set aside.

In a wok or large frying pan, heat the oil, add the ginger and garlic and stir-fry for 15-20 seconds, then add the chicken and continue to stir-fry for further 2-3 minutes until the chicken is cooked. Add the spring onions, beans, carrot and pepper (capsicum) and stir-fry for 1 minute. Add the noodles and beansprouts and stir-fry for 30 seconds, then add the marinade mixture and stir-fry until the sauce thickens and coats the ingredients. Serve immediately.

Serves 4.

CHICKEN & BLACK BEAN SAUCE

1 teaspoon cornflour
4 teaspoons light soy sauce
2.5 cm (1 in) piece fresh root ginger, finely chopped
1 clove garlic, crushed
350 g (12 oz) skinned and boned chicken breasts
1 green pepper (capsicum), deseeded
8 canned water chestnuts, drained
4 spring onions
2 tablespoons vegetable oil
55 g (2 oz/½ cup) cashew nuts
5 tablespoons dry sherry
175 g (6 oz) bottle black bean sauce

In a bowl, mix together the cornflour, soy sauce, ginger and garlic. Slice the chicken into thin strips and coat in the cornflour mixture and leave to stand for 10 minutes. Dice the green pepper (capsicum), cut the water chestnuts in half and slice the spring onions into 2.5 cm (1 in) lengths; set aside.

In a wok or large frying pan, heat the oil, add the chicken and stir-fry for 2 minutes, then add the pepper (capsicum), spring onions and water chestnuts and stir-fry for a further 1 minute. Add the cashew nuts, sherry and black bean sauce and stir-fry until sauce thickens.

Serves 4.

ARABIAN POUSSIN

3 teaspoons olive oil
1 small red onion, finely chopped
225 g (8 oz/1¼ cups) couscous
350 ml (12 fl oz/1½ cups) chicken stock
25 g (1 oz) no-need-to-soak dried apricots, finely
    chopped
15 g (½ oz/2 tablespoons) raisins
grated rind and juice of ½ lemon
25 g (1 oz/¼ cup) toasted pine nuts
1 tablespoon chopped fresh mint
4 poussins
salt and pepper
150 ml (5 fl oz/⅔ cup) dry white wine
2 teaspoons mint jelly

Preheat oven to 180C (350F/Gas 4). In a pan, heat 1 tablespoon oil and gently fry the onion until soft. Put the couscous into a bowl and add 225 ml (8 fl oz/1 cup) of the stock, the fried onion, apricots, raisins and the lemon rind and juice and leave to stand for 15 minutes. Stir in the pine nuts and mint. Loosen the skin around the breast of each poussin and carefully push the stuffing round the meat, securing the skin in place with a wooden cocktail stick. Use any excess stuffing to place under the poussins in a roasting tin.

Brush the poussins with the remaining oil and sprinkle with salt and black pepper. Roast in the oven for 50-60 minutes, basting occasionally. Remove the poussins from the roasting tin and set aside. Pour the remaining stock, wine and mint jelly into the pan and stir together over a high heat, bring to the boil and spoon over the poussins.

Serves 4.

TIKKA KEBABS

150 ml (5 fl oz/⅔ cup) natural yogurt
1 tablespoon grated fresh root ginger
2 cloves garlic, crushed
1 teaspoon chilli powder
1 teaspoon ground cumin
1 teaspoon tumeric
1 tablespoon coriander seeds
juice of 1 lemon
½ teaspoon salt
2 tablespoons chopped fresh coriander
350 g (12 oz) chicken meat, cubed
RAITA:
150 ml (5 fl oz/⅔ cup) natural yogurt
2 teaspoons mint jelly
85 g (3 oz) finely chopped cucumber
2 spring onions, finely chopped

Blend the first 10 ingredients in a blender or food processor until smooth. Pour into a bowl. Stir in the cubed chicken, cover and allow to stand overnight in the refrigerator.

Preheat grill. Thread chicken onto skewers and cook under the hot grill for 15-20 minutes, turning frequently and brushing with any remaining marinade. In a bowl, mix together the raita ingredients. Serve the kebabs on a bed of pilau rice, garnished with sprigs of coriander and lemon wedges. Hand the raita separately.

Serves 4.

CHICKEN BIRYANI

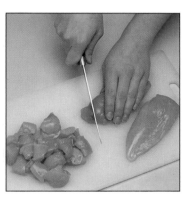

8 tablespoons vegetable oil
1 stick cinnamon
8 cloves
6 cardamom pods, bruised
2.5 cm (1 in) piece fresh root ginger, finely chopped
700 g (1½ lb) skinned and boned chicken, cubed
2 cloves garlic, crushed
1 teaspoon chilli powder
300 ml (10 fl oz/1¼ cups) natural yogurt
150 ml (5 fl oz/⅔ cup) chicken stock
pinch of saffron strands
4 tablespoons boiling water
350 g (12 oz/2¼ cups) basmati rice
4 tablespoons sultanas
4 tablespoons flaked almonds
1 onion, sliced

Preheat oven to 190C (375F/Gas 5). In a flameproof casserole, heat 4 tablespoons oil and add the spices and fry for 15 seconds. Add the chicken, garlic and chilli and fry for 4 minutes. Add the yogurt, 1 tablespoon at a time, stirring between each addition until yogurt is absorbed by the spices. Add the stock and simmer for 20-25 minutes. Transfer to a bowl. Soak the saffron in the boiling water and put to one side. Wash the rice under cold running water until the water runs clear, then cook in boiling, salted water for 3 minutes and drain.

Put 2 tablespoons oil in the casserole, spoon in a layer of rice, sprinkle with a little of the saffron water and cover with a layer of chicken. Repeat, ending with a layer of rice. Add any cooking juices left from the chicken, cover tightly and cook in the oven for 25-30 minutes. In a pan, heat the remaining oil and fry the sultanas and almonds until golden; remove. Fry the onions until crisp and golden. Sprinkle the biryani with the almonds, onions and sultanas.

Serves 4.

MUGHLAI CHICKEN

6 cloves garlic, peeled
85 g (3 oz) blanched almonds
2.5 cm (1 in) piece root ginger, peeled and chopped
6 tablespoons vegetable oil
1 kg (2¼ lb) chicken pieces
9 whole cardamom pods
1 stick cinamon
6 whole cloves
1 onion, finely chopped
2½ teaspoons ground cumin
1 teaspoon cayenne pepper
150 ml (5 fl oz/⅔ cup) natural yogurt
300 ml (10 fl oz/1¼ cups) double (thick) cream
1 tablespoon sultanas
1 firm, ripe banana
½ teaspoon each garam masala and salt

Put the garlic, almonds, ginger and 4 tablespoons water into a blender and blend to form a paste. Cube chicken. Heat the oil in a flameproof casserole or saucepan and fry the chicken on both sides until golden. Set aside. Put the cardamom, cinnamon and cloves into the pan and fry for a few seconds. Add the chopped onion and fry until beginning to turn golden brown. Add the paste from the blender together with the cumin and cayenne and fry for 2 minutes or until the mixture is lightly browned.

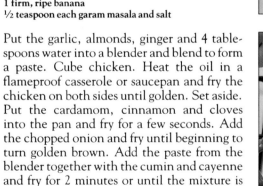

Still on the heat, add 1 tablespoon yogurt and cook for about 20 seconds, then add another tablespoon. Continue adding yogurt in this way until it has all been added. Put the chicken pieces and any juices into the pan with the salt and cream and gently bring to a simmer, stirring. Cover and leave to cook gently for about 20 minutes. Add the sultanas and banana and cook for a further 10 minutes or until the chicken is tender. Stir in the garam masala and salt.

Serves 4.

CACCIATORE

2 tablespoons olive oil
4 large chicken breasts, with bones
175 g (6 oz) red onion, thinly sliced
2 cloves garlic, thinly sliced
150 ml (5 fl oz/⅔ cup) red wine
150 ml (5 fl oz/⅔ cup) chicken stock
400 g (14 oz) can chopped tomatoes
3 teaspoons tomato purée (paste)
1 red pepper (capsicum), deseeded and sliced
1 yellow pepper (capsicum), deseeded and sliced
2 tablespoons chopped fresh basil
salt and pepper
pinch of sugar
pasta noodles, to serve

Preheat oven to 180C (350F/Gas 4). In a pan, heat the oil and fry the chicken breasts all over until golden brown, then transfer to a shallow casserole. Gently fry the onion and garlic in the pan without browning, add the wine, stock, tomatoes, tomato purée (paste), pepper (capsicum), 1 tablespoon of the basil, salt and pepper and the sugar and bring to the boil.

Pour over the chicken, cover and cook in the oven for 45 minutes. Serve on a bed of pasta noodles and sprinkle with the remaining basil and plenty of black pepper.

Serves 4.

CIDER APPLE CHICKEN

pared rind of 1 lemon plus 1 teaspoon juice
½ cinnamon stick
1 onion, quartered
1.5 kg (3¼-3½ lb) chicken
salt and pepper
85 g (3 oz/⅓ cup) butter
1 tablespoon oil
3 tablespoons brandy
450 g (1 lb) eating apples, peeled and cored
150 ml (5 fl oz/⅔ cup) cider
300 ml (10 fl oz/1¼ cups) crème fraîche
1 tablespoon each chopped fresh chives and parsley

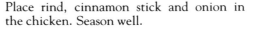

Place rind, cinnamon stick and onion in the chicken. Season well.

Preheat oven to 180C (350F/Gas 4). Heat 55 g (2 oz/¼ cup) butter and the oil in a flameproof casserole and brown the chicken on all sides. Pour over the brandy and ignite. Thinly slice one of the apples and add to the casserole once the flames have died down. Add the cider to the casserole, bring to the boil, cover and cook in the oven for 1¼ hours.

Melt the remaining butter in a pan, cut the remaining apples into thick slices and sauté until just cooked. Remove the chicken from the casserole and place on a warmed serving platter and surround with the sautéed apples. Add the crème fraîche and lemon juice to the casserole, stir well and boil to reduce slightly. Season well and pour over the chicken. Sprinkle with the chopped herbs and serve at once.

Serves 4-6.

CHICKEN & VEGETABLES

1 tablespoon oil
115 g (4 oz) smoked bacon, chopped
2 cloves garlic, peeled
12 shallots, peeled
1 stick celery, cut into 2.5 cm (1 in) lengths
2 small turnips, peeled and quartered
2 carrots, peeled and cut into matchstick strips
225 g (8 oz) button mushrooms
150 ml (5 fl oz/⅔ cup) dry white wine
150 ml (5 fl oz/⅔ cup) chicken stock
1.35 kg (3 lb) corn-fed chicken, without giblets
55 ml (2 fl oz/¼ cup) double (thick) cream
juice of ½ lemon
salt and pepper

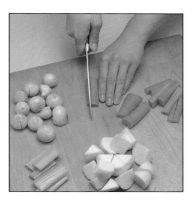

Preheat oven to 200C (400F/Gas 6). In a flameproof casserole, heat the oil, add the bacon, garlic and shallots and fry for 2-3 minutes. Add the remaining vegetables and fry for a further 2-3 minutes until the bacon is starting to turn golden brown. Pour the wine over the vegetables and boil rapidly to reduce the liquid by half. Add the chicken stock. Remove the casserole from the heat and add the chicken. Cover and cook in the oven for 45-55 minutes.

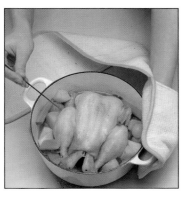

To check if the chicken is cooked, pierce the leg with a skewer: it is ready if the juices run clear; if not return to the oven for a further few minutes before testing again. When cooked, remove the chicken and vegetables to a serving dish. Cover and keep warm. Return the casserole to the heat, skim off any fat and boil vigorously to reduce to just over 150 ml (5 fl oz/⅔ cup). Add the cream and simmer for 2 minutes; add the lemon juice and salt and pepper. Serve hot with the chicken.

Serves 4.

CASSOULET

225 g (8 oz/1¼ cups) haricot beans, soaked overnight
700 ml (25 fl oz/3¼ cups) chicken stock
2 tablespoons olive oil
8 chicken thighs
115 g (4 oz) smoked rindless bacon, cut into strips
1 large onion, thinly sliced
2 cloves garlic, thinly sliced
150 ml (5 fl oz/⅔ cup) dry white wine
200 g (7 oz) can chopped tomatoes
2 tablespoons tomato purée (paste)
1 bouquet garni
salt and pepper
225 g (8 oz) chorizo sausage, cut into large chunks
25 g (1 oz/6 teaspoons) butter
55 g (2 oz/1 cup) fresh white breadcrumbs
2 tablespoons chopped fresh parsley

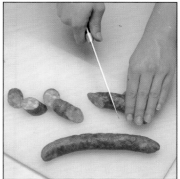

Drain the beans and put into a large pan with 550 ml (20 fl oz/2½ cups) of the stock and enough water to cover. Bring to the boil and simmer for 50 minutes. Preheat oven to 180C (350F/Gas 4). Heat 1 tablespoon oil and fry the chicken until golden, then remove from the pan and set aside. Fry the bacon until browned, then add the onion and garlic and continue cooking until softened. Drain the beans and return to the pan with the wine, remaining stock, tomatoes, tomato purée (paste), bouquet garni and seasonings. Bring to the boil, then stir in the bacon mixture.

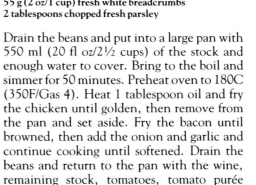

Transfer half the bean mixture to a flameproof casserole. Arrange the chicken and chorizo on top and cover with the remaining beans. Cover and bring to the boil, then transfer to the oven and cook for 1 hour. Melt the butter and remaining oil in a frying pan and fry the breadcrumbs until golden. Stir in the parsley. Uncover the casserole, sprinkle over the breadcrumbs and return to the oven. Cook for a further 15-20 minutes. Serve with bread and a salad.

Serves 4.

MOROCCAN CHICKEN

3 cloves garlic, crushed, or 1 tablespoon garlic paste
1 teaspoon each paprika and ground ginger
½ teaspoon ground cumin
4 tablespoons olive oil
4 skinned and boned chicken breasts
1 large onion, finely chopped
4 tablespoons chopped fresh parsley
pinch of saffron threads
150 ml (5 fl oz/⅔ cup) chicken stock
12 green olives
finely grated rind and juice of ½ lemon
salt and pepper

Mix the garlic, paprika, ginger and cumin with 3 tablespoons olive oil.

Place the chicken portions in a shallow dish and pour over the oil and spices and leave to marinate for 3-4 hours. Heat the remaining oil in a pan, add the onion and cook gently for 2-3 minutes. Add the chicken pieces and the marinade to the pan and brown the chicken slightly. Add the parsley, saffron and chicken stock; cover and simmer for 30 minutes or until the chicken is cooked.

Remove chicken from the pan and keep warm. Add the olives and lemon rind and juice and season with a little salt and pepper. Bring to the boil and boil rapidly until reduced to approximately 150 ml (5 fl oz/ ⅔ cup). Pour over the chicken and serve immediately.

Serves 4.

LENTIL-BAKED CHICKEN

225 g (8 oz/1¼ cups) green lentils
25 g (1 oz/6 teaspoons) butter
1 tablespoon olive oil
1.5 kg (3¼-3½ lb) chicken
175 g (6 oz) smoked streaky bacon
12 shallots, halved
4 cloves garlic, thickly sliced
150 ml (5 fl oz/⅔ cup) dry white wine
300 ml (10 fl oz/1¼ cups) chicken stock
1 bouquet garni
chopped fresh parsley, to garnish

Preheat oven to 200C (400F/Gas 6). Place the lentils in a pan of salted water, bring to the boil and simmer for 15 minutes.

In a flameproof casserole, heat the butter and oil and brown the chicken on all sides, then remove from the casserole and set aside. Cut the bacon into thick strips and add to the casserole with the shallots and garlic and cook for 2-3 minutes. Drain the lentils and stir into the bacon mixture, place the chicken on the bed of lentils, pour over the wine and stock and add the bouquet garni. Bring to the boil, cover and cook in the oven for 50 minutes.

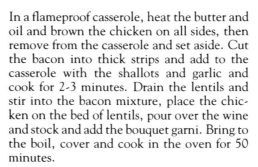

Remove the lid of the casserole, add a little water if the lentil mixture is looking too dry and return to the oven, uncovered, for a further 35-40 minutes until the juices of the chicken run clear when pierced. Remove the bouquet garni and garnish with chopped fresh parsley.

Serves 4-6.

FAMILY CHICKEN PIE

700 g (1½ lb) chicken pieces
1 large onion, thickly sliced
85 ml (3 fl oz/⅓ cup) dry white wine
200 ml (7 fl oz/¾ cup) chicken stock
1 bouquet garni and salt and pepper
25 g (1 oz/6 teaspoons) butter
175 g (6 oz) button mushrooms, halved
25 g (1 oz/¼ cup) plain flour
225 g (8 oz) can sweetcorn kernels
2 tablespoons chopped fresh parsley
1 teaspoon lemon juice
4 tablespoons double (thick) cream
1 kg (2 lb) potatoes
115 ml (4 fl oz/½ cup) hot milk
85 g (3 oz/¾ cup) grated Cheddar cheese
25 g (1 oz) salted potato crisps, crushed

Place the chicken, onion, wine, stock and bouquet garni in a large pan and bring to the boil. Reduce the heat and simmer for 25-30 minutes until the chicken is tender. Drain the liquid and reserve for the sauce. Discard the bouquet garni and remove skin and bones from the chicken; coarsely chop the flesh. Melt the butter in a pan and gently fry the mushrooms, then stir in the flour and cook for 1 minute. Add the reserved poaching liquor and onion.

Return to the heat and bring to the boil, stirring continuously. Stir in the chicken, sweetcorn, parsley, lemon juice and cream and season to taste with salt and pepper. Cook the potatoes and mash with the milk and 55 g (2 oz/½ cup) of the cheese and season to taste. Preheat grill. Spoon the chicken mixture into a flameproof dish and cover with creamed potato. Mix the crisps with the remaining cheese. Sprinkle over the potato crisps and grill until golden.

Serves 4.

CHICKEN & HAM PIE

25 g (1 oz/6 teaspoons) butter
225 g (8 oz) sweetcure ham, cut into 2.5 cm (1 in) cubes
350 g (12 oz) skinned and boned chicken, cut into 2.5 cm (1 in) cubes
1 onion, chopped
225 g (8 oz) leeks, trimmed and sliced
175 g (6 oz) button mushrooms, sliced
25 g (1 oz/¼ cup) plain flour
300 ml (10 fl oz/1¼ cups) chicken stock
150 ml (5 fl oz/⅔ cup) single (light) cream
finely grated rind of ½ lemon
salt and pepper
225 g (8 oz) shortcrust pastry
2 tablespoons grated Parmesan cheese
milk for glazing

Preheat oven to 200C (400F/Gas 6). In a pan, melt the butter, add the ham and chicken and cook for 2-3 minutes. Remove from the pan and reserve. Add the vegetables and cook for 2-3 minutes until starting to soften. Return the ham and chicken to the pan, stir in the flour and cook for 1-2 minutes until vegetables are starting to soften. Remove from the heat and gradually add the chicken stock and the cream. Return to the heat and, stirring, cook for 2 minutes until thickened. Add the lemon rind and season with salt and pepper.

Transfer the chicken and ham mixture to a 1 litre (35 fl oz/4½ cup) pie dish. Mix the pastry with the Parmesan, then roll out on a floured surface 2.5 cm (1 in) larger than the pie dish. Cut off a 2.5 cm (1 in) strip to fit the edge of the dish. Brush the edge with a little water, then cover with the pastry lid. Pinch the edges together to seal and brush the pie with milk to glaze. Bake in the oven for 25-30 minutes or until the pastry is golden brown.

Serves 4.

CHICKEN & MUSHROOM COBBLER

25 g (1 oz/6 teaspoons) butter
1 small onion, finely chopped
225 g (8 oz) button mushrooms, sliced
25 g (1 oz/¼ cup) plain flour
200 ml (7 fl oz/¾ cup) chicken stock
200 ml (7 fl oz/¾ cup) single (light) cream
450 g (1 lb) cooked chicken, diced
salt and pepper
2 tablespoons chopped fresh parsley
FOR THE SCONE DOUGH:
115 g (4 oz/1 cup) plain flour
55 g (2 oz/¼ cup) butter
25 g (1 oz/¼ cup) grated Cheddar cheese
3 tablespoons cold milk

Preheat oven to 190C (375F/Gas 5). In a large pan, heat the butter, add the onion and mushrooms and cook for 2-3 minutes until the vegetables start to soften. Sprinkle over the flour and cook for 1 minute. Gradually blend in the stock and the cream. Return the pan to the heat and cook for 2 minutes, stirring until the sauce thickens.

Add the chicken, season and add the parsley; mix well. Transfer to an ovenproof dish. Sift the flour into a bowl, rub in the butter finely, then stir in the cheese and mix with enough milk to form a soft, but not sticky, dough. On a floured surface, roll the dough out to a thickness of 2.5 cm (1 in) then, with a fluted cutter, cut out 12 rounds. Arrange these around the edge of the dish and brush with a little milk. Bake in the oven for 35-40 minutes until golden. Serve hot.

Serves 4.

CHICKEN & FETA PIE

225 g (8 oz) cooked minced chicken
350 g (12 oz) frozen spinach leaves, defrosted, well drained and chopped
175 g (6 oz) feta cheese
1 teaspoon finely grated lemon rind
2 teaspoons lemon juice
¼ teaspoon freshly grated nutmeg
freshly ground black pepper
6 sheets filo pastry
45 g (1½ oz/9 teaspoons) butter, melted

Preheat oven to 200C (400F/Gas 6). In a large bowl, mix together the chicken, spinach, feta, lemon rind and juice, nutmeg and pepper.

Brush one of the sheets of filo pastry with butter and press it gently into a 27.5 x 17.5 cm (11 x 7 in) non-stick tin, allowing the ends of the pastry to overlap the tin. Repeat with a second sheet of pastry, placed at a 90° angle; repeat with 2 more sheets of pastry, brushing with butter each time.

Spoon the spinach filling into the filo case and bring the overlapping pastry sides over the filling. Crumple the remaining pastry and arrange loosely on top of the pie. Brush lightly with any remaining butter and cook in the oven for 25-30 minutes until golden and crisp.

Serves 4-6.

CHICKEN PASTIES

350 g (12 oz/3 cups) plain flour
salt and pepper
85 g (3 oz/⅓ cup) butter
85 g (3 oz/⅓ cup) solid vegetable fat
1 tablespoon fresh chopped thyme
1 tablespoon vegetable oil
½ onion, chopped
55 g (2 oz) rindless streaky bacon, chopped
1 carrot, peeled and diced
1 large potato, peeled and diced
350 g (12 oz) chicken breast, minced
85 g (3 oz) mushrooms, chopped
½ tablespoon plain flour
150 ml (5 fl oz/⅔ cup) chicken stock
beaten egg or milk for brushing

Preheat oven to 190C (375F/Gas 5). Sift the flour and a pinch of salt into a bowl, add fats and rub in finely until mixture resembles breadcrumbs. Add the chopped thyme and 3 tablespoons iced water and mix together to form a dough. Wrap in cling film and refrigerate for 30 minutes. Heat the oil in a frying pan and add the onion, bacon, carrot and potato and fry for 2-3 minutes until the onion starts to soften. Add the chicken and mushrooms and fry for a further 3-4 minutes. Add the flour and cook for 1 minute.

Gradually add the stock, return to the heat and, stirring, cook for 2 minutes until the sauce thickens. Season and leave to cool. On a floured surface, roll out the pastry and cut out eight 15 cm (6 in) rounds. Place 2 tablespoons of the cold mixture in the centre of each round, brush the edges with a little beaten egg or milk and fold the pastry over to enclose the filling. Pinch the edges together to seal. Glaze with egg or milk and place on a baking sheet. Bake for 20-25 minutes until golden.

Serves 4.

STUFFED CHICKEN PARCELS

4 skinned and boned chicken breasts
115 g (4 oz) duck liver pâté
1 teaspoon finely grated orange rind
3 teaspoons orange juice
5 sprigs of thyme
salt and pepper
25 g (1 oz/6 teaspoons) butter
2 teaspoons olive oil
350 g (12 oz) ready-made puff pastry
1 large egg, beaten
1 teaspoon poppy seeds

Preheat the oven to 200C (400F/Gas 6). Cut a small incision in each chicken breast to make a pocket.

Mix together the pâté, orange rind and juice, 1 sprig of finely chopped thyme and seasoning. Transfer the mixture to a piping bag fitted with a plain nozzle and pipe a quarter of the mixture into each pocket and seal with a wooden cocktail stick. In a frying pan, heat the butter and oil and seal the chicken quickly on both sides until well browned. Remove from the heat, drain and cool, then chill. Thinly roll out the pastry and cut into long 4 cm (1½ in) wide strips. Discard the cocktail sticks from the chicken and top each breast with a sprig of thyme.

Brush the pastry strips with egg and wind the strips, egg-side in, around the breasts, overlapping very slightly to enclose the chicken completely. Place on a lightly dampened baking sheet, brush with remaining egg and sprinkle with poppy seeds. Make a small hole in the top of each one and bake in the oven for 35-40 minutes until golden. Serve with buttered new potatoes and an orange salad.

Serves 4.

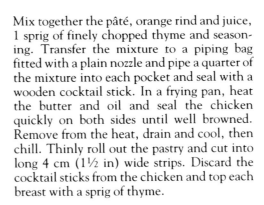

PUFF PASTRY ROLLS

1 tablespoon oil
2 shallots, finely chopped
1 clove garlic, crushed
115 g (4 oz) mushrooms, finely chopped
1 tablespoon chopped fresh sage
1 tablespoon chopped fresh thyme
225 g (8 oz) skinned and boned chicken
2 tablespoons Greek yogurt
2 tablespoons grated Parmesan cheese
salt and pepper
175 g (6 oz) ready-made puff pastry
1 egg, beaten

Preheat oven to 200C (400F/Gas 6). Heat the oil in a small pan, add the shallots, garlic and mushrooms and fry for 3-4 minutes until soft. Add the chopped herbs and put to one side to cool. Finely mince the chicken, transfer to a bowl and add the yogurt, 1 tablespoon Parmesan cheese, the shallot and mushroom mixture and season with a little salt and pepper; mix well. On a floured surface, roll out the puff pastry to a rectangle measuring about 30 x 40 cm (12 x 16 in) and cut into 4 strips lengthways.

Place spoonfuls of the mixture along the length of each strip. Brush the edges with a little beaten egg and fold the pastry over to enclose the filling. Pinch the edges of the pastry together to seal. Brush with a little more beaten egg and sprinkle with the remaining Parmesan cheese. Cut into 5 cm (2 in) lengths and make 2 slashes in each roll. Place on a greased baking sheet and bake in the oven for 15-20 minutes or until golden brown.

Serves 4.

CHICKEN & TOMATO PIE

225 g (8 oz/2 cups) plain flour
pinch of salt
55 g (2 oz/¼ cup) unsalted butter, chilled and cubed
55 g (2 oz/¼ cup) white vegetable fat, chilled and cubed
2 tablespoons iced water
450 g (1 lb) cooked chicken, skinned and boned
6 tomatoes, sliced
300 ml (10 fl oz/1¼ cups) thick sour cream
3 tablespoons pesto sauce
salt and pepper
beaten egg or milk for glazing

Preheat oven to 190C (375F/Gas 5). To make the pastry, sift the flour and salt into a bowl, add the butter and vegetable fat and rub in finely until the mixture resembles breadcrumbs. Add the water and mix together with a knife until the dough forms a ball. Wrap in cling film and refrigerate for 30 minutes. Cut the chicken into slices and layer with the tomatoes in a 20 cm (8 in) dish, filling almost to the top. Mix together the thick sour cream and pesto, season with a little salt and pepper and pour over the chicken and tomatoes.

Roll out the pastry and, using the pie dish as a guide, cut out a piece slightly larger than the dish. Roll out the trimmings, and cut a strip to place on the rim of the pie dish, then brush with a little water. Place the pastry lid on top. Pinch the edges together to seal and brush the surface of pie with a little beaten egg or milk to glaze. Cook in the oven for 25-30 minutes or until the pastry is golden and crisp. This pie is delicious eaten cold.

Serves 4.

ROQUEFORT VERONIQUE

25 g (1 oz/6 teaspoons) butter
1 tablespoon oil
4 skinned and boned chicken breasts
1 leek, trimmed and chopped
2 teaspoons plain flour
175 ml (6 fl oz/¾ cup) milk
70 g (2½ oz) Roquefort cheese
85 ml (3 fl oz/⅓ cup) single (light) cream
150 g (5 oz) seedless green grapes, skinned
chopped fresh parsley, to garnish

In a frying pan, heat the butter and oil and cook the chicken on all sides until golden.

Reduce the heat, stir in the chopped leek, cover and continue cooking for 30 minutes until the juices of the chicken run clear when pierced. Remove the chicken from the pan and set aside on a warmed serving plate.

Sprinkle the flour into the pan and cook for 1 minute, remove from the heat and gradually add the milk. Return to the heat and stirring bring to the boil and cook for 2 minutes until thickened. Add the cheese, cream and grapes and cook for a further 5 minutes, stirring all the time. Pour over the chicken and garnish with chopped fresh parsley.

Serves 4.

CHICKEN STROGANOFF

450 g (1 lb) skinned and boned chicken breasts
55 g (2 oz/¼ cup) butter
1 tablespoon olive oil
2 onions, thinly sliced
175 g (6 oz) button mushrooms, sliced
2 teaspoons Dijon mustard
55 g (2 oz) gherkins, sliced
200 ml (7 fl oz/¾ cup) thick sour cream
salt and pepper
noodles or rice, to serve
chopped fresh parsley and paprika, to garnish

Place the chicken between 2 sheets of cling film. Use a rolling pin to flatten. Slice into 1 x 4 cm (½ x 1½ in) strips.

In a frying pan, heat the half the butter and oil and cook the onions until softened. Add the mushrooms and cook for a further 5 minutes Remove from the pan and set aside.

Heat the remaining butter and oil in the pan and fry the chicken over a high heat, turning frequently, for 6-8 minutes until cooked. Return the onions and mushrooms to the pan, stir in the mustard, gherkins, cream and seasonings and heat through gently for 3-4 minutes. Serve on a bed of noodles or rice and garnish with chopped parsley and paprika.

Serves 4.

CHICKEN MOUSSELINE

FOR THE MOUSSE:
85 g (3 oz) watercress leaves
85 g (3 oz) chicken breast
salt and pepper
150 ml (5 fl oz/⅔ cup) double (thick) cream
8 chicken thighs, skinned and boned
FOR THE SAUCE:
1 tablespoon vegetable oil
1 shallot, finely chopped
150 ml (5 fl oz/⅔ cup) dry white wine
150 ml (5 fl oz/⅔ cup) chicken stock
55 ml (2 fl oz/¼ cup) double (thick) cream
1 teaspoon chopped fresh tarragon or basil
1 teaspoon lemon juice

Preheat the oven to 190C (375F/Gas 5). Lay the chicken thighs on a board, season the insides with salt and pepper and add spoonfuls of the mousse. Roll the flesh around the mousse to enclose it and wrap each thigh in a square of oiled kitchen foil, sealing each one well. Place on a baking sheet and cook in the oven for 20-35 minutes or until the chicken is cooked and the mousse is firm.

To make the mousse, blanch the watercress in boiling, salted water for 15 seconds, drain and refresh under cold water. Drain again and squeeze as dry as possible.

Meanwhile, make the sauce. In a saucepan, heat the oil and gently fry the shallot until softened. Increase the heat, add the wine and boil rapidly until the quantity is reduced by half. Add the chicken stock and continue to boil to reduce the liquid until just under 150 ml (5 fl oz/⅔ cup) of stock remains.

Put the watercress into a food processor, add the chicken breast and season with a little salt and pepper. Process the mixture until very smooth. Gradually pour in the double cream while the processor is still running, taking care not to over-beat the mousse or the cream will separate and spoil the texture.

With the stock at boiling point, add the cream and simmer for 3-4 minutes, stirring all the time, until the sauce starts to thicken. Add the tarragon and lemon juice and season with salt and pepper. Remove the chicken thighs from the foil and spoon over the sauce.

Serves 4.

SMOKED CHICKEN KEDGEREE

25 g (1 oz/6 teaspoons) butter
1 teaspoon coriander seeds, crushed
1 onion, sliced
1 teaspoon ground coriander
2 teaspoons ground cumin
85 g (3 oz/½ cup) long-grain rice
85 g (3 oz/½ cup) red lentils
550 ml (20 fl oz/2½ cups) chicken stock
350 g (12 oz) smoked chicken, coarsely chopped
juice of ½ lemon
115 ml (4 fl oz/½ cup) natural Greek yogurt
2 tablespoons chopped fresh parsley
2 hard-boiled eggs, coarsely chopped
1 lemon, sliced, to garnish
mango chutney and poppadoms, to serve

In a large pan, melt the butter, add the crushed coriander seeds and the onion and cook over a gentle heat until slightly softened, then stir in the ground coriander, cumin, rice and lentils and coat well with the butter. Pour in the stock, bring to the boil, then cover and simmer for 10 minutes.

Remove the lid, add the chicken and continue cooking for a further 10 minutes until all the liquid has been absorbed and the rice and lentils are tender. Stir in the lemon juice, yogurt, parsley and chopped hard-boiled eggs, and heat through gently. Spoon into a warmed serving dish and garnish with lemon. Serve with mango chutney and poppadoms.

Serves 4.

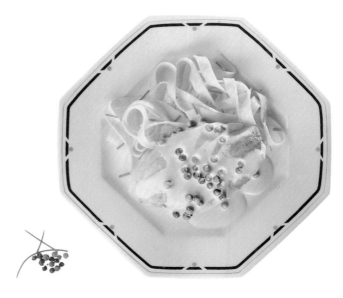

POULET AU POIVRE

25 g (1 oz/6 teaspoons) butter
1 tablespoon olive oil
4 skinned and boned chicken breasts
3 tablespoons brandy
250 ml (9 fl oz/1 cup) double (thick) cream
3 teaspoons pickled green peppercorns
3 teaspoons pickled pink peppercorns
pinch of sugar
salt

In a large frying pan, heat the butter and oil and fry the chicken breasts over a high heat to seal them all over.

Reduce the heat, cover and continue cooking for a further 25 minutes, turning regularly. Remove the chicken from the pan and set aside on a hot serving dish. Pour the brandy into the pan and ignite it using a lighted taper.

When the flames have died down, stir in the cream, peppercorns, sugar and salt, bring to the boil and simmer for 2-3 minutes. Pour over the chicken and serve at once.

Serves 4.

-CHICKEN WITH CHEESE SAUCE-

PAELLA

3 tablespoons vegetable oil
1 small onion, finely chopped
350 g (12 oz) chicken breast, sliced
150 g (5 oz) chestnut mushrooms
20 g (¾ oz/9 teaspoons) plain flour
150 ml (5 fl oz/⅔ cup) dry white wine
150 ml (5 fl oz/⅔ cup) chicken stock or water
2 x 78 g (2¼ oz) Boursin cheeses with herbs and garlic
2 tablespoons chopped fresh parsley
salt and pepper
450 g (1 lb) fresh pasta

25 g (1 oz/6 teaspoons) butter
1 tablespoon oil
4 chicken drumsticks or thighs
1 large onion, sliced
2 cloves garlic, crushed
1 red pepper (capsicum), deseeded and sliced
1 green pepper (capsicum), deseeded and sliced
175 g (6 oz/1¼ cups) long-grain rice
2 teaspoons paprika
550 ml (20 fl oz/2½ cups) chicken stock
pinch of saffron strands
175 g (6 oz) peeled prawns
175 g (6 oz) mussels, cleaned
85 g (3 oz) frozen peas
salt and pepper
chopped fresh parsley and lime wedges, to garnish

Heat 2 tablespoons oil and cook the onion until soft. Add the chicken and fry for 2 minutes. Add the mushrooms.

In a paella pan, heat the butter and oil and fry the chicken until golden, then remove from the pan and set aside. Add the onion, garlic and peppers (capsicums) and cook until slightly softened, then stir in the rice and the paprika. Bring the stock to the boil in another pan, add the saffron and pour onto the rice mixture, return the chicken to the pan and simmer gently for 15-20 minutes.

Fry for a further 2 minutes or until the chicken is cooked. Sprinkle over the flour and stir until all the fat is absorbed. Remove from the heat and slowly add the white wine and stock or water. Return the pan to the heat and bring to the boil, stirring, then reduce the heat and cook for 2 minutes, stirring until the sauce thickens.

Cut the cheese into cubes and add to the sauce, stirring until it has melted. Add the chopped parsley and season with a little salt and pepper. Cook the pasta in plenty of boiling salted water to which you have added the remaining tablespoon of oil (this prevents the pasta sticking together as it cooks) until just tender (*al dente*). Drain the pasta well and serve with the chicken sauce.

Serves 4.

Add the prawns, mussels and peas and cook gently for a further 10 minutes or until all the liquid has been absorbed. Discard any mussels which remain closed. Season with plenty of salt and pepper and garnish with chopped parsley and wedges of lime.

Serves 4.

MUSHROOM RISOTTO

55 g (2 oz/¼ cup) butter
1 onion, finely chopped
225 g (8 oz) raw chicken meat, sliced into strips
55 g (2 oz) Parma ham, cut into strips
225 g (8 oz) mixed mushrooms, sliced
3 sprigs of rosemary
300 g (10 oz/2 cups) risotto rice
150 ml (5 fl oz/⅔ cup) white wine
850 ml (30 fl oz/3¾ cups) chicken stock
150 g (5 oz/1¼ cups) grated Mozzarella cheese
55 g (2 oz/½ cup) grated Parmesan cheese
salt and pepper

In a large pan, melt the butter and gently fry the onion until softened. Add the chicken and fry to seal quickly on all sides, then stir in the ham, mushrooms, rosemary and rice and cook until the rice is transparent.

Add the wine and cook, stirring continuously, until it has been absorbed. Pour in the stock, about 150 ml (5 fl oz/⅔ cup) at a time, stirring until it is absorbed. Continue adding the stock in this way until all the stock has been used up and the rice is creamy. Stir in the Mozzarella and continue cooking for a further 5 minutes. Serve at once, sprinkled with grated Parmesan and black pepper.

Serves 4.

STUFFED BRIOCHES

25 g (1 oz/6 teaspoons) butter
1 clove garlic, crushed
6 spring onions, coarsely chopped
1 teaspoon pickled green peppercorns, drained
85 g (3 oz) baby button mushrooms, sliced
4 teaspoons dry vermouth
150 ml (5 fl oz/⅔ cup) thick sour cream
115 g (4 oz) cooked chicken, sliced
1 small red pepper (capsicum), deseeded, skinned and sliced
salt and cayenne pepper
1 tablespoon chopped fresh chervil
6 individual brioches, tops removed and filling scooped out

Preheat oven to 180C (350F/Gas 4). In a frying pan, melt the butter and gently sauté the garlic, onions, peppercorns and mushrooms until slightly softened. Stir in the vermouth and allow to boil, then add the thick sour cream and simmer until reduced and thickened. Stir in the chicken and pepper (capsicum) and cook for a further 5 minutes. Season with salt and cayenne pepper and stir in the chervil.

Spoon the chicken filling into the brioches, replace the tops, place on a baking sheet and cover with foil. Bake in the oven for 10 minutes. Serve warm, garnished with sprigs of chervil.

Serves 6.

CHICKEN ITALIENNE

4 boned and skinned chicken breasts
8 slices Parma ham
bunch of fresh sage
175 g (6 oz) dolcelatte cheese, cut into 4 slices
freshly ground black pepper
2 tablespoon olive oil

Cut each chicken breast in half and flatten slightly by beating between 2 sheets of grease-proof paper with a rolling pin.

Lay the slices of Parma ham on a board. Put a piece of chicken in the middle of each slice and place 2 or 3 fresh sage leaves on the chicken and top with a slice of dolcelatte. Season with pepper. Wrap the Parma ham around the chicken to form a parcel.

Heat the oil in a frying pan, add the chicken and fry for 3-4 minutes on each side until the chicken is cooked and the cheese has melted.

Serves 4.

CHICKEN PROVENÇALE

25 g (1 oz/6 teaspoons) butter
1 tablespoon oil
6 cloves garlic, unpeeled
4 chicken joints, cut in half
115 ml (4 fl oz/½ cup) medium sherry
400 g (14 oz) can chopped tomatoes
2 tablespoons tomato purée (paste)
2 tablespoons chopped fresh herbs
salt and pepper

In a large pan, heat the butter and oil, add the garlic and the chicken, skin-sides down, and cook for 15 minutes on one side until the chicken is half cooked.

Add the sherry to the pan and boil rapidly until reduced by half. Turn the chicken pieces over and continue to boil until the sherry is reduced to a syrup.

Add the tomatoes and tomato purée (paste) and continue cooking for a further 15 minutes until the chicken is tender and the sauce has reduced to a glaze. Add the chopped herbs and season with a little salt and pepper. Serve with saffron rice and French beans.

Serves 4.

CHICKEN FRICASSÉE

4 boned and skinned chicken breasts
15 g (½ oz/3 teaspoons) butter
½ tablespoon oil
12 small shallots, halved
175 g (6 oz) shiitake mushrooms, sliced
1 tablespoon plain flour
55 ml (2 fl oz/¼ cup) dry white wine
150 ml (5 fl oz/⅔ cup) chicken stock
150 ml (5 fl oz/⅔ cup) double (thick) cream
1 tablespoon chopped fresh chervil or parsley
juice of ½ lemon
salt and pepper

Cut each chicken breast into 4 pieces. In a pan, heat the butter and oil, add the chicken and fry over a high heat until golden.

Remove from the pan and put to one side. Add the shallots to the pan and fry for 3-4 minutes until starting to turn golden. Add the mushrooms and cook for a further 2 minutes. Sprinkle over the flour and cook for 1 minute. Gradually add the white wine and chicken stock. Bring to the boil, stirring, and cook for 2 minutes until the sauce thickens slightly.

Return the chicken and any juices to the pan. Add the cream and simmer for 10-12 minutes until the chicken is tender. Add the chervil or parsley, lemon juice and salt and pepper. Serve hot.

Serves 4.

SPINACH & RICOTTA CHICKEN

1 shallot, chopped
2 tablespoons olive oil
1 teaspoon fennel seeds
55 g (2 oz) ricotta cheese
25 g (1 oz) pine nuts, toasted and chopped
115 g (4 oz) finely chopped, cooked spinach
4 chicken breasts
salt and pepper
8 rashers bacon, rinds removed
1 clove garlic, crushed
400 g (14 oz) can chopped tomatoes
2 teaspoons tomato purée (paste)
2 teaspoons sugar
2 tablespoons chopped fresh basil

In a small pan, gently fry the shallot in 1 tablespoon oil until transparent. Add the fennel seeds and cook for 30 seconds. Remove from the heat. Mix the shallot and fennel seeds with the ricotta and pine nuts. Drain the spinach well and add to the mixture; reserve. Lay the chicken breasts on a board and slice each one through the centre leaving one edge uncut so that each breast can be opened like a book. Season with salt and pepper. Spread 2 tablespoons of the spinach mixture over each breast, then roll up.

Wrap 2 rashers of bacon around each chicken breast and secure with cocktail sticks. Place in a small greased ovenproof dish and cook for 15-20 minutes. Grill for 2-3 minutes to crisp the bacon. Meanwhile, add remaining oil to a pan and cook the garlic for 30 seconds. Add the tomatoes, tomato purée (paste), sugar, and salt and pepper and simmer for 15 minutes until thicker. Adjust the seasoning and add the basil. Spoon over the chicken.

Serves 4.

TARRAGON CHICKEN

25 g (1 oz/6 teaspoons) butter
1 tablespoon oil
4 large, corn-fed chicken breasts, skinned
2 large leeks
2 tablespoons tarragon vinegar
150 ml (5 fl oz/⅔ cup) dry white wine
225 ml (8 fl oz/1 cup) chicken stock
1 large carrot, peeled
150 ml (5 fl oz/⅔ cup) crème fraîche
1 teaspoon cornflour
1 teaspoon Dijon and tarragon mustard
2 teaspoons chopped fresh tarragon
salt and pepper
tarragon sprigs, to garnish

In a frying pan, heat the butter and oil and fry the chicken until golden on both sides, remove from the pan and allow to drain on absorbent kitchen paper. Coarsely chop one leek and fry gently until slightly softened, add the vinegar and boil rapidly until the quantity is reduced by half. Pour in the wine and stock and return the chicken to the pan, then cover and simmer for 25 minutes. Cut the remaining leek and the carrot into matchstick strips and cook for 4-5 minutes in separate pans of boiling, salted water; drain and refresh under cold water, then drain again.

Remove the chicken from the pan and arrange on a warmed serving dish. Strain the cooking liquor into a clean pan and bring to the boil. In a bowl, whisk together the crème fraîche, cornflour, mustard and 2 tablespoons of the pan juices. Return the mixture to the pan and add the carrots, leeks and tarragon. Heat gently until the sauce thickens and season to taste. Spoon over the chicken breasts and garnish with sprigs of tarragon.

Serves 4.

CHICKEN WITH YOGURT

150 ml (5 fl oz/⅔ cup) dry white wine
2 teaspoons English mustard
3 tablespoons chopped fresh tarragon
4 skinned and boned chicken breasts, cut into strips
1 tablespoon oil
1 tablespoon cornflour
3 tablespoons brandy
150 ml (5 fl oz/⅔ cup) Greek yogurt
salt and pepper

In a bowl, mix the white wine with the mustard and tarragon. Add the chicken, mix well, cover and refrigerate for 3-4 hours. Drain and reserve the marinade.

Heat the oil in a pan and cook the chicken quickly without browning. Mix the cornflour to a paste with a little water and add to the pan with the brandy and the reserved marinade.

Cook over a medium heat for 12-15 minutes until the chicken is cooked through. Add the yogurt, heat through and season with a little salt and pepper. Serve hot.

Serves 4.

MARSALA LIVERS

450 g (1 lb) chicken livers, cores removed
1 tablespoon well-seasoned plain flour
25 g (1 oz/6 teaspoons) butter
2 teaspoons olive oil
1 red onion, thinly sliced
115 g (4 oz) button mushrooms, sliced
55 g (2 oz) Parma ham, cut into thin slices
2 teaspoons fresh thyme leaves, plus sprigs to garnish
85 ml (3 fl oz/⅓ cup) Marsala
225 ml (8 fl oz/1 cup) chicken stock
1-2 teaspoons Worcestershire sauce
2 teaspoons tomato purée (paste)
salt and pepper
tagliatelle, to serve
150 ml (5 fl oz/⅔ cup) thick sour cream
cayenne pepper

Toss the chicken livers in the flour. In a pan, heat the butter and oil and gently fry the onion until softened. Remove from the pan and set aside. Increase the heat and fry the floured livers until well browned, then reduce the heat, return the onions to the pan and add any remaining flour, the mushrooms, Parma ham and thyme and stir well.

Pour in the Marsala and stock and bring to the boil, stirring continuously. Stir in the Worcestershire sauce and tomato purée (paste) and season to taste. Cook the tagliatelle, drain and arrange on a warmed serving plate, top with the livers and spoon over the thick sour cream. Sprinkle with a little cayenne pepper and garnish with sprigs of thyme.

Serves 4.

CHICKEN WITH CRAB

4 skinned and boned chicken breasts
175 g (6 oz) white and brown crabmeat
2 spring onions, finely chopped
1 teaspoon tomato purée (paste)
salt and pepper
15 g (½ oz/3 teaspoons) butter
1 shallot, finely chopped
4 tablespoons brandy
1 tablespoon plain flour
2 tablespoons dry white wine
115 ml (4 fl oz/½ cup) chicken stock
175 g (6 oz) cooked peeled prawns
4 tablespoons crème fraîche
1-2 tablespoons lemon juice
1 tablespoon chopped fresh dill

Preheat oven to 200C (400F/Gas 6). Lay the chicken breasts between 2 sheets of greaseproof paper and beat out with a rolling pin to about 0.5 cm (¼ in) thick. Mix the crabmeat with the spring onions and tomato purée (paste) and seasoning. Place 2-3 tablespoons of the crab mixture along the length of each breast and roll up to enclose the filling. Cut squares of foil larger than each chicken breast. Brush with oil and roll tightly around each breast, twisting the ends to seal. Place in an ovenproof dish and bake for 12-15 minutes until cooked.

Melt the butter in a small pan and fry the shallot for 2 minutes. Add the brandy and boil rapidly to reduce the liquid by half. Stir in the flour, then gradually add the wine and stock and bring to the boil, stirring until the sauce has thickened. Add the prawns and crème fraîche and simmer for 2 minutes. Add the lemon juice, dill and seasoning. Remove the chicken from the foil, adding any juices to the sauce. Slice the chicken breasts, fan out and spoon over the sauce.

Serves 4.

INDEX

Picture this: the artist as illustrator

the artist

Edited by Sylvia Backemeyer

Central Saint Martins College of Art & Design

Picture this:
as illustrator

with essays by Martin Baker, Andrew Hall, Marie McLoughlin, Paul W Nash, Alan Powers, Paul Rennie, Roger Sabin & David Wootton

in association with The Herbert Press

First published in Great Britain 2005

The Herbert Press
an imprint of A&C Black Publishers
37 Soho Sqaure
London W1D 3QZ

www.acblack.com

ISBN-10: 0-7136-7160-2

ISBN-13: 978-0-7136-7160-5

Design by Phil Baines & Catherine Dixon

Printed and bound in China by C & C Offset Printing Co. Ltd.

1/ Sylvia Backemeyer
Introduction:
a century of creativity

Sylvia Backemeyer is Head of
the Central Saint Martins Museum
Collection and is responsible for the
research project, which has resulted in
this publication and an exhibition. She
has written a number of publications
based on the collection including *Making
their Mark: art, craft and design at the
Central School 1896–1966* (Herbert Press,
2000).

This book of essays is a celebration of illustration in all its manifestations as taught at Central Saint Martins in the last hundred years. Many people, including many illustrators, feel that as an art form it does not receive the attention it deserves. The purpose of this book is to address this by highlighting the contribution made by one of this country's most influential art schools. As part of my research for the book I have been privileged to interview a number of alumni from both founding colleges and this introduction focuses to a large extent on their memories of the people who taught them and the significance of that teaching.

Early history

Looking at prospectuses from the two colleges for the same year in the mid 1960s it is interesting to note the different way in which the illustration course is described. St Martin's has a separate course on illustration 'designed to assist those students who wish to produce subjects of a story-telling or illustrative nature, either in black and white or colour'. The Central School still has illustration firmly imbedded in the School of Book Production: 'Illustrations are made as an integral part of the printed page'. In both Schools at that time illustration was something in which you could choose to specialise in your third year, having previously studied a range of related subjects: calligraphy, life drawing, typography, advertisement design, and a range of techniques for drawing and printmaking.

At the Central School, Noel Rooke initiated black and white book illustration as part of the Book Production Course in 1905. The initial medium used was wood engraving and in the following 30 years most British wood engravers had been taught by him or come under his influence indirectly. Although most of them went on to produce single prints and commercial art work of different types, the origin of their wood engraving technique was for books: Clare Leighton, John Farleigh, Ray Marshall (later Garnett), Lynton Lamb and Margaret Pilkington all learnt their technique from Rooke. One of his earliest and most

1 John O'Connor, Wood engraving for Dorothy Rutter, ed., *We happy few: an anthology by O. Rutter*, Golden Cockerel Press, 1946.
Courtesy Reading University.

distinguished pupils, Robert Gibbings, founded the Society of Wood Engravers. Other Rooke students worked for or founded private presses.[1] Wood engraving continued to be taught at the Central School until 1966, John Farleigh having taken over from Rooke in 1937 and Gertrude Hermes from Farleigh in 1947. Hermes also briefly taught wood engraving at St Martin's in the late 1930s. At St Martin's probably the most distinguished teacher of wood engraving was Clifford Webb (1945–65). He was followed by John O'Connor who taught the subject for a further ten years.[1]

At this time all art schools employed practising artists and designers for one or two days a week while they worked as freelance artists the rest of the time. The students were in constant contact with working artists many of whom were among the most distinguished practitioners in their field. They mostly worked across the board, doing commercial work for magazines such as *Lilliput* and *Radio Times*, posters for London Transport and the GPO, publicity for companies, designs for postage stamps, and illustrations for books. There are too many artists to cover in detail but those teaching at the Central School and St Martin's who have influenced illustrators up to the present

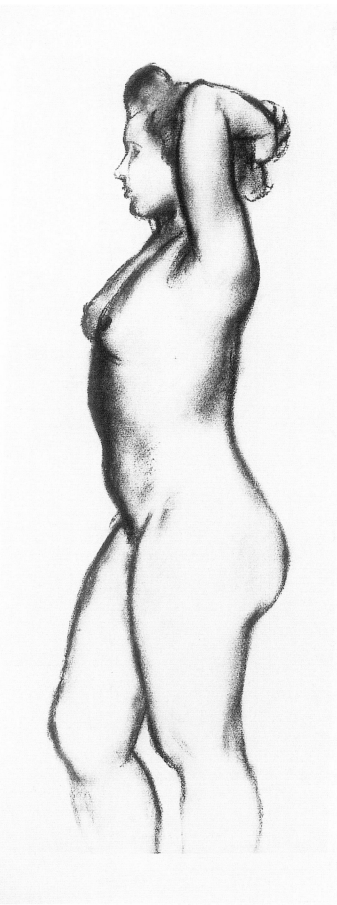

2 Lynton Lamb, Drawing for Lydia Avilov, *Chekhov in my life*, John Lehman, 1950.
Central Saint Martins Museum Collection.

3 Bernard Meninsky, Standing female nude, charcoal, 1926–28, in John Russell Taylor, *Bernard Meninsky*, Redcliffe Press, 1990.
Central Saint Martins Museum Collection.

day include Bernard Cheese, Anthony Gross, Gertrude Hermes, Paul Hogarth, Walter Hoyle, Clarke Hutton, Harold Jones, Lynton Lamb [2], John Minton, Mervyn Peake, Keith Vaughan, Clifford Webb and Fritz Wegner.

Fashion illustrators worked in a similar way teaching part-time and freelancing for magazines and newspapers. They are covered in a separate chapter, as is the work done in specific areas such as commercial art, book illustration, book jackets, and comics and cartoons.

It is important to remember that before 1970 very few illustrators were able to specialise, especially early in their careers. Names will often occur in more than one chapter with an artist working for example for the *Radio Times* and London Transport as well as illustrating books. When they did eventually specialise, most of them chose book illustration, usually children's book illustration, and they often wrote the books as well.

Teachers

For the purposes of this book I have chosen a few tutors who seem to have had the greatest significance for their students as illustrators, and tried to capture a sense of why that was. Susan Einzig speaking of the period 1939 to 1942

4 Morris Kestelman, 'The bareback rider', colour lithograph. Commissioned by Noel Carrington in 1937 for *The circus in England* which was never published due to the outbreak of war. Central Saint Martins Museum Collection. Copyright courtesy of Boundary Gallery.

mentions the wonderful atmosphere in what was the 'most famous craft-orientated school in London'. The sense of being taught by the greatest experts in their field made a life-long impression on her.[2]

Bernard Meninsky, an extremely talented artist and member of the London Group, taught life drawing, a discipline all students had to acquire at that time, and an invaluable skill for illustrators.[3] He had a profound effect on his students. Judith Kerr remembers him as a 'dazzling draughtsman'. Margaret Levetus writes:

> Bernard Meninsky always had something to say and was always encouraging, leaving you with something definite to aim for and the conviction you would eventually achieve it.[3]

Morris Kestelman knew Meninsky both as a student and fellow teacher.[4]

> As a teacher he made a great impression on many students for he was gifted with brilliant powers of demonstration accompanied by lucid exposition of what he was about. What held me was the intensity of his concentration in the act of drawing. It was a fascinating exercise to watch, and it related to you as a student. He talked very well, constructively and clearly, and would establish a strong personal relationship, watching your reaction.[4]

Leonard Rosoman has possibly the most vivid memories of Meninsky who taught him life drawing from 1938 to 1939.[5] For Rosoman, Meninsky was

> probably the greatest influence on me ever. After about three weeks studying in his class I remember him sitting down beside me and saying 'I've been looking at your work and I want to talk about it'. He had waited for some time as he had wanted to see how my drawing developed without interrupting the flow, in order to make a particular point. He said my work was full of promise but it was a little bit tight and controlled. He thought I needed to break it down a little bit, becoming more receptive and responsive to the model we were drawing. This approach was most unusual at the time and also very interesting. It made a great impression on me and was the beginning of an involved and interesting friendship. I got to know him and his family very well, going to his home for meals and discussing things in great depth. I was aware at the time that the treatment I was getting was most unusual, quite unlike any criticism and discussion I had ever had before and it made a considerable impact on me and my work.[5]

Meninsky taught life drawing and painting from 1913 to 1950 when he tragically committed suicide. Students taught by Meninsky include Lynton Lamb, Morris Kestelman, Clarke Hutton and John Farleigh, all of whom went on to teach.

5 Leonard Rosoman, Frontispiece for Thomas Mann, *The magic mountain*, Folio Society, 2000. Private collection.

TULIP

Habit de Noce, feathered   Habit de Noce, flamed   Adonis

John Farleigh was an early student of Noel Rooke and used wood engraving to illustrate many books. He went on to teach book illustration at the Central School and was an inspired tutor and a great practical support to his students. Peggy Fortnum, first illustrator of Paddington Bear, remembers him undertaking to find her a first job, a book jacket or book to illustrate, to tide her over those worrying first weeks after leaving college.[6]

As an all-round freelance illustrator working across many fields Farleigh shared his own working experience on a day-to-day basis with his students; he would often use the School presses to print his own work. It must have been fascinating for students to watch him work on the illustrations for Bernard Shaw's *The adventures of the black girl in her search for God* or Sitwell's *Old fashioned flowers*.[7] This latter book, published by Country Life in 1939, was one of the most ambitious experiments in autolithography, breaking new ground in print quality. Students remember Farleigh drawing his flower pictures directly on to the stone in the studios.

His close links with the publishing world – he was an editor at the Sylvan Press – gave many students a start. It

6 Peggy Fortnum, 'Paddington Bear', From the Paddington Bear books by Michael Bond, illustrated by Peggy Fortnum. Paddington & Company, c.2005.

7 John Farleigh, 'Tulips', auto lithograph for Sir Sacheverell Sitwell, *Old fashioned flowers*, Country Life, 1939. Central Saint Martins Museum Collection.

was through John Farleigh that Noel Carrington came to the Central School. Carrington had worked with Farleigh while he was an editor for Country Life as well as meeting him regularly in professional contexts such as the Double Crown Club dinners. Other Central staff and Farleigh's recent students were delighted to work on some of the early Puffin Picture Books. Students and staff involved in Puffins include S.R. Badmin, Clarke Hutton, Pearl Binder, Kathleen Hale, Phyllis Ginger and James Holland. Farleigh's autobiographical textbook *Graven image*,[6] as well as going into some detail on subjects such as 'illustrating a book' uses both his own work and work by his students to illustrate the points he is making.

Clifford Webb was also a wood engraver, but not in the Noel Rooke tradition. He taught wood engraving at St Martin's from 1945 to 1965, not as part of book production but as one of the options available to students on the print-making course, although Webb himself is probably best known for the eight books he illustrated for the Golden Cockerel Press.[9] Many of his students would have also used it for book illustration, including Simon Brett who was taught by Webb in the early 1960s.[7] [10] Reminiscing on Webb as a teacher Brett recalls the group of eight to ten students working away in the basement of St Martin's; boxwood was provided free in those days.

> Clifford Webb taught engraving in a faded blue smock, which he climbed into and fastened at the neck. It made him look like one of Courbet's peasants, but was just part of his impeccable but unfussy craftsmanship.[8] Webb's engravings are marked by a feeling for the surface of the block … Rediscovery of the surface was an important part of being modern, and in Britain, the re-establishment of engraving as a medium for artists. Webb's avoidance of 'minuteness' in engraving and espousal of a conscious grandeur in the disposal of tonal variety is perhaps the core of his artistic personality. He warned students against the exquisite and nudged their attention away from the imitative and back to more basic principles, the responsibility that is, to design fully, the responsibility to the decorative impact of the surface as a whole. I think I never heard him mention Bewick.[9]

Webb also taught zoological drawing, taking groups of students to London Zoo, a common practice in art schools at that time. He enjoyed drawing animals himself and produced a number of books for children in pen and ink and pen and wash.[8] John O'Connor took over wood engraving from Webb in 1965.

Gertrude Hermes taught wood engraving at the Central School at the same time as Webb was teaching at St

8 Clifford Webb, from *The friendly place*, written and illustrated by Clifford Webb, Frederick Warne, 1962. Private collection.

9 Clifford Webb, 'Boy with serpent', wood engraving for Eurof Walters, *The serpent's presence*, Golden Cockerel Press, 1954. Courtesy Reading University.

10 Simon Brett, 'Brother Cockerel', wood engraving for Brendan O'Malley, *The animals of Saint Gregory*, Paulinus Press 1981. Winner of the Francis Williams Illustration Award, 1981. Central Saint Martins Museum Collection.

Martin's.[11] She was one of the teachers William Johnstone brought with him from Camberwell when he was made Principal of the Central School in 1947. She not only taught wood engraving but also life and zoological drawing at St Martin's. She is however most remembered for her evening classes in wood engraving. She almost certainly modelled her teaching on her experiences at the Leon Underwood School of Art where 'the students were treated as artists from the beginning and it was up to them to find their own way forward'. The last thing she would have wanted was a recognisable 'Hermes School' of wood engravers. The most she would have felt necessary was to provide the 'gen' on the use of tools as she and Blair Hughes-Stanton had done for Agnes Miller Parker in 1926, and to instil a workmanlike approach to the presses.[10]

John Lawrence was her student from 1955 to 1957 and remained a friend for life.[12] For him her classes were 'the most important thing of all'. He remembers her as quietly supportive.

> We learned through example. I suppose it was a sort of osmosis; you tuned into her wave-length. She was incredibly generous, inviting him to use the press in the basement of her house in Danvers Street. Her recent work, at that time mainly big linocuts, would be spread out on a huge table. Sometimes they would talk about her work and ideas, her feeling for landscape, and organic structure, and the loose way you could use wood with quite a lot of 'fireworks' in the cutting. She was always very encouraging.[11]

She and Hughes-Stanton remained on good terms after their divorce and both taught at the Central School. Several students remember them sitting together on the stairs, discussing their work in deep and friendly conversation.

Another tutor who greatly influenced John Lawrence was Keith Vaughan who taught illustration from 1948 to 1957.[13] Vaughan would bring in copies of the short story magazine *Argosy*, give each student a story, and get them to illustrate it. They would work in black and white, dip-pen and ink. Vaughan would spend at least 20 minutes analysing each student's drawing, looking at aspects of black and white tonality, he analysed each one more as a little drawing or painting than as a narrative illustration. Vaughan was essentially a painter rather than an illustrator and that came through in his teaching. He would also bring in illustrations by John Minton, with whom he was very close, especially current work from the *Radio Times*. John Minton's work was one of the greatest influences on students at that time and it was, in a way, as if Minton was teaching them through Vaughan.[12]

11 Gertrude Hermes, 'Solomon's seal', wood engraving for I. Gosse, *A florilege*, The Swan Press, Chelsea, 1931. Central Saint Martins Museum Collection.

12 John Lawrence, 'Winter', wood engraving for Susan Hill, *The magic apple tree: a country year*, Hamish Hamilton, 1982. Central Saint Martins Museum Collection.

John Vernon Lord, a postgraduate student at the Central School in 1960 and 1961 and subsequently an illustrator, writes in a memoir about the effect Mervyn Peake had on him.[**14, 15**] Peake taught illustration from 1951 to 1962. When John Lord encountered him he was suffering from Parkinson's disease and was often in a bad way but Kestelman continued to employ him, in part because of the insights he was still able to give students.

He made me think more deeply about the subject of illustration. I can recall him saying to me once, 'It is not only how you draw but what you draw, what you choose to put in the picture and what you decide to leave out'. He was the first teacher to emphasise the power of atmosphere and content in pictures and how we should aim to create a mood in our illustrations that made the content live. Peake made some interesting comments about drawing in his little manual *The craft of the lead pencil*. What he says in it is very characteristic of what he would say during my brief encounters with him at the Central. In a section on clumsiness he says that being clumsy as a draughtsman is 'no bar to excellence, it is less hampering than too dextrous a hand. To find it difficult to be expressive forces the tyro to be scrupulous in deciding what it really is that he wants to express. Hurried drawings are worse than useless', he wrote, 'for they can become a habit. Your hand must follow not precede your idea.' He emphasises that 'the aim' in drawing is 'to be expressive', that a drawing should be 'the embodiment of the idea, the experience'. What interests us about what we see or imagine should be communicated through our drawings. He goes on, 'It is for you to leave the spectator no option but to see what you liked; the curves, or the jaggednesses, the outline shape, or the shadowy patterns, the sense of movement, or stillness, the contrasting of flatness with solidity, dark with light, smooth with rough – whatever it may have been – the drawing must be about that – your choice; give him none.'[13]

13 Keith Vaughan, *The adventures of Tom Sawyer* by Mark Twain, Paul Elek, 1947. Central Saint Martins Museum Collection.

14 John Vernon Lord, 'The old man of Sark', pen and ink drawing for *The nonsense verse of Edward Lear*, Methuen, 1984. Central Saint Martins Museum Collection.

15 Mervyn Peake, 'The ancient mariner', drawing for Samuel Taylor Coleridge, *The rime of the ancient mariner*, Chatto and Windus, 1943. Central Saint Martins Museum Collection

Fritz Wegner was employed at St Martin's as a visiting teacher in illustration and taught on a regular basis one day a week from 1961 to 1984. During this period he taught many of our foremost illustrators including Nicola Bayley, Patrick Benson, Glynn Boyd Harte, Jill Barklem and Sara Midda. He was one of the most influential teachers at St Martin's as well as being a prolific book illustrator himself.

Detailed, precise and witty, Wegner's drawings define perfectly the meaning of the words 'to illustrate', which is to illuminate or make clear.[14]

Andrew Dodds, who taught part-time at St Martin's for nearly 20 years, describes how Wegner would bring in his own work-box of brushes and paints and work his way round the room spending time individually with each student.[16]

He was an excellent teacher. He had a gift to make everyone feel that at that moment they were the most important person in the world and their needs were special. The students loved it of course.[15]

Students are fulsome in their praise for his teaching methods and the support he gave them. Patrick Benson, a student of Wegner from 1956, describes him as

16 Andrew Dodds, Fritz Wegner, sketch made in the 1960s. Published in Andrew Dodds, *London then*, Jardine Press 1994. Central Saint Martins Museum Collection.

17 John Minton, Frontispiece for Reginald Arkell, *Old Herbaceous*, Michael Joseph 1950. Central Saint Martins Museum Collection.

Emotional, sensitive and imaginative. Gentle and encouraging, he helped students find their individual style and way of working. He introduced me to artists who inspired me and who I could identify with, for instance the American artist Edward Gorey. I owe him an enormous debt.[16] [**18**]

Wegner made himself available to his students long after they had graduated, continuing to give them advice and support.

Andrew Dodds had a foot in both camps. He was a student at the Central School from 1947 to 1950 studying under John Farleigh, Bernard Meninsky, John Minton, Keith Vaughan and S.R. Badmin. Dodds describes the atmosphere at the Central School in those immediate post-war years as 'hardworking and committed'. A large proportion of students were ex-service men as were many of the younger staff, and there was a sense of equality in their relationships. He was particularly impressed by John Minton, who was a brilliant and inspiring teacher and a charming person.[17] [**17**]

In 1953 Dodds got a job at St Martin's teaching illustration and remained until 1972. Morss, the then Principal, had previously been Principal at Colchester School of Art where Dodds had taken his Foundation Course. At St Martin's he spent a day a week teaching illustration while also working as a freelance illustrator. He liked his students to keep sketch books, insisting they drew something every day that had impressed them in some way and he would look at them each week. 'This was a tip I got from Ardizzone; it's a great discipline.'[18] Students taught by Dodds include Sara Midda, Glynn Boyd Harte [**19**] and Michael Foreman.

Sketch books were very much the thing in the 1960s. Michael Foreman remembers that when Gordon Ransome, Head of Graphics, invited him back to teach he insisted Foreman bring back his sketch books. '"Keep up your sketch books" was the mantra of all teachers at that time.'[19]

Michael Foreman remembers with gratitude Walter Hoyle who taught him at St Martin's. As part of his freelance work Hoyle did watercolour poster designs for the Post Office. He had one ready for delivery at their office at Kew and asked Foreman to take it there for him.

'Take your portfolio along, maybe they will give you something', he said. And they did, they gave me a poster, so he kind of started me off. I did five or six for them over a period of two to three years. They paid me a hundred guineas for that poster and that paid for my summer.[20]

18 Patrick Benson, *The sea-thing child* by Russell Hoban, Walker Books, 1999. Winner of the V&A Illustration Award, 2000. Central Saint Martins Museum Collection.

19 Glynn Boyd Harte, *Mr Harte's holiday*, written and illustrated by Glynn Boyd Harte, Sinclair-Stevenson, 1990. Private Collection.

War time

During the war and in the immediate post-war years both colleges benefited from talent from the continent.

Fritz Wegner came to London from Vienna as a refugee aged 14 in 1939.[20] His talent for drawing was recognised and he was found a place at St Martin's.

Val Biro, a young Hungarian was sent by his father to study at the Central School in 1939. He undertook the usual range of subjects taught to Commercial Art students at Central at the time: life drawing, wood engraving, calligraphy, typography, and illustration. Biro became a prolific illustrator working for journals and newspapers and illustrating many books, including his own 'Gumdrop' books. His Hungarian heritage with its baroque flourishes is particularly evident in his early work for *Radio Times*.

Susan Einzig was a refugee from Berlin in 1939. She also attended the Central School and was evacuated in 1940 to Northampton where the full-time students from the Central School, St Martin's and some other art schools were evacuated during the war.[21] In this small, close-knit community she got to know people from other disciplines whom she otherwise would not have met, such as Jeannetta Cochrane, the costume designer, and Bernard Adeney, the painter and textile designer, and his artist wife Noel who gave her a home with his family. Susan Einzig became known for her sensitive and imaginative book illustrations, especially those for *Tom's midnight garden* and *In the window seat*.[21] She links her love of illustration to her love of reading and says her illustrations are the product of a rich imaginative life. She was influenced as an artist by her relationship with John Minton whom she met while teaching at Camberwell School of Art. She also taught illustration for many years at Chelsea where her students included Emma Chichester Clarke and Hannah Firmin.

Judith Kerr was another refugee from Berlin, escaping with her parents and brother in 1933, living first in Switzerland and then Paris before arriving in London in 1936.[22] During the war she attended both the Central and St Martin's as an evening student.[22] Her passion was life drawing and she attended as many evening classes as she could. Classes went on all through the war, including some on Sundays, except during the worst of the Blitz. It was sometimes very cold and in the winter of 1947 (the coldest winter for many years and a time of coal shortages and rationing) the models couldn't take their clothes off. After the war she was awarded a scholarship. Because she had to earn her living she had to have it converted to a 'trade scholarship'. This meant she worked two days in her

20 Fritz Wegner,
*The wicked tricks of Till
Owly Glass*, by Michael
Rosen, Walker, 1989.
Short-listed for an Emil
award 1989.
Private collection.

21 Susan Einzig,
In the window seat by
Gillian Avery, Oxford
University Press, 1960.
Artist's collection.

22 Judith Kerr, *Mog's
bad thing*, written and
illustrated by Judith
Kerr, Collins, 2000.
Courtesy of Harper
Collins.

chosen 'trade', textile design, and three days at the Central School. Strictly speaking she should have studied textiles but such was the flexibility of the day Kerr was allowed to concentrate primarily on life drawing and painting. Because she virtually ignored 'illustration' as a subject while at college, she failed the Central School Diploma which had come in to being in 1948 – rather an irony for someone who became the successful illustrator of so many children's books.

Post war

After the war and national service another influx of talent enrolled at Central and St Martin's, including John Burningham who arrived at Central in 1956 to study illustration, and Michael Foreman who came to St Martin's in 1958 to study commercial art. They have become two of our most talented and prolific book illustrators, winning numerous awards and both achieving success with a first book. Foreman illustrated *The General* [**24**] which he produced with his first wife, Janet Charters, while still at the RCA, in 1961.[23] Burningham wrote and illustrated *Borka, the adventures of a goose with no feathers*, which won the Kate Greenaway medal in 1963.[24] [**23**] They both initially combined book illustration with teaching at the Central, St Martin's, and in Foreman's case, the RCA. Foreman was made an RDI in 1985 for his work as a travel illustrator. Both have won numerous prizes for book illustration.

Nicola Bayley was another early success story. She was encouraged to apply to the RCA by her tutor Fritz Wegner and her work was spotted by Tom Maschler of Jonathan Cape, which led to her being commissioned to produce *Nicola Bayley's book of nursery rhymes* in 1975.[25] She has fond memories of St Martin's in the 1960s. 'On the edge of Soho was absolutely it!'[26] She was a contemporary of Glynn Boyd Harte who was also much influenced by Fritz Wegner. It was Bayley who gave him a set of crayons and got him to experiment with colour; all his work up to then had been in black and white.[27]

Jill Barklem, another of Wegner's students in the late 1960s, was already working on the idea for her Brambly Hedge books while she was at St Martin's. Their potential was recognised by Collins in 1980 and, as well as the books, china and other products based on the illustrations have been produced.

Even in the 1960s student memories are still of Central as a rather serious, work-orientated place. St Martin's was a different story. Michael Foreman observed

> You could always tell St Martin's students, they had paint on their shoes. The 1960s was a marvellous time to be at art

23 John Burningham, *Borka, the adventures of a goose with no feathers*, written and illustrated by John Burningham, Cape, 1963. Winner of the Kate Greenaway Medal, 1963. Central Saint Martins Museum Collection.

school. On Fridays we had life drawing and Quentin Crisp was often the model. After lunch many of the group came back rather the worse for wear. It was very entertaining. Staff and students mixed across the departments; there was great fluidity. I met all sorts of people – Joe Tilson, Elizabeth Frink, Anthony Caro – we would all meet and drink together.[28]

Central Saint Martins' illustrators did not only influence by teaching and through their own work. Many wrote 'how to do it' books, some of which are still in print and many still used, e.g. Anthony Gross, Simon Brett, Paul Hogarth, Mervyn Peake, Lynton Lamb and John O'Connor. Laurence Scarfe edited *The Saturday Book* for many years. They also contributed to the new journals on design, illustration and printing; *Signature*, *Motif* and *Image*, which flourished after the war. The famous debate in *Motif* 1 and 2 in 1958-59 in which Edward Ardizzone and Lynton Lamb discuss the merits of their different approaches to illustration is of perennial interest. Ardizzone in *Motif* 1, November 1958, writes about 'The born illustrator', advocating drawing from memory and seeing it as an imaginative process. Lamb, in *Motif* 2, February 1959, talks about 'The true illustrator' in which he advocates drawing from life or failing that from the best possible reference sources. Lamb is known for the extensive research he did for his books. Other illustrators teaching at the Central and St Martin's who wrote articles in these and other journals, such as *Graphis* and the *Penrose Annual*, or were written about, are Laurence Scarfe[25], Barnett Freedman, Paul Hogarth, Mel Calman, and many more.

The 1950s and 1960s were a golden period for illustrators. Magazines and advertising still relied on illustration as did all types of book – fiction and non-fiction.

Speaking about her early career Faith Jaques, who left the Central School in 1948, writes

So much work available at this period – photography has taken most of it now. Advertising was much more fanciful and imaginative. I did decorative menus, borders and ornaments for Shell and ICI; half-page newspaper illustrations for J. Arthur Rank; drawings for the Central Office of Information, the Gas Board, the Electricity Board, the Milk Board, the Cheese Board; full colour illustrations for Horniman's Tea, decoration for Fortnum & Mason's, exhibition work, Portmeirion mugs, Post Office posters and, later, commemorative stamps, educational film-strips, and so on. I worked for most of the advertising agents of the time, and earned quite a lot.[29] [26]

A number of students who had trained as theatre designers or textile designers or fine artists also ventured

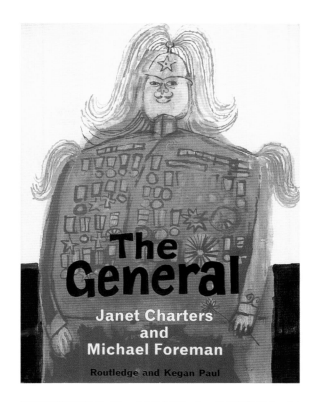

24 Michael Foreman, *The General*, written and illustrated by Janet Charters and Michael Foreman, Routledge & Kegan Paul, 1961. Private collection.

25 Laurence Scarfe, Illustration for 'Abbey', article on Westminster Abbey, written and illustrated by Laurence Scarfe, *Motif* 4, 1960. Central Saint Martins Museum Collection.

Two sons of Henry Lord Norris, 1601

into book illustration. Matthew Rice and Sheila Jackson from Theatre Design both produced illustrated books.[27]

The colour supplements started in the 1960s and in the early years were yet another outlet for the illustrator. Children's libraries flourished both in public libraries and in schools; they provided a ready market for the books that were pouring out of the publishers, and lots of work for illustrators. At that time there was a huge category of fiction specifically aimed at the adolescent. OUP had a large number of such titles; books by Rosemary Sutcliffe, Alan Garner and Philippa Pearce were published – all illustrated with black and white illustrations.

They generated a literature of their own with *Growing Point*, *Junior Bookshelf* and *Books for Keeps*, all reviewing books for children, including illustrated books. Margery

Faith Jaques

26 Faith Jaques, 'Snug & Selena go to town', from *Tales of the little brown mouse* by Alison Uttley, Heinemann, 1984. Courtesy Chris Beetles Gallery.

27 Sheila Jackson, *Music time: a book of easy tunes* by Prudence Hemelryck, Puffin Book 80, Penguin, 1947. Central Saint Martins Museum Collection.

Fisher in *Intent upon reading* wrote about 'children's books as "literature"', an original concept at that time, and of course book illustrators benefited from this too.[30]

From the 1960s a number of publishers had children's book editors who began to promote and publish a range of imaginative innovative work. The publication of the work of Brian Wildsmith by the legendary Mabel George, children's book editor at OUP from 1956, was considered by many to be a turning point for children's book illustration, paving the way for a surge of imaginative and colourful illustrators of children's books including many from Central and St Martin's. Tom Maschler of Cape published work by Nicola Bayley and John Burningham; and Julia MacRae, who had a very big impact on the children's book world, first as part of Hamish Hamilton and later under

her own imprint [**29**], published John Lawrence and Michael Foreman. Sebastian Walker started Walker Books in the late 1970s. Among the Central Saint Martins alumni published by them are Helen Oxenbury, John Lawrence, Nicola Bayley, Colin McNaughton, Nick Sharratt and Fritz Wegner, with Helen Oxenbury designing their logo.[**30**]

Book illustration is currently promoted and kept in the public eye by specialist galleries such as Chris Beetles and the Illustration Cupboard in London, the planned Centre for Children's Book Illustration in Newcastle, and the many prizes and awards for book illustration.

Both colleges established postgraduate courses in graphic design in the 1970s with options in illustration. Celia Berridge, a postgraduate student on the Central School graphic design course, writes warmly about the training she got and the skills she learnt. She was awarded the Francis Williams Award in 1977 while still a student on the course for her picture book *Runaway Danny* (André Deutsch 1977).[**28**] She produced 'Drawing matters', an animated film which was accepted in lieu of a dissertation. This together with the practical skills she learned on the MA course helped her get a commission with the BBC to produce a TV animated series, *Postman Pat,* for which she did the illustrations (later to be taken over by other illustrators and produced in book form).[31] [**31**] St Martin's had a Film and Video Unit which illustration students were

28 Celia Berridge, *Runaway Danny*, written and illustrated by Celia Berridge, Andre Deutsch, 1975. Winner of the Francis Williams Illustration Award, 1975. Artist's collection.

29 John Lawrence, Logo for Julia MacRae Books, 1984. Private collection.

30 Helen Oxenbury, Logo for Walker Books, 1986. Adapted from the original design of the late 1970s. Private collection.

31 Celia Berridge,
*Postman Pat and
Greendale Farm*, press-
up pack, devised and
illustrated by Celia
Berridge for Andre
Deutsch, *Postman
Pat*©1986
Entertainment Rights
PLC.
Artist's collection.

encouraged to use. Patrick Benson spent much of his final fourth year working with film and animation.

The final essay in the book, 'All change!' by Andrew Hall, is a personal view of the changes brought about by the coming of the new technology and the way St Martin's and, from 1989, Central Saint Martins, rose to the occasion with a new generation of students finding different ways of producing a range of exciting and innovative work. Illustration still continues to be taught in the college at both BA and MA level, and remains a force for communication, pleasure and entertainment.

Copyright © 2005 Sylvia Backemeyer

Notes

1   For further information on this subject see Joanna Selborne, 'Making an impression', in Sylvia Backemeyer ed., *Making their mark: art, craft and design at the Central School 1896–1966*, Herbert Press, 2000, pp.18–31.
2   Interview with Susan Einzig, 30 January 2004.
3   'A student at the Central School of Arts and Crafts, 1936–1940' by Margaret Till, in Sylvia Backemeyer ed., *Making their Mark*, Herbert Press, 2000, p.124.
4   Morris Kestelman, 'Reminiscences', in *Bernard Meninsky: 1891–1950*, Museum of Modern Art, Oxford, 1981, pp.18–23.
5   Interview with Leonard Rosoman, 24 May 2004.
6   John Farleigh, *Graven image: an auto-biographical textbook*, Macmillan, 1940.
7   Interview with Simon Brett, 14 May 2004.
8   Introduction by Simon Brett to *Clifford Webb: retrospective exhibition*, Leicester University, 1982.
9   *ibid.*
10 Judith Russell, *The wood engravings of Gertude Hermes*, Scolar Press, 1993, p.10.
11 Interview with John Lawrence, 17 May 2004.
12 *Ibid.*
13 From a unpublished memoir by John Vernon Lord, 'Student at the Central School of Arts and Crafts 1960–61', which includes quotations from Mervyn Peake, *The craft of the lead pencil*, Alan Wingate, 1946.
14 Joanna Carey, 'A certain magic', in *The magic pencil: children's book illustration today*, British Library, 2003, p.24.
15 Interview with Andrew Dodds, May 2004.
16 Telephone conversation with Patrick Benson, March 2004.
17 Interview with Andrew Dodds, May 2004.
18 *Ibid.*
19 Interview with Michael Foreman, March 2004.
20 *Ibid.*
21 Philippa Pearce, *Tom's midnight garden*, Oxford University Press, 1958.
22 Judith Kerr wrote three fictionalised accounts of her life as a refugee, *When Hitler stole Pink Rabbit*, 1971; *Bombs on Aunt Dainty*, 1975; and *A small person far away*, 1978. In 1989 these were published in one volume by Harper Collins as *Out of the Hitler time*.
23 Janet Charters and Michael Foreman, *The General*, Routledge & Kegan Paul, 1961.
24 John Burningham, *Borka: the adventures of a goose with no feathers*, Cape, 1963.
25 Nicola Bayley, *Nicola Bayley's book of nursery rhymes*, Cape, 1975.
26 Interview with Nicola Bayley, March 2004.
27 Obituary (Glynn Boyd Harte) in the *Guardian*, 19 December 2003.
28 Interview with Michael Foreman, March 2004.
29 Faith Jaques, quoted in Douglas Martin, *The telling line*, Julia MacRae, 1989, pp.65–66.
30 Margery Fisher, *Intent upon reading: a critical appraisal of modern fiction for children*, Brockhampton Press, 1961.
31 Notes sent by Celia Berridge to the author, June 2004.

2/ David Wootton
Book illustration

David Wootton is a writer and researcher on British art of the nineteenth and twentieth centuries. Particularly interested in the relationship between word and image, he has developed an expertise in various aspects of illustration through his close association with the leading London art dealer, Chris Beetles. He is currently training to teach English at secondary level

During the first half of the 20th century, the Central

School was much more important than St Martin's as an institution for nurturing illustrators. A generation of innovative teachers included Noel Rooke, A. S. Hartrick and W. P. Robins, with John Farleigh, Lynton Lamb and Anthony Gross numbered among their outstanding students.

At St Martin's School, just before the turn of the century, Mabel Lucie Attwell and her husband-to-be Harold Earnshaw had met while studying together.[1] However, their work was influenced less by their teachers than by the broad and populist look promoted by the members of the London Sketch Club. By the 1920s, Attwell was a household name as a result of her highly successful annuals and the many objects that carried her designs.

St Martin's came into its own after 1945 when Gertrude Hermes, Clifford Webb and Harold Jones were among the major figures to join the teaching staff. From that time a cross-fertilisation took place between the two colleges, long before they were officially united.

Noel Rooke and his importance as a teacher of wood engraving

Book Illustration as a subject at the Central School of Arts & Crafts originated through the person of Noel Rooke. Between 1900 and 1905 Rooke attended evening classes at the recently-founded school in order to supplement his studies at the Slade School of Art. Additionally, he received private tuition from its founder, William Lethaby, and its teacher of lettering, Edward Johnston, as well as from his father, the Pre-Raphaelite painter, Thomas Matthews Rooke.

From his time as a student, Rooke gained much experience as an illustrator, and decided to turn to wood engraving as he became increasingly dissatisfied with the quality of photo-mechanical reproduction. Wood engraving had thrived through the 19th century as a reproductive medium, but Rooke wished to revive its creative potential,

1 Mabel Lucie Attwell, 'Good fun', from *Lucie Attwell's annual*, Dean & Son. © Lucie Attwell Ltd 2005. Courtesy Chris Beetles Gallery.

LUCIE ATTWELL'S ANNUAL

LUCIE ATTWELL'S ANNUAL

DEAN & SON LTD

GOOD FUN!

DEAN

emulating such earlier designer-engravers as Bewick and Blake.

Among Rooke's teachers, Johnston proved most important in influencing this direction. He taught that 'the form of a letter was determined by the form of the tool used to make it'[1] and Rooke applied this principle to wood engraving. He made his first small engravings in 1904, alongside his fellow student, Eric Gill.

In 1905, Rooke joined the staff of the Central School to teach 'Book Illustration, Lettering, Black and White, etc.'. Then, a year later, he paid homage to Johnston in using wood engraving to illustrate his teacher's seminal volume, *Writing and illuminating and lettering* (John Hogg 1906). However, he was not allowed to teach wood engraving until at least 1908, as it continued to be generally considered as no better than an outdated method of reproduction. Once he became the full-time Head of Book Production in 1914, he had a much greater degree of influence, but much less time to pursue his own work. As a result, he is better remembered as a teacher than as an illustrator. And to mention Robert Gibbings, John Farleigh and Clare Leighton as being among his many students is to indicate how important a teacher he was.

Gibbings and Farleigh, in particular, had significance for the histories of illustration and wood engraving beyond their own achievements as illustrators. Gibbings (student 1911–13) stood alongside Rooke as one of the founders of the Society of Wood Engravers in 1920; and, as the owner-manager of the Golden Cockerel Press between 1924–33, he published Rooke's four wood-engraved illustrations to *The birth of Christ according to Luke* in 1925. Farleigh (student 1919–22) went on to teach at the Central School and, in 1947, succeeded Rooke as the Head of Book Production.

Turning to their most acclaimed illustrations, Farleigh appears to be an interpreter of literature, and Gibbings more an interpreter of landscape. Early in his career, Farleigh illustrated editions of the classical authors Pindar (Blackwell 1928–30) and Homer (Shakespeare Head Press 1930–31) in cool semi-abstraction. However, he made his name through association with the contemporary writers George Bernard Shaw and D. H. Lawrence. *The adventures of the black girl in her search for God* (Constable1932) created a sensation through both Shaw's agnostic text and Farleigh's images, which are at once beautiful in form and satirical in intent.[2] The artist responded so sympathetically to the author's suggestions – even sketches – that they developed a collaboration, which lasted seven years. Yet Farleigh would have preferred to be remembered for a less popular book by another author, D. H. Lawrence's *The*

2 John Farleigh,
The adventures of the black girl in her search for God, Constable, 1932.
Central Saint Martins Museum Collection
(photo Phil Baines).

man who died (Heinemann 1935); for his striking illustrations in black and red, depicting Christ after his death, sit so harmoniously with the typeface, designed by J.H. Mason, also on the staff of the Central School.

Of the early productions of Gibbings, published at his Golden Cockerel Press, it is perhaps the 1924 volume of work by Henry Thoreau, the American naturalist, that is most prescient. For Gibbings is remembered as a traveller and countryman, and remembered as such because of his ability to combine memoir and observation in books which he both wrote and illustrated. Central to these is a series of eight river books beginning with *Sweet Thames run softly* (Dent 1940).[3]

3 Robert Gibbings, Wood engraved frontispiece for *Sweet Thames run softly*, Dent, 1940 Courtesy Reading University.

4 Clare Leighton,
'The September apple
pick', wood engraving
for *The farmer's year*,
1933.
Courtesy David
Leighton.
Central Saint Martins
Museum Collection.

Clare Leighton (student *c*.1920) was similarly attracted to the rural environment, and managed to surpass early expectations that she would spend her career illustrating boys' adventures written by her father. She signalled her preferred direction in 1929 by working on an edition of Thomas Hardy's *The return of the native* (Macmillan 1929). However, as with Gibbings, she came into her own in illustrating her own texts. Inspired in part by H.N.Brailsford, the Marxist editor of *The New Leader*, she published *The farmer's year* (Collins 1933) in which she described the stark poverty of British agricultural workers in the great depression.[2][4] The twelve full-page engravings, representing the months of the year, support her view in being monumental, even heroic, in character. The success of this volume not only spurred Leighton herself to produce *Four hedges* (Gollancz 1935) and *Country matters* (Gollancz 1937) – but initiated a trend, though one that tended to greater optimism.

The tradition established by Noel Rooke at the beginning of the century was sustained by his direct heir, John Farleigh, at the Central School, and also influenced St Martin's: John O'Connor studied at the Central and taught at St Martin's, while Blair Hughes-Stanton and his former wife Gertrude Hermes taught at both schools. John Lawrence was a student of Hermes at the Central; Clifford Webb taught Frank Vernon Martin and Simon Brett at St Martin's.

A.S.Hartrick and his importance as a teacher of lithography

If Rooke's influence was manifested principally through the wood engravers among his students, then leading illustrators in other media can be identified with his contemporary teachers at the Central School. A.S.Hartrick headed a school of lithographers, while W.P. Robins did the same for etchers and engravers.

When Archibald Standish Hartrick began to teach at the Central School in 1914 he was an established magazine illustrator, known particularly for his association with *The Graphic*. While a student in Paris in the 1880s, he had met Gauguin, Toulouse-Lautrec and Van Gogh, and so brought a Continental breadth to his art, treating illustration as just one of several activities. This attitude seems to be suggested by the title of his manual, *Lithography as a fine art*, published in 1932 by OUP, two years after his retirement from the Central School. His breadth and his expertise in depicting working men would both be echoed by a number of his students.

James Fitton studied under Hartrick in evening classes at the Central School from 1925 and, eight years later, returned to give evening classes in lithography, mostly to his own contemporaries. Significant among these were Pearl Binder, James Boswell, James Holland and Edward Ardizzone. Ardizzone used lithography most memorably for his own children's books, and so will be discussed below; but the others can be treated as a group, in the use that they made of their art to oppose Fascism.

Fitton's class in lithography was instigated in 1933, in the same year that the Artists International Association was founded, and the four artists considered here were central to both. Indeed, lithography was a means by which they could generate a popular art to promote a left-wing, anti-militarist message. Fitton and Boswell explored Camden Town and the East End together, while Binder actually lived in the East End, and all drew on observations of working-class life in preparing their lithographs. Initially, the results appeared more in periodicals than books: the 'three Jameses', as the men were known collectively, contributed cartoons to *Left Review*; Binder contributed images of the English social scene to *New Masses*. However, from the very early 1930s, Binder also used lithography to produce book illustrations of significance, both artistic and social. She followed work on Thomas Burke's *The real East End* (Constable 1932), and P. Godfrey's *Backstage* (Harrap 1932) with the first of her own books, *Odd jobs: stories and drawings* (Harrap 1935), which was described by one of her obituarists as comprising portraits from life carried out with humour and economy.[3][5] Later demonstrations of her political engagement included exhibiting in the USSR, and living among miners in South Wales.

More than a decade on, this class of lithographers – Ardizzone included – would reunite through their contributions to a gentler periodical, *Lilliput*, as a result of commissions from James Boswell, its art editor from 1947 to 1950.

Fitton's evening class seems to have supplemented the course led by Clarke Hutton, for it was Hutton who succeeded Hartrick as Instructor in Lithography in 1930, after spending three years as his student. He may have lacked the political glamour of the 'three Jameses' but he contributed considerably to the development of book illustration, especially through colour lithography. While his illustrations to John Bunyan's *The pilgrim's progress* (SCM 1947) are often singled out as among his most successful, he is perhaps best remembered for his children's books, including a number of Puffin Picture Books and the Picture History series for the Oxford University Press, in the 1940s and 1950s.[6]

Lynton Lamb studied lithography alongside Hutton at the Central School, and 'of all his teachers, remembered

THE STORY OF TEA

By Anne Skibulits and Clarke Hutton

Puffin Picture Book Number 72 * A Penguin Publication

5 Pearl Binder,
Theatre dressmaking
lithograph for
Backstage, by
P.Godfrey. Harrap,
1933.
Produced while she
was a student at the
Central School.
Central Saint Martins
Museum Collection.

6 Clarke Hutton
Book cover for *The
story of tea* by Anne
Skibulits and Clarke
Hutton.
Colour lithograph,
Puffin Picture Book,
no 72, 1948.

Hartrick with most affection'[4]. At the same time, it was perhaps Lamb who, of all Hartrick's students, most emulated the master's versatility. He became a painter, designer and writer, as well as an illustrator; and his illustrations were produced in a variety of media that included wood engraving and pen and ink, as well as forms of lithograph.

On leaving the Central School, Lamb took up a position as Production Adviser to the Oxford University Press, and the experience and expertise that he gained throughout this career made him an able teacher: back at the School of Book Production of the Central School in the late 1930s, and as Head of Lithography at the Slade School (1950–71), as well as at other institutions.[7] Many of his commissions as an illustrator came from the OUP, while it also published his most important didactic writings, including *Drawing for illustration* (1962).

The edition of Anthony Trollope's *Can you forgive her?*, which OUP published in 1948, must represent the breadth of Lamb's achievement. These two volumes comprised Lamb's illustrative contribution to the Oxford Illustrated Trollope, of which he was also art editor, a role which made him 'responsible for the typography and appearance of the books, and for the choice of illustrators'[5]. His attempt to interest such artists as Rodrigo Moynihan in the project, while unsuccessful, shows how he enacted his belief that 'painting is the source of our graphic tradition'[6]. His own illustrations demonstrate both his devotion to research and his ability to employ a range of techniques. He believed that illustration should be based on extensive research. He describes this at length in his book *Drawing for illustration*. His theoretical opposition to Ardizzone is famous, but did not affect their friendship or ability to work together: Ardizzone contributed two volumes, *The Warden* (1952) and *Barchester Towers* (1953), to this series. The sixteen lithographs for Anthony Trollope's *Can you forgive her?* (OUP 1948) were drawn on two stones. It is a measure of his professionalism that all the drawings were completed without alteration. Since it is a technically difficult thing to do on stone, Lamb ensured by the means of meticulous studies and tracings beforehand that none was needed.

Lamb's understanding of the relation of painting and illustration stood him in good stead when commissioning artists to illustrate the Oxford Trollope. His own wide range of skills and versatility enabled him to work in pen and ink, chalk drawn on lithographic stones, and chalk on zinc plates. He did the drawings on stone for George Eliot's *Silas Marner* (Limited Editions 1953) and on zinc plates for Wilkie Collins' *The woman in white* (Folio Society 1956).

7 Lynton Lamb, *Can you forgive her?* by Anthony Trollope, OUP, 1948. Private Collection.

His skill in wood engraving learned from Noel Rooke and employed in the 1930s should be mentioned as in need of reassessment.

W.P. Robins and his importance as a teacher of etching and engraving

William Palmer Robins was a protégé of Sir Frank Short who, from the late 19th century, had helped revive an interest in etching in Britain. Robins taught printmaking at St Martin's School and then at the Central School and, between these periods of teaching, published the treatise *Etching craft* (Batsford 1922). His wide influence on illustrators and other artists is here represented by the figure of Anthony Gross, who studied in his evening classes at the very outset of his career.

While at school at Repton, Anthony Gross had gained an 'early familiarity with the materials and tools of printmaking'[7]. In 1923, at the age of eighteen, he took up a place at the Slade School of Fine Art and, during the summer term, strengthened his printmaking skills by studying at the Central School with Robins, who provided 'a strict course of instruction in traditional methods of working'[8]. A focus for this brief but seminal course was a series of drawings that Gross had made in Normandy and which Robins encouraged him to turn into etchings. The results were so successful that the Abbey Gallery agreed to handle his etchings, and two years later mounted his first solo show.

In the meantime, however, Gross decamped to Paris, and joined the engraving class of C.A. Waltner at the Ecole des Beaux-Arts. Led from that point by his Francophilic disposition, his development as an artist, and his subsequent career, changed direction. Yet the technical training he had gained under Robins remained with him and carried him forward. As his skill as an etcher was recognised in France, so Gross was elected to La Jeune Gravure Contemporaine and given the commission to illustrate a limited edition of Jean Cocteau's *Les enfants terribles* (1936), a number of years before the author produced his own illustrations. His contribution to the project was at once extensive and strikingly modern.

The close of Gross's career is marked as emphatically by another set of etched and engraved illustrations, to his own *The very rich hours of Le Boulvé* (1980). It was he who conceived this celebration of the village in the Lot that, from 1955, had provided him with a home, and he who, in 1978, suggested its publication to the Rampant Lions Press in Cambridge. In his text, he surveyed all aspects of Le Boulvé past and present, as a portrait of France in miniature, and so provided himself with a wealth of material

8 Anthony Gross *The Forsyte Saga* by John Galsworthy, six colour lithograph. Heinemann, 1950. Courtesy artist's estate and the Redfern Gallery.

to depict. The twenty-six copper etchings provide a
summation of his career, as is suggested by the comment
that they are 'rooted in the spirit of the classicism of the
thirties in France ... also rooted in an ideal of the engraving
as a separate art'[9].

Between these two etched volumes stands a major work
of illustration in other media; this was the first illustrated
edition of John Galsworthy's *The Forsyte saga*, containing
twelve colour lithographs, and a further seventy-two pen
and ink drawings which were photographically
reproduced.[8] The work was commissioned from Gross in
1948, the year that he began to teach at the Central School,
and published by Heinemann two years later. Assessing
that the project would take him eighteen months to
complete, he spent the first six in full-time research, a
dedication which is reminiscent of Lynton Lamb, and
which was praised by him in *Drawing for illustration*. The
fruits of this approach are indicated by Edward Hodnett:

> Gross was assiduous in documenting the gradually changing
> scene with such details as chandeliers and cruets at formal
> dinners by gaslight, an oasis of quiet in Cheapside ... and the
> arrival of the motorcar on carriage springs.[10]

Equivalent care was taken with the technical aspects of
the book, as is evocatively described by Alan Horne:

> the illustrations have an ethereal quality, the freely applied
> lithographic colouring giving the effect of light washes
> contrasting with areas of textural interest. The elegant
> tail-pieces and ... chapter headings were originally working
> sketches.[11]

If Hodnett's words imply a distinction between the
artist's approaches to his English and French subjects,
those of Horne suggest the common ground between
them. Though only intermittently an illustrator, Gross
became a master in the field, modifying his distinctively
fluid line to suit each particular text, while underpinning
all with a technical integrity learned early from Robins.

Children's book illustrators before 1945

While the attainment of specific skills aided the careers of
many illustrators, others made their names through association with a particular genre. This is well demonstrated
by the seminal achievements of children's book illustrators who emerged from the Central School before the war,
and whose rich talents presaged those of many later
students of both the Central and St Martin's.

Children's book illustrators are often their own authors,
and are likely to live on through the characters that they
create or develop. So it is with some leading alumni of the
Central School, who established themselves in the 1930s.

Alfred Bestall is almost synonymous with 'Rupert Bear', as is Kathleen Hale with 'Orlando the Marmalade Cat'. And, while Edward Ardizzone was more versatile, and his work more ubiquitous, he is still held in affection as the father of 'Little Tim'. Yet equally gifted illustrators are sometimes associated with the more famous writers with whom they collaborate. So the Moreton-Sales are remembered in conjunction with the much-loved Eleanor Farjeon.

Alfred Bestall attended evening classes at the Central School from 1919 and intermittently through the 1920s. These prepared him for what seemed likely to be the varied career of a jobbing artist-illustrator. However, in 1935, he was chosen to succeed Mary Tourtel as the illustrator of 'Rupert Bear', the strip she had created for the *Daily Express*, and so focused his energies on this one popular project. In so doing, he followed many of the suggestions of Stanley Marshall, the children's editor of the paper and the founder of the high-minded Rupert League.

Bestall developed a more concrete imaginative world, peopled with many interesting new characters, and also evolved Rupert's canonical appearance. Indeed, though he had not created Rupert, he made him very much his own, particularly from 1940, when the annual, which collected the strips, was first published in full colour. Though professional colourists completed the narrative illustrations, Bestall produced the evocative covers and endpapers, and continued to do so until 1973.

John Morton-Sale and Isobel Lucas were contemporaries of Bestall in the School of Book Production, and became engaged in 1920, while still students. John and Isobel developed similar skills and complementary approaches, he concentrating on landscape and she on figures, so that when they graduated, and married, in 1924, their talents fitted neatly together. A decade later, when they began to collaborate closely, with Mary Grigg's *The yellow cat* (1936), their illustrative achievements seemed the natural results of joint efforts.

Consequently, the Morton-Sales were introduced to Eleanor Farjeon by Sir Robert Lusty, of the publishers Michael Joseph, as the ideal illustrators for her latest book, *Martin Pippin in the daisy field*. This was to be the sequel to *Martin Pippin in the apple-orchard* (1921), the romantic fantasy which had made Farjeon's name, though aimed more directly at young readers. When the volume appeared in 1937, it was sufficiently successful to seal the partnership – and friendship – between artists and author. Their second joint project, *Sing for your supper*, was published in 1938, and others followed, including *Cherrystones* (Michael Joseph 1942).[9] Much later, in

9 Isobel and John Moreton Sale, *Cherry stones* by Eleanor Farjeon, Michael Joseph, 1942. © Chris Beetles Ltd., St.James, London.

1952, the Morton-Sales turned away from illustration to found the Parnassus Gallery, which specialised in the publication of high-quality fine art prints.

When Kathleen Hale enrolled at the Central School in 1928, she was a mature – and married – woman, already establishing herself as an artist. Yet, while she had trained at Manchester School of Art and Reading University, she had never formally studied oils, and so took lessons at the Central under Bernard Meninsky. Like many fellow students, she greatly valued his instruction (as outlined in the introduction to this volume), but he failed to gauge her potential. Indeed, it would take another decade for her talent to flower properly, but when it did, with the Orlando books, she was proved to be a true artist.

Hale found that her two sons responded to a fairly limited range of children's books: Edward Ardizzone's 'Little Tim', Jean de Brunhoff's 'Babar' and, from an earlier age, the tales of Beatrix Potter. So she began to tell her own stories based around a real ginger cat, one of several family pets. A friend, the philosopher and linguist C.K. Ogden, encouraged her to turn these into books, and she showed the results to Geoffrey Smith, of the printers, Cowells of Ipswich. In turn, they were shown to Noel Carrington, children's book editor at Country Life, who accepted them for publication. So *Orlando the marmalade cat: a camping holiday* and *a trip abroad*, the first two of eighteen titles, appeared in 1938.[10] Orlando's afterlife, if not as varied as Rupert's, included a radio serial and a ballet.

Hale's characters are undoubtedly endearing, and their adventures equally engaging. But, as with many of the best children's books, the stories live as much through the distinction of their illustrations, and the way those illustrations are presented. Hale achieved a great deal through rich colour and almost oriental design, so that the images are at once immediate and highly sophisticated, humorous and elegant. She also involved herself in their lithographic reproduction, 'the printing firm, Cowell, providing her with some rudimentary training in drawing directly onto the printing plates'.[12] While this occurred for reasons of economy, it also suggests her artistic dedication.

While introducing a distinct look in her books, Hale undoubtedly emulated such recent models as Ardizzone's 'Little Tim'.[11] *Little Tim and the brave sea captain*, the first of Ardizzone's delightful series, had appeared in 1936, two years before the first Orlando books, and helped establish his reputation. Though he produced the manuscript in pen and watercolour, incorporating a hand-written text as well as speech bubbles, the book was printed in what was the fairly new medium of offset lithography. Ardizzone attended James Fitton's lithography classes at the Central

10 Kathleen Hale *Orlando the marmlade cat, his silver wedding,* written and illustrated by Kathleen Hale, Country Life, 1944. Private collection.

11 Edward Ardizzone *Little Tim's last sea voyage,* written and illustrated by Edward Ardizzone, Bodley Head, 1972. © Laura Cecil Literary Agency.

12 Susan Einzig, *Tom's midnight garden* by Phillipa Pearce, OUP, 1958. Artist's collection.

School (see above), possibly in order to understand the process by which his new work would be reproduced. While its apparent spontaneity suggests his immediate control of the medium, the strength of many later books, posters and independent prints demonstrates how masterly a lithographer he would become.

Mention should be made here of Harold Jones, a contemporary of these illustrators who taught at St Martin's during the 1940s, and so provides a bridge to the later period, in which St Martin's came into its own. While he made his name with his lithographed illustrations to Walter de la Mare's *This year, next year* (Faber 1937), he is best remembered for his work on *Lavender's blue* (OUP 1954), a book of nursery rhymes compiled by Kathleen Lines. It won an American Library Association Award and was included in the honours list for the Hans Christian Andersen Award. One obituarist noted that it best exemplified his 'obviously ambiguous style, apparently simple but with a sophisticated sense of design'.[13]

Children's book illustrators post 1945

In his book *The telling line*, Douglas Martin gives the year *c.*1962 as the date which may be taken as the crossover point separating the black and white era from the full-colour one which succeeded but did not entirely supplant it.[14] But, pertinent to this present volume, that approximate date also marks the point at which St Martin's finally emerged as the full equal of the Central School. Despite the achievement of certain alumni, notably children's book illustrators, Central might be broadly associated with black and white and St Martin's with colour.

After the Second World War many artists known equally well for their work as painters and printmakers were employed to illustrate books. These books were aimed at the flourishing readership of older children and were mainly illustrated in black and white. For example Paul Elek produced the Camden Classics Series, from 1947, using well-known contemporary artists to illustrate each volume. These included Anthony Gross and the neo-romantics Keith Vaughan and John Minton – all teachers at the Central School.

Susan Einzig was one of the artists trained at the Central School whose dreamy, romantic illustrations perfectly captured the spirit of the books she illustrated. In particular her black and white pen and ink drawings for *Tom's midnight garden* (OUP 1958) remain to this day a perfect evocation of the spirit of place.[12] This book won the Carnegie Medal for the best children's book of 1958 and although this is not specifically for illustration, it is

difficult to think that Einzig's illustrations were not a contributing factor.

Peggy Fortnum was another prolific illustrator, who trained under John Farleigh and worked mainly in black and white from the late 1940s. 'She has illustrated some eighty children's books mostly with line drawings delightfully evocative of the situations and feelings which she is portraying.'[15] She produced the first-ever illustrations for Paddington Bear, the Michael Bond series of books aimed at younger children, and illustrated eleven titles in the period 1958–73.[13] The work was then taken over by Fred Banbery (another Central student 1938-1940), who produced his illustrations in colour.[14]

Faith Jaques, another student of John Farleigh, was one of the most prolific illustrators, with at least seventy children's books to her credit, mainly in black and white. It wasn't until the late 1970s with *Tilly's house* (Heinemann 1979), the first book she both wrote and illustrated, that she moved into colour.[15] Most of her illustrations were for books written by other people and she liked to work closely with each author, taking great pains to study his or her intentions and undertaking extensive research. For her last book, *The Orchard book of nursery rhymes*, published after her death in 1990, she provided a fascinating introduction, in which she wrote about the rhymes and why she illustrated them in the way she did.[16]

Two Central School alumni – both students during and immediately after the Second World War – made a pioneering use of colour. Val Biro first established himself as a prolific black and white illustrator before using wash as well as pen for his own series 'Gumdrop', from 1966, featuring a vintage car.[16] Judith Kerr has almost always

13 Peggy Fortnum, Paddington bear. From The Paddington Bear books by Michael Bond, illustrated by Peggy Fortnum. © Paddington & Company Ltd, 2004.

14 Fred Banbery Book cover for *Paddington at the circus* by Michael Bond, with illustrations by Fred Banbery. Collins, 1973. © Chris Beetles Ltd, St. James, London

15 Faith Jaques *Tilly's House* written and illustrated by Faith Jaques, Heinemann/Atheneum 1979. Private collection

worked in full colour, writing and illustrating her first children's picture book, *The tiger who came to tea* (Collins), in 1968.[17]

As is clear from this essay, the Central School produced the majority of illustrators before and immediately after the Second World War, but from 1960 the illustration course at St Martin's became a force to be reckoned with and nurtured a number of talented artists.[17] The teacher who seems to have influenced all of them is Fritz Wegner, himself a student at St Martin's whose work features in several chapters in this book. Wegner has been illustrating books for over fifty years and while working in a variety of media his preferred medium is pen and ink.

> He draws with a wiry spring-loaded line, full of energy and perfectly controlled with a celebratory enjoyment of detail and an easy way with formal flourishes and decorative devices and hand-lettering. Always there is a sense of spatial awareness which adds great depth to his illustrations; figures are brilliantly drawn and he excels at crowd scenes: even on the smallest scale, each figure has an expressive individuality.[18] [18]

It is likely that his intricate and detailed drawings influenced several of his students: Nicola Bayley, Sara Midda, Jill Barklem, Patrick Benson.

Cats predominate in the work of Nicola Bayley whose intense, brilliant, jewel-like compositions are usually on a very small scale, e.g. Antonia Barber's *The mousehole cat* (Walker Books 1990), [21] William Mayne's *The patchwork cat* (Cape 1981), and Gretchen Woelfle's *Katje, the windmill cat* (Walker Books 2001). Her intimate knowledge of cats and their ways is captured in the loving detail with which they are portrayed in these books.

Sara Midda, a student at St Martin's in the 1970s, combined her skills as a watercolourist with detailed drawing. She is best known for *In and out of the garden* (Sidgwick & Jackson 1981) which combines precise yet delicate and detailed watercolour drawings of garden plants and flowers with recipes and country lore lettered alongside them.[19] Her work is very popular in Japan and she has a long-standing contract with Mitsukoshi, the Japanese department store for which she has designed a range of over six hundred items including baby wear and linen, crockery and glasses, and gift wrap.

Jill Barklem has produced immensely detailed and delicately drawn ink and wash illustrations for her own series of books, 'Brambly Hedge' (Collins 1980).[20] This series is about a world of mice existing in the hedgerows, and was already being planned by the artist on her long daily journeys through the countryside to college. The characters of

16 Val Biro, *Gumdrop and the dinosaur* written and illustrated by Val Biro, Hodder 1988. Artist's collection.

17 Judith Kerr, *The tiger who came to tea*, written and illustrated by Judith Kerr, Collins, 1968 Courtesy Harper Collins.

the miniature world of Brambly Hedge have also generated a range of decorated china, cards, gift wrap and other products.

Patrick Benson cites Wegner as one of his most significant influences. Benson has mostly illustrated other people's books, around twenty-five in all, with authors such as Roald Dahl, William Mayne, Russell Hoban and Kenneth Grahame.[22] He won the Mother Goose Award in 1984 as The Most Promising Newcomer in Children's Book Illustration for his illustrations to William Mayne's *Hob stories* (Walker Books 1984). In an interview for *The magic pencil*, the book accompanying the exhibition of the same name at the British Library in 2003, Benson says about his work:

> I think the most important thing an illustrator can do is to provide lots of visual clues, bits of information – rather like snapshots – that will act as a sort of springboard for the imagination and help the child to visualise the surroundings in which the story is happening.

Michael Foreman was at St Martin's from 1958 to 1959 studying Commercial Art with Bernard Cheese, Walter Hoyle and John Hadley Rowe. He then went to the Royal College where he was taught by Ardizzone and Edward Bawden. He is an extremely prolific illustrator and has illustrated around 190 books.[25] He illustrates both his own texts and those by other people, including many classics ranging from Shakespeare to Kenneth Grahame's *The wind in the willows*[23] (Pavilion Books 2001). He has won many awards for illustration for individual books as well as being elected RDI for travel illustration. Indeed travel is one of his obsessions and he feels strongly that basing his images on first-hand experience of places is essential for readers of all ages. He himself is 'a prodigious traveller, who heads for Heathrow rather than to the reference library in search of authenticity'.[19]

John Lawrence was a student at the Central School from 1955 to 1957. He was taught wood engraving by Gertrude Hermes who was a tremendous influence on him. His first colour wood-engraved book illustrations were for Defoe's *Colonel Jack*, which was published by the Folio Society in 1967 and won him a Francis Williams Award. He has been described as 'the Rowlandson of the 20th-century engraving school. His engravings are tightly packed, highly charged and with the exact number of burin thrusts where, when he so chooses, he splits the form through from the black to white poles'.[20]

He has used his engraving skills with some effect in books for children and in particular *Rabbit and pork, rhyming talk* (Hamish Hamilton 1975), a volume of

18 Fritz Wegner, 'The man sneezed', from *The sneeze* by David Lloyd, Walker Books, 1986. Central Saint Martins Museum Collection.

rhyming slang with hand-coloured wood engravings. More recently he has produced two picture books for young children with vinyl engravings: *This little chick* (2000), and Martin Waddell's *Tiny's big adventure* (2004), both published by Walker Books. He has also worked in a variety of other media, producing a large number of children's books for all ages working with many distinguished authors, e.g. Richard Adams's, *Watership down* (Kestrel Books 1976) and Philippa Pearce's *Emily's own elephant* (Julia MacRae 1987).

John Burningham and Helen Oxenbury met when they were students at the Central School in the 1950s. Burningham was on the illustration course, and Oxenbury studied Theatre Design. John Burningham became established as a children's book illustrator only a few years after graduating with his picture book *Borka, the adventures of a goose with no feathers*, which was published by Cape in 1963

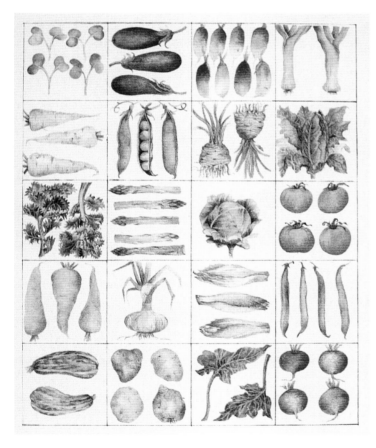

19 Sara Midda, 'The vegetable garden' from *In and out the garden* by Sara Midda, Sigdwick & Jackson, 1981. Winner of the Francis Williams Award for 1982.
Central Saint Martins Museum Collection.

20 Jill Barklem, 'Autumn' from *The complete Brambly Hedge*, written and illustrated by Jill Barklem, Collins, 1980.
Central Saint Martins Museum Collection.

21 Nicola Bayley, *The mousehole cat* by Antonia Barber, Walker Books, 1990. Winner of the British Book Award for the Illustrated Children's Book of the Year, 1990. Artist's collection.

and for which he won a Kate Greenaway Medal. Except for a very few early titles and his very successful interpretation of Kenneth Grahame's *The wind in the willows* (Kestrel 1983), [24] Burningham both writes and illustrates his own books.[26] His style as an illustrator has developed considerably from the brilliant, full colour images of Borka to the simpler line drawings both with and without colour in *Mr Gumpy's outing* (Cape 1970), another Kate Greenaway Medal winner. Brian Alderson, writing about this book, says

> The gradual pile-up of creatures in Mr Gumpy's boat, the inevitable disaster and the concluding tea party have a naturalness in both the telling and the illustration which goes a long way to support the claim that perfection in picture books is not to be sought in the predominance of one element over another but in the easy interlocking of all the parts. [21]

22 Patrick Benson, *The Minnipins* by Roald Dahl. Cape, 1991. Central Saint Martins Museum Collection.

Helen Oxenbury published her first book in 1967 and rapidly became as successful a children's illustrator as her husband, winning the Kate Greenaway Medal for her vision of Edward Lear's *The Quangle Wangle's hat* and Lewis Carroll's *The hunting of the Snark* (Heinemann 1969). Oxenbury illustrates both her own stories and other people's writing. She has worked in a range of styles and media. In the early 1980s she was asked to develop some books for very young children by Walker Books, a new imprint, and her work is now very much associated with this publisher. Perhaps because she has illustrated books throughout her own children's childhood, the children Helen Oxenbury draws have a very contemporary feel.

It is the robust reality of the children that heightens the fantasy element in *We're going on a bear hunt* (Michael Rosen, Walker Books 1989).[27] This is a wonderful evocation of a light-hearted, imaginative family outing in the countryside to look for a bear – and a breathless stampede back to the house when they find one. [22]

The recent years have been a period of great creativity for alumni of the Central School and St Martin's. In addition to those already mentioned Colin NcNaughton (Central School from 1970) has created a number of exuberant picture books including the Kurt Maschler Award winner *Guess who's just moved in next door?* (Walker Books 1991), while Nick Sharratt (St Martins 1980s) works very successfully using computer-aided design, demonstrating the willingness of Central Saint Martin's to embrace new media.

Conclusion

Through the 20th century the students and teachers of Central Saint Martins have proved themselves vital practitioners of book illustration. An understanding of the book as a whole, and an ability to master specific media, marked out these illustrators from an early date. They have offered masterly interpretations of classic and contemporary literature, especially English, for both adults and children; but they have also frequently revealed active imaginations, through their own creations, from Ardizzone's Little Tim books to Barklem's inhabitants of Brambly Hedge, and from Leighton's country subjects to Gross's vision of France. Whether it be the traditional black and white of a private press or the latest computer-generated palette, Central Saint Martins has been an influential presence.

23 Michael Foreman, *The wind in the willows* by Kenneth Grahame, Pavilion Books, 2001. Central Saint Martins Museum Collection.

24 John Burningham, 'Mole goes fishing' from *The wind in the willows* by Kenneth Grahame, Viking Press, 1983. Artist's collection.

25 Michael Foreman,
'He bore himself like a
monarch,' from
Shakespeare stories by
Leon Garfield,
Gollancz, 1985.
Artist's collection.

Notes
1 Edward Johnston, *Writing and illuminating and lettering*, The
 Artistic Crafts Series, John Hogg, 1906.
2 Clare Leighton's obituary, *The Guardian*, 8 December 1989.
3 Pearl Binder's obituary, *The Daily Telegraph*, 27 January 1990.
4 George Mackie, *Lynton Lamb*, illustrator, Scolar Press, 1978,
 p.xviii.
5 Mackie, *op. cit.*, p. xxii.
6 Mackie, *op. cit.*, p.xxv.
7 Graham Reynolds, 'The prints', in Mary and Peter Gross, editors,
 Anthony Gross, Scolar Press, 1992, pp.59-76.
8 Graham Reynolds, *op. cit.*, p.59.
9 Jane Lee, *op. cit.*, p 25.
10 Edward Hodnett, *Five centuries of English book illustration*,
 Scolar Press, 1988, p.293.
11 Alan Horne, editor, *The dictionary of 20th century book illustrators*, Antique Collectors' Club, 1994, p.231.
12 *Kathleen Hale: artist illustrator*, London, The Gekoski Gallery,
 Frederick Warne, 1995, pp.12–13.
13 Harold Jones' obituary, *The Times*, 13 June 1992.
14 Introduction to Douglas Martin, *The telling line: essays on fifteen
 contemporary book illustrators*, Julia MacRae Books, 1989, p.23.
15 Alan Horne, editor, *The dictionary of 20th century book illustrators*, Antique Collectors' Club, 1994, p.196.
16 'Faith Jaques writes about the rhymes', in Faith Jaques and Zena
 Sutherland, *The Orchard book of nursery rhymes*, Orchard Books,
 l990, pp.82–6.
17 For example, Violet Drummond (St Martin's 1930s) was the
 second person to be awarded the Kate Greenaway Medal, for
 Mrs Easter and the storks (Faber 1957).
18 'A certain magic', in Joanna Carey, *The magic pencil: children's
 book illustration today*, the British Council/British Library, 2003,
 p.23.
19 'Michael Foreman', in Douglas Martin, *The telling line: children's
 book illustration today*, Julia MacRae Books, 1989, pp.303–4.
20 Albert Garrett, *A history of wood engraving*, Bloomsbury Books,
 1978, p.296.
21 Brian Alderson, quoted in the entry on John Burningham in Alan
 Horne, editor, *The dictionary of 20th century British book illustrators*, Antique Collectors' Club, 1995.
22 'A certain magic', in Joanna Carey, *The magic pencil: children's
 book illustration today*, British Council/British Library, 2003,
 pp.19–20.

26 John Burningham,
Mr Gumpy's outing,
written and illustrated
by John Burningham,
Cape, 1970.
Winner of the Kate
Greenaway Medal,
1970.
Central Saint Martins
Museum Collection.

27 Helen Oxenbury,
'Splash splosh' from
*We're going on a bear
hunt* by Michael Rosen
Walker Books, 1989.
Central Saint Martins
Museum Collection.

3/ Marie McLoughlin
Drawing dreams: fashion illustration

Marie McLoughlin studied Fashion at St Martin's in the early 1970s and Design History at Winchester in the early 1990s, where her MA dissertation was on Utility clothing. She is currently researching Muriel Pemberton and the development of fashion education at Brighton University.

Fashion

at Central Saint Martins is internationally famous but few realise it began as an evening class in fashion drawing in 1931. The central importance of drawing to the course, and the artist who founded it and ran it for the next four and a half decades, Muriel Pemberton, gave it a unique strength and character. In 1931 Muriel Pemberton had just graduated from the Royal College of Art with its first ever diploma in fashion. She had written her own curriculum[1] with the help, amongst others, of James Laver, then Keeper of Prints & Drawings at the Victoria and Albert Museum. The three major strands of her studies were historical costume, pattern cutting (which she learnt at the Katinka School of Pattern Cutting in Knightsbridge in exchange for drawing lessons), and fashion drawing. These were to form the backbone of the St Martin's course, beginning with drawing.

The first three decades of the 20th century were a golden age for fashion illustration. In 1908 Poiret's exotic oriental fashions drifted weightlessly across pages illustrated by Iribe, followed in 1911 by the *Gazette du Bon Ton*.[2] [1] Drawing clothes far from the corsets and frou-frou of the *Belle Époque*, Iribe, Barbier and Lepape captured the new age. Pre-war Paris was at the centre of a revolution in the visual arts; cubism, abstraction, fauvism and the exoticism of Diaghilev's Ballets Russes must all have been known to these young artists and their increasingly stylised drawings created a fantasy world of simplicity, light and colour that still evokes the modernism of the beginning of the century. When war broke out in 1914 the *Gazette* was forced to suspend publication. The artists were then employed by Condé Nast, a publisher who in 1909 had bought an ailing American East Coast society magazine called *Vogue*, adding a British edition in 1916 and a French one in 1920. In 1921 he bought up the *Gazette*. When it finally closed, the artists, now including Benito and Mourgue, remained with *Vogue*; this French School enjoyed a near monopoly of the covers throughout the twenties despite talented American artists such as Helen

1 S. Barbier, 'La fontaine de coquillages', *Gazette du Bon Ton*, 1914. Central Saint Martins Museum Collection.

2 Elizabeth Suter, Fashion drawing illustrating fabrics, with swatches attached, mixed media, 1970s. Artist's collection.

Dryden and George Plank who had worked for *Vogue* since before the war.

Those glossy covers, depicting a world of luxury and elegance, were not the domain of the average fashion artist. Most were technicians working to very strict rules. Writing in London in 1932 Eliot Hodgkin describes a typical challenge for the fashion artist employed to do a full-page newspaper advertisement for a world famous department store.

> He (rarely she) is required to produce 23 full-length adult ladies, 4 misses, 2 half ladies (blouses), 2 half ladies (petticoats), 4 heads wearing hats, 2 pairs of unoccupied shoes, 2 pairs of gloves and a dinner table fully laid with linen and glass. An equal number of eyes right and left are required so that the page can be balanced and there are to be no tennis racquets or parasols with which the table of glass and linen might be demolished. In addition he must liaise with the buyer, probably the only person to have seen the originals in Paris, on presentation details such as the position of the hemline, the tilt of the hat and so on.[5]

Whilst work of this sort has been almost totally superseded by the photograph there is still a place today for the descriptive rather than the creative fashion drawing [2], for example as an explanatory or technical drawing of a garment that does not yet exist, as in Elizabeth Suter's drawings, for the Queen, of Hardy Amies designs, or instructive drawings as in Margaret Woodward's scaled pattern diagrams in Norah Waugh's *The cut of women's clothes*.

The St Martin's drawing class which began (in 1931) the year before Hodgkin described the lot of the commercial fashion artist so graphically, was no doubt aimed at precisely the jobbing artist he describes. At that time it was the only real route into fashion, as he explains:

> There is in England, so far as I know, no scope whatsoever for the girl who designs fashions by drawing them. Dressmaking houses that do not confine themselves to copying French dresses have their own designer who is either a cutter or the head of the firm; someone, at any rate, so identified with the policy and reputation of the house that no beginner with a portfolio of designs could hope to be allowed to compete.[4]

This was also the year before *Vogue* started to replace the cover drawing with a photograph. So as the class began, the role of the fashion artist was changing as photography became increasingly important in the straightforward depiction of clothes. However advertisers and magazine editors wanted to be able to draw people into the lifestyle those clothes represented and this is where the artist

could use his or her creativity. The leading British artists of this period were Francis Marshall, the only Briton to work regularly for *Vogue*, and in the forties Gertrude Ettinger, 'ett', who was also art director of *The Ambassador*. Writing in *Fashion drawing*, Marshall says: 'The difficulties in fashion drawing ...[are] the dearth of teachers and proper training ... Many art schools have no fashion courses: often those that do are overcrowded.'[5]

Whilst teaching, Muriel Pemberton was also working as an illustrator, and her first drawing for *Vogue* appeared around 1933: it was an advertisement for a furriers in Carlos Place.[6] She went on to work for *Vogue Export* and *The Ambassador*, and in 1947 she was sent to draw Christian Dior's New Look collection for the *News Chronicle*. She recalls the thrill, after a long period of wartime austerity, of seeing the full, swirling skirts as they brushed against the faces of the audience and swept over the ashtrays.[7] [3–6]

At Burslem School of Art, Pemberton had been their youngest ever scholarship student, entering the college at 13 years 11 months. She went on to the RCA as a painting student in 1927. The Principal of the Royal College and Head of the Painting School at that time was William Rothenstein, a portrait painter.[8] After a year at the college, mindful of the need to earn a living afterward, she transferred to the School of Design, headed by Professor Tristam. This department did not teach design and making as the Central School of Arts & Crafts did, but was largely concerned with fine printmaking, illustration and mural painting. Paul Nash was a tutor and watercolour artists such as Bawden and Ravilious were recent graduates. Pemberton's self-styled fashion curriculum reflected the fine art and illustration bias of the department, and she carried this bias into her future fashion teaching.

Pemberton's original evening class at St Martin's was part of the commercial art department headed by John Hadley-Rowe, who later became Vice-Principal and, in 1941, Pemberton's husband. Additional classes in pattern cutting and museum studies were added and gradually this developed into a complete fashion course. In 1938 Pemberton became the government art inspector with responsibility for dress[9] and, by the time the new St Martin's building was opened in Charing Cross Road in the same year, fashion was well established. The brochure for the opening states: 'For fashion designing and fashion drawing new and better equipment and accommodation are provided'.[10]

Drawing was a fundamental skill that all students were expected to master at St Martin's. In addition to learning the discipline of observational drawing, which also took

3 & 4 Muriel Pemberton, fashion drawing for the *News Chronicle*, 1940s. Reproduced by permission of St Peter's House Library, the University of Brighton, and Liz Griffiths and family.

5 & 6 Muriel Pemberton, drawings of 'Antoinette', 1950s, mixed media. Collection of Liz Griffiths.

place in the Victoria and Albert Museum, the emphasis on the clothed figure, the way the limbs moved, the way weight was distributed, the angle of the hips and the shoulders, gave students a clear understanding of the form of the body and how clothes would sit and hang, or pull and swing, when worn. Once it came to designing clothes, students were able to see beyond the manufacture of an exquisite decorative carapace and to see dress design as both a kinetic and three-dimensional art form.

Immediately after the war St Martin's had more students than any other art school in the country but only the Dress and Painting departments offered classes at advanced level.[11] In the second post-war reorganisation of art education following the Coldstream Report,[12] only nine fashion courses were recognised at degree level in 1963. The previous year the St Martin's course was renamed Dress Design & Fashion Drawing making it the only one to offer a drawing specialism. The RCA, which as a postgraduate institution was not part of the reorganisation, did not offer fashion illustration either, stating in its course introduction throughout the 1960s: 'Fashion drawing is not included, as it is felt that in the past much confusion has arisen between fashion drawing and fashion designing'.

Initially St Martin's won approval for the DipAD courses in Dress and in Illustration that had been set up by Muriel Pemberton and her husband John Hadley-Rowe, but had to re-submit an application for Fine Art approval the following year. According to the application form submitted in Autumn 1961, the dress department had only one full-time member of staff at this time, Miss Muriel Pemberton ARWS, ARCA, WIAC, but 21 part-time tutors are also listed. Pemberton retired from her post as Head of Department at St Martin's in 1975 but continued to paint, draw and exhibit, and to teach drawing at Brighton School of Art.

When Pemberton joined St Martin's it was very much an art school. The Central School of Arts & Crafts was the premier college for practical design studies, surpassing the Royal College with which a merger was suggested at one point.[13] Fundamental to the Arts & Crafts movement was the idea that skilled craftsmanship was integral to pleasing and successful design so the Central School should have been the natural crucible for a successful course in fashion and dressmaking. At the beginning of the century it had a strong textile strand with embroidery classes taught by May Morris and Mrs A.H. Christie.[14] Out of the embroidery classes there developed a dress class and by 1919 there was a School of Textiles & Costume. In 1930, the year before Pemberton started teaching, this divided again, creating a School of Costume headed by Jeannetta Cochrane. Her

interests took the course in an increasingly theatrical direction with much emphasis on historical costume. Before the war all classes associated with contemporary dress were outsourced to the Shoreditch Technical School. In his advice to prospective fashion artists Hodgkin could easily have been describing an early Central class:

> Another disadvantage of the fashion class as against the life class is that the former is often little better than a dressmaking class, combined with instruction in embroidery, research into the costumes of the ancients, and the designing of theatrical costumes.[15]

He urged them to join one of the excellent LCC evening classes in drawing instead.

From the outset Central had a much more academic approach to design studies than St Martin's and its staff regularly produced textbooks on their subjects which still have value today. Much emphasis was placed on the cut and construction of clothes with great historical accuracy. In 1954 Norah Waugh produced *Corsets and crinolines* followed in 1964 by *The cut of men's clothes: 1600–1900*, both published by Faber & Faber. She was to have gone on to write *The cut of women's clothes: 1600–1930* (also published by Faber & Faber) but her untimely death meant that it was written almost entirely from Waugh's notes by Margaret Woodward.[7] It was published under Norah Waugh's name in 1968 with a note from Woodward explaining that she had completed and seen the book through the press

> out of a deep personal affection and respect for the work of my colleague the late Miss Norah Waugh, who died suddenly, at Easter 1966.

Waugh had started teaching at Central in the 1930s and apart from a brief wartime spell in Moscow[16] remained there until her death. Her books are illustrated by Woodward with technically accurate scale drawings and cutting diagrams. The series deliberately began at 1600 because Woodward, a medieval specialist, was to have written the volume for the earlier period. Sadly she too died unexpectedly, in 1973, before she was able to write her own book. Her drawings exemplify the fundamental differences between the two colleges in illustrating fashion.

However by the post-war period the two colleges regarded themselves as complementary, and Woodward and Pemberton were external assesors to each other's courses. The colleges merged in 1989 to form Central Saint Martins.

From 1953 the guiding force in the Costume Life Room at St Martin's was Elizabeth Suter. Tall, elegant and *sportif* in the Katherine Hepburn mould, in stark contrast to the short and bubbly Pemberton, she began her art studies

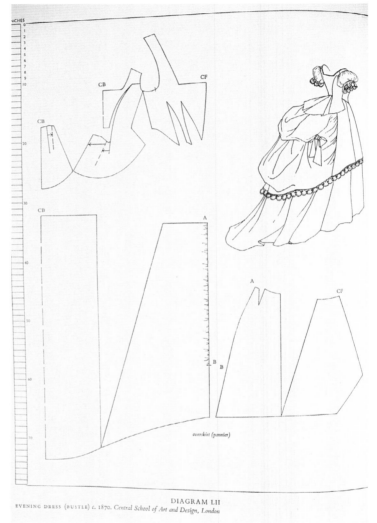

DIAGRAM LII

EVENING DRESS (BUSTLE) c. 1870. *Central School of Art and Design, London*

7 Margaret Woodward, drawing of pattern cutting details for Norah Waugh, *The cut of women's clothes 1600–1930*, Faber & Faber, 1968. Central Saint Martins library.

8 & 9 Elizabeth Suter, drawings of Paris collections, ink, 1978. Artist's collection.

DeLuca. 78.

WAR. BADGES.

Kilts. Open at side. Punk de Luxe

Chateau 78

Corduroy.

drawing with Meninsky at Central School in 1943, and was delighted when Meninsky remarked 'I suppose you want to be a fashion artist'. Suter says candidly she 'only ever wanted to draw, she didn't want to become a painter as there was nothing she particularly wanted to say'. Central School was full after the war so after a spell in the WRNS at Bletchley she joined a small private art school in Chelsea,[17] where she feels she learnt most of her drawing skills from Sam Rabin. He had studied at the Slade under Tonks, Professor of the hugely successful Painting School that Rothenstein had consciously set out to emulate when he took over at the RCA in 1920. Tonks had been a surgeon and an anatomist before becoming a painter and the importance of the body, the bones, the stance, the distribution of the weight, are all key to Suter's approach to drawing the figure; this corporeal solidity can be seen in the work of all who studied with her.

Throughout her years at St Martin's, which spanned three decades, Elizabeth Suter worked as an illustrator for Jaeger, Simpsons and Libertys and for newspapers and magazines including *The Times*, *Good Housekeeping* and *Country Life*, covering the Paris collections four times a year.[**8, 9**] She travelled with a writer and a photographer and each trip would last a week with three or four shows a day of two hundred garments. Drawing at the shows was strictly forbidden so she devised a personal code, noting details such as the position of the belt and the number of buttons and would do the drawings later in the day, a day often followed by dinner with a client, a punishing schedule. She covered the weddings of both Princess Anne and the Princess of Wales for *Country Life*.[**10**] The morning of the Wales' wedding was spent rushing around the various couturiers collecting details and swatches of the dresses of all the principals. This was followed by an afternoon of drawing whilst the television coverage played, and the whole lot – a grand set piece of the wedding party and individual drawings of the Queen, the Queen Mother and other prominent Royals – was rushed off to the printer to reach the news-stands the next day. A copy was sent to the honeymooning couple on the Royal yacht, 'to their undoubted delight', as she remarked wryly. When she left St Martin's, although asked to join other colleges she concentrated on drawing, working extensively for Hardy Amies, in particular preparing sketches of possible outfits for H.M. The Queen. She recalls with some amusement a palace comment on the drawings: 'there is no need to make them look like me'.

One of the first students to pass through Suter's class was Jo Brocklehurst. She had joined the college when she was only fourteen and recalls a broad curriculum from

10 Elizabeth Suter, double-page spread of the wedding of the Prince and Princess of Wales for *Country Life*, July 1981. Artist's collection.

anatomy classes to opera outings. After two years she spent a year at Woolwich Polytechnic then returned for a further two years study when she met Elizabeth Suter. Although she has worked for the press, she prefers the independence of doing her own drawings, and has become the unofficial chronicler of club culture both in the UK and in Europe, Berlin and Amsterdam in particular. Her large vibrant drawings epitomise the energy of the club scene.[11] She does not like to be described as an illustrator, a definition she finds too confining, preferring painter or draughtsperson. Following a recent period in America she has returned to England and in a deliberate move to reaffirm her personal roots and look back at her work in the English club scene she has used the world of Carroll's Alice, or rather Dodgson's Alice, to create a series of drawings: Brocklehurst through the Looking Glass. With these she has made an installation, a drawing room which fuses Victoriana and the dance world of the club scene, tightly corseted Duchesses, reminiscent of elderly aunts, and a mischievous White Rabbit in fetishistic garb.

Models are very important to the artist. Suter favoured dancers, encouraging students to capture the way the figure moves and to understand what the body is happy doing. Some young models were later to become famous, like Chrissie Hynde and Sid Vicious ('Absolutely terrifying' said Suter), but best remembered are Marjorie Butler, who had been a model when Suter was studying with Meninsky and looked as if she had stepped out of a Lautrec painting, and Antoinette, muscular, supple and able to hold the most extraordinary poses.

I recall as a raw young student in the seventies being somewhat taken aback by these two middle-aged characters who seemed to have so little to do with fashion: Marjorie, soft and round with white hair piled on her head, dressed in purple tights and Edwardian underwear, pouting and flirtatious; and Antoinette, unsmiling, dressed in black T-shirt and tights accentuating extraordinarily knobbly knees, hair fashioned into alarming bunches and with a masculine strength and angularity.[12–14] However the classes were in some ways a discourse on the nature of fashion itself. Clothes are important in the costume life class and Antionette and Marjorie, supremely confident in their eccentric garb, were able to adopt such imperious poses that any sense of fancy dress was banished. Fashion was no longer about clothes but about the state of mind in which clothes were worn; it was created by attitude and flair rather than fabrics and sewing. Anyone who drew Marjorie in feather boa and lacy pantaloons was left in no doubt that she believed she looked beautiful and such was her conviction that it was impossible to see her as anything

11 Jo Brocklehurst, drawing of punks, mixed media, 1982. Artist's collection.

12 Jo Brocklehurst, drawing of Marjorie Butler, c.1970. Artist's collection.

13 Jo Brocklehurst, drawing of 'Antoinette', 1970. Artist's collection.

14 Howard Tangye, drawing of 'Antoinette', 1970s. Artist's collection.

16 Colin Barnes, drawing of the designer Bruce Oldfield, mixed media, 1970s. Private collection.

17 Elizabeth Suter, drawing of Colin Barnes, coloured pencils, 1970s. Artist's collection.

15 Gladys Perint Palmer, cover illustration for the Japanese magazine *Trendsetter*, March 2002. Artist's collection.

Trendsetter

FASHION BUSINESS & MARKETING MAGAZINE　　　BIMONTHLY

75

2002
MARCH

特集○不振から再生へ、復調の要因を探る
変わる
都心型百貨店

else. It was an object lesson in that all-important skill: to dress women so that they believe they are beautiful.

Pemberton and Suter were different in many ways. Pemberton loved to work with great swathes of colour whilst Suter was the master of wash and line; however they did share one very important quality: they always encouraged their students. Gladys Perint Palmer, later a visiting lecturer at St Martin's herself, said Pemberton was the first tutor she ever had who praised rather than preached: Miss Pemberton's ducks are all swans. Upon completing the beginner's course at St Martin's GPP had decided she wanted to specialise in illustration and just before the summer break was instructed to come back in September with sketchbooks full of drawings. As it was a glorious summer she went to the beach and did not do a stroke of work. Too scared to go back to illustration she went to fashion instead. However she did spend the major part of her time drawing in Suter's classes, avoiding design altogether. Towards the end of the course she worked on her sketchbooks and designs at a table in the corner; if Pemberton knew she said nothing. In fact GPP says: 'She prepared us for life by encouraging us to learn the rules, break the rules and never get caught.' (She also advised them to eat apples and cabbages.) GPP recalls Pemberton's exuberant use of clashing colours (she has been compared to Matisse, admittedly by Jeffrey Archer[18]), and her Bloomsbury flat, where the furniture was upholstered in a medley of the painting colours and there were masses of pillows, each a different hue. One of the most useful things she learned from Pemberton, she says ruefully, is to always mix up plenty of paint as you will never match the colour again. Sadly colour reproduction was not commonplace when Pemberton was at her most active as an illustrator. Pemberton later became well known for her vibrant water-colours, particularly her flower paintings. She was a regular exhibitor at the Royal Academy's Summer Show from 1937, had her first one-woman show at the Leicester Galleries in 1951, another at Brighton Polytechnic in 1980, and a major retrospective at Chris Beetles in the spring of 1993. She was made a Fellow of the Royal Society of Watercolourists in 1974 and Senior Fellow of the Royal College of Art in 1985.

Gladys Perint Palmer's career has taken her around the world. Born in Hungary but educated in England she spent the early years of her career in Hong Kong where she worked regularly for the *South China Morning Post* and taught a drawing class at the University of Hong Kong. Currently Executive Director of Fashion at the Academy of Art University in San Francisco, where she employs Pemberton's maxim 'hire the best people and let them get

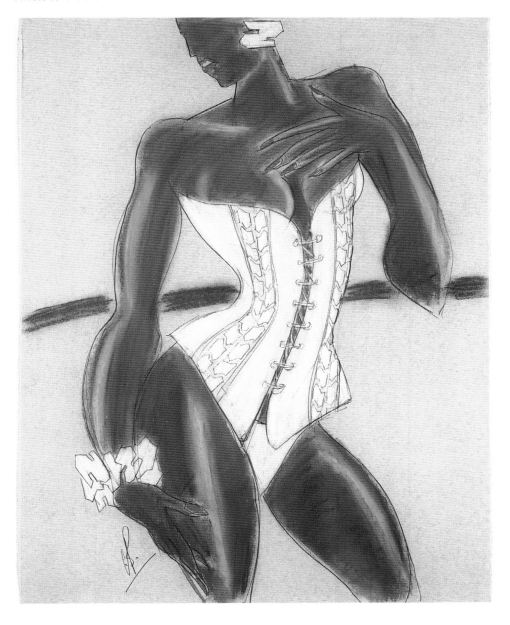

18 Colin Barnes, drawing for the Pirelli Girls calendar series, mixed media, 1970s. Private collection.

on with it', she is still a very active freelance illustrator. For *Vogue* alone she has produced editorial work for the American, British, Italian, Japanese, German, Spanish and Australian editions; she has also done editorial work for *The New York Times*, *San Francisco Examiner* (where she was fashion editor), *Washington Post*, *Los Angeles Times*, *New Yorker*, *Elle* and *The Sunday Times* in the UK.[15] She has had countless advertising clients, appears in Phaidon Press' *The fashion book*, 1998, as one of five hundred people of influence since 1860, and her 2003 book of satirical drawings with scurrilous comments on the principal players and hangers-on in the world of couture, *Fashion people*, was published in English and French by Assouline. She has an Honorary Doctorate from the University of San Francisco.

Describing Pemberton as part visionary, part inspiration, part mother, she muses on how Pemberton would have viewed the virtual revolution had she lived to see it. She thinks she may have said man can draw; a mouse can't.[19] However, the pupil to whom she said one day 'You'll be in the top ten Gladys' ('I was amazed she even knew my name') has designed a virtual drawing course. Backed up with text, images, audio and slide shows, her university creates video demonstrations in its own film studios that are mailed to students on CD-ROM. Students post internet images for group critiques.[20]

Central Saint Martins has always taken a broad mix of students including part-time and overseas students. Colin Barnes, one of the most commercially successful of St Martin's fashion artists, came to the school, like so many, by a very circuitous route.[16, 18] Evacuated from Singapore as a child he trained initially as an actor at RADA. Whilst resting – working in Heals' bed department – he met Claire Wallis, a textile and later graphic designer who, when he expressed a desire to study fashion drawing, recommended he speak to Margaret Woodward, who in turn sent him to Muriel Pemberton. Upon being asked whether they should take this mature student or not, Suter shrugged and replied 'Why not?' Not the most auspicious start to what was to become a lasting friendship and a successful career.[17]

Tall and lanky as a young man, urbane and full of fun, Barnes absorbed everything until Suter confessed 'There is nothing more I can teach you'. He worked for many major companies and magazines including *Cosmopolitan*, Harrods, *Vogue* and *Vogue Homme*, GAP and *Elle* in Paris, and his drawings from the eighties in particular epitomise the opulence and colour of that period. The Pirelli Girls series depicts glossy and voluptuous women who fill the page with glamour.

19 Shari Peacock, drawing of Vivienne Westwood collection, watercolour, 1983. Private collection.

A part-time lecturer at St Martin's in 1988 he wrote *Fashion illustration: the techniques of fashion drawing* (McDonald Orbis 1988), with an introduction by Elizabeth Suter. As well as examples of past and contemporary drawings it contains exercises recognisable from Suter's classes, such as the single line exercise where the pencil is never lifted from the paper, and the moving figure exercise where the model is drawn repeatedly as she moves forward, shifting weight from foot to foot. At the time of his sudden and untimely death in 1994 he had studios in both London and Paris.

Another artist whose work is very evocative of the eighties is Shari Peacock. An Iranian born in Sofia, Bulgaria, where all her education had been in Russian, she had come to London to study architecture. 'Early one evening, bored with the routine of school, work, home, home, school, work, I wandered into an art school in Charing Cross Road.'[21] She joined a St Martin's evening class in drawing, taught briefly by Barnes then by Tangye, and decided to make illustration her career. She won the Cecil Beaton Award, sponsored by *Vogue*, acknowledging her debt to her tutor Howard Tangye, and worked for many publications including *Vogue*, *The Guardian*, *The Independent*, and *Ms London*. Her fluid watercolours of Vivienne Westwood designs capture the bohemian layered look of the fashion at that time.[19]

Whilst her fanatical devotion to creativity was inspirational to friends and students alike[22] her creative drive and restless spirit made almost impossible demands upon her friends and upon herself. She moved from illustration to write a novel, *English as a foreign language*, a semi-autobiographical stream of consciousness written in English with a striking virtuosity. Her relish in the use of the language shines through. '... there was a method in my madness, a manner, a mode, *modus operandi*, nay *vivendi*, for I had to live, survive ...', an extraordinary tour de force by someone whose first languages were Bulgarian, Farsi and Russian. Not content with this third career she decided, at the age of 40, to embark on a fourth and train as a dancer. In 1999 she enrolled at the Eurythmie School in Hamburg, first learning German and convincingly giving her date of birth as 1965 rather than 1956. Within a few days of her arrival in Germany she became ill and was taken to hospital where she died in her sleep. Her friends and family were shocked to hear that she had had lung cancer.

Howard Tangye was a close personal friend of Shari Peacock, indeed he has befriended many of his former students. Like so many others his entry to St Martin's was unorthodox. Coming to London from his native Australia he was directed to Muriel Pemberton who, as so often

20 Howard Tangye, Dior invitation, 2001. Artist's collection.

21 Howard Tangye, drawing for Yves Saint Laurent, make-up, pen and ink, 1970s, Artist's collection.

22 Howard Tangye, portrait of Natalie Gibson, fashion print lecturer at Central Saint Martins, mixed media, 2004. Artist's collection.

when she spotted outstanding talent, and with her usual disregard for the admissions formalities, said 'we must have you'. After a year as a special student, a typical Pemberton ploy, he transferred via the normal channels to the three-year degree course where Elizabeth Suter remembers him fondly as the first to arrive and the last to leave each day, working, working, working.[23] Graduating with a first in 1974 he worked briefly for Zandra Rhodes before taking up the exchange scholarship St Martin's enjoyed with Parsons School of Design in New York where he found himself drawing five days a week. Parsons had had a professional programme in fashion design since 1896 and from 1954 to 1970 fashion illustration had been a department in its own right.[24] This unusual stress on drawing was something it shared with St Martin's. Tangye worked successfully as an illustrator in New York for several years, even after his return to London. In the late seventies there was still plenty of work; the *New York Times* was full of famous artists and all the big stores still had in-house illustrators (Saks department store had Antonio), often with an associated house-style. He was bemused to get repeated commissions for Henri Bendel, for which he was paid, even though they were never published. They sought confirmation of consistency before using an artist, an approach that seems wildly extravagant today, but once hired illustrators were expected to turn their hand to anything associated with fashion and, before computer aided design, this called for technique and discipline.[20, 21]

Always a good all rounder in Elizabeth Suter's words, he won dress design awards for Echo Industries and, in 1981, Courtelle Fabrics, and in the eighties worked again for Zandra Rhodes as assistant designer and illustrator. He has continued to draw ceaselessly, pushing the boundaries of fashion illustration with drawings for the windows of Voyage, the hyper-exclusive fashion shop which operated a locked door policy, admitting only those it deemed fit to wear its clothes, occasionally turning away celebrities like Madonna to the delight of the press.

With a mixed portfolio of teaching, design and illustration he contributed to several books on illustration in the late eighties and early nineties and (like Eliot Hodgkin half a century earlier) urged students, if unable to take a full-time course, always to choose a life class in preference to a fashion class.[25] In another unconventional illustration assignment in 1995 he created the paintings and drawings for Cruella de Ville's studio in Disney's *101 Dalmatians*. A regular exhibitor over the last 20 years, his often Schiele-like drawings, almost always on paper in mixed media, depict elegant and beautiful sitters without resort to those

23 Claire Smalley, unpublished drawing from John Galliano's collection, 1987. Marc Vaulbert de Chantilly. Estate of Claire Smalley.

fashion artist clichés of the slightly enlarged eyes or the pouting mouth.[22]

Currently Senior Lecturer for Womenswear for the Fashion BA at Central Saint Martins, slight and self-possessed, Tangye exudes an inner calm and like his predecessors Pemberton and Suter, he gives his students the confidence to achieve to their optimum. He continues to run drawing classes at Central Saint Martins, often teaching himself, sometimes with Jo Brocklehurst as a visiting lecturer, but admits with chagrin that drawing no longer enjoys the prominence it once had.

Claire Smalley was another exceptional St Martin's student. Graduating with a first in 1986, she could have made a career out of design but chose illustration. Her drawings for Galliano (1987–9) capture the languor and decadence of his early London work.

Before making a drawing, in addition to the usual Polaroids and sketches, she would ask many questions and

24 Julie Verhoeven, 'Can you spot the logos?', *Dazed & Confused*, 2001.

take copious written notes. This intellectual and intelligent approach, together with an understanding of the weight and hang of different materials and a knowledge of fashion history gave her an empathy with Central Saint Martins' trained designers,[26] and she worked tirelessly to capture the mood their clothes evoked. However the drawings she produced were sensual and instinctive rather than cerebral. These introspective qualities could have been a hindrance at the manufacturing end of the fashion trade, but she seemed to enjoy the autonomy of the freelance illustrator, refusing to draw anything that did not interest her. Before her premature death in 2003 she was working for *View*, a fashion forecast journal which predicts fashion trends up to three years ahead.[23] These drawings and paintings, which turn abstract concepts about future fashion moods into visual images, are far removed from traditional fashion drawings of dress and model and perhaps indicate the direction her future work might have taken.

Julie Verhoeven is often cited as one of the artists symptomatic of a renaissance in illustration.[27] [24 –26] With both parents working in the field, one as a graphic designer, the other as an illustrator, she was encouraged to learn to type. However at 16 she enrolled at Medway College in Kent to do a fashion diploma. There she was taught drawing by Tangye who encouraged her to join his St Martin's drawing class. She continued attending drawing classes, with evening classes taught by Shari Peacock and summer school by Jo Brocklehurst, even after she started working for John Galliano, another former Tangye student; indeed Galliano paid her fees for the summer school. She went on to work in Paris, and works both as a designer, with work for Louis Vuitton and her own collections for Gibo amongst others, as well as working as an artist, video artist, illustrator and occasional visiting lecturer at Central Saint Martins. Her style is graphic and two-dimensional and her drawings have been used as textile prints in her collections; they have a whimsical, erotic quality. She starts each season by developing the face or the character for that collection; wide-eyed, gentle creatures reminiscent of the sixties but exuding a contemporary sexuality. She published *Fat bottomed girls* in 2003, following her similarly titled exhibition, and in March 2004 had a one-woman show of paintings, 'Farewell, my lovely', at the Taché-Lévy Gallery in Brussels. Quiet and self-effacing, her work is difficult to categorise.

In recent years the importance of fashion drawing both within CSM and within the fashion industry has been on the wane. Whilst it is true that style magazines like *The Face* and *Dazed & Confused* have commissioned more illustrations recently and that there has been a vogue for retro,

25 & **26** Julie Verhoeven, 'Inventive ways of illustrating make-up', from *Dazed & Confused*, 2001. Artist's collection.

naive, felt-tip drawings in fashion retailing, photography, despite being much more expensive, still dominates. 'It's very boring, very repetitive, and you can't see the clothes', according to Tangye.[28] Perhaps part of the problem is simply that, just as the intensive drawing training that Tangye experienced at St Martin's and especially Parsons, no longer exists, art directors, commissioning editors and the general public no longer have the experience of reading interpretive drawings, finding a photograph much easier to understand.

The second half of the 20th century was a tough time for fashion artists. The public's unshakeable belief in the truth of the photographic image and a period of radical change in the art world have both helped make figurative work on paper unfashionable, which makes the work of the artists featured here all the more commendable.

Notes
1 John Russell Taylor, *Muriel Pemberton*, Chris Beetles, 1993, pp. 29–31.
2 Founded by Lucien Vogel and Michel de Brunhoff it was an exclusive magazine illustrating the clothes of the Parisian haute-couture.
3 Eliot Hodgkin, *Fashion drawing*, Chapman & Hall, 1932, p.13.
4 Eliot Hodgkin, *Fashion drawing*, Chapman & Hall, 1932, p.7.
5 Francis Marshall, *Fashion drawing*, Studio, 3rd edition 1948, p.77. First published in 1942 whilst he was in the Navy.
6 She was employed to draw the furs for advertisements and catalogues. John Russell Taylor, *Muriel Pemberton*, Chris Beetles, 1993, p.31.
7 Muriel Pemberton talking to Lou Taylor in the BBCs *Through the Looking Glass*, broadcast from November 1989 on BBC 2. See also Elizabeth Wilson and Lou Taylor, *Through the Looking Glass*, BBC Books, 1989, p.148.
8 Rothenstein had studied in Paris where he had met Lautrec and been much influenced by Whistler. Pemberton clearly felt her association with him important enough to mention in the introduction to a one-woman show she had at the Leicester Galleries in 1951.
9 The government art inspectorate was a panel of 12 and included Sutherland, McKnight-Kauffer and Pemberton's recent teacher Rothenstein. Public Record Office (PRO) ED 146/152.
10 *LCC programme on the Opening of Saint Martins School of Art and Technical Institute for the Distributive Trades*, Charing Cross Road, by the Rt. Hon. Herbert Morrison JP, MP, Leader of the Council. Wednesday 3 May 1939, CSM Archive.
11 There was a two-year general art course similar to the present-day foundation course called Intermediate and from 1946 the more advanced National Diploma in Design (NDD) which St Martin's offered in Dress & Painting.
12 Following the First Coldstream Report of 1960 the two-year NDD was replaced with a three-year Diploma in Art & Design, Dip AD, which aimed to provide a broad liberal arts-based education equivalent to a university degree. Much emphasis was placed on drawing skills and complementary and historical studies. Muriel Pemberton was a member of the specialist Textile Panel that decided which colleges would be able to award the new qualification.
13 Public Record Office (PRO) ED 146/152: 1936. *Report of the Committee for Advanced Art Education in London.*
14 Mrs Christie wrote *Embroidery and tapestry weaving* in 1906 as part of Lethaby's Artistic Crafts series of Technical Handbooks.
15 Eliot Hodgkin, *Fashion Drawing*, Chapman & Hall, 1932, p.3.
16 Biographical note on the dust jacket of *Corsets and crinolines*, Batsford, 1954. During the war she worked for the Ministry of Information and the Press Office of the British Embassy in Moscow.
17 Peter Lewis Crown and Pauline Stevenson, both later lecturers at St Martin's, also attended this art school.
18 'The greatest compliment you can pay to an artist is to buy their pictures ...which is why I possess three books on Matisse and three paintings by Muriel Pemberton'. Jeffrey Archer, quoted in John Russell Taylor, *Muriel Pemberton*, Chris Beetles, 1993, p.7.
19 Gladys Perint Palmer, *Fashion people*, Assouline, 2003, p.396.
20 For more details visit www.academyart.edu
21 Shari Peacock, *English as a foreign language*, Sofia, 1998, p.59.
22 In email correspondence with her ex-husband Jeremy Peacock, 29 April 2004.
23 Interview with Elizabeth Suter, 20 January 2004.
24 Melanie Brooks, *Fashion illustration in Britain and New York, 1960–1988.* Unpublished MA dissertation, V&A/RCA History of Design, May 2000.
25 Ian Simpson, ed., *The new guide to illustration*, Phaidon, 1990, p.142.
26 Claire illustrated for Joe Casely-Hayford, Jenny Packham and Russell Thompson's knitwear company Artifice & Guile. All are CSM graduates. She also worked for Jasper Conran and others.
27 Fashion illustration has enjoyed a revival over the past five years, thanks to a new wave of young, funky artists such as Jason Brooks, Graham Routhwaite and Julie Verhoeven.
28 Kate Quill, 'Artistry left out of the picture', *The Times*, 9 February 2004.

4/ Roger Sabin
Comics and cartoons

Dr Roger Sabin lectures in Cultural Studies at Central Saint Martins College of Art and Design. He is the author of several books including *Comics, comix and graphic novels* (Phaidon 1996). He writes for specialist publications such as *Eye* and *Image and Narrative* and has an occasional review column in the *Observer*.

There is a scene in Dan Clowes' now-classic comic strip 'Art School Confidential', a loosely autobiographical account of life at art college, where the depressed and edgy narrator turns to the reader and advises: 'Never mention cartooning in art school because it is mindless and contemptible and completely unsuitable as a career goal!'[1]

But when we look at the history of the Central School/ St Martin's/ Central Saint Martins, and the number of top-flight cartoonists that have passed through their doors, any assumptions about 'career goals' start to look a bit hollow. Alumni have been responsible for penning, at one time or another, such stars of the form as Batman[1], Judge Dredd, Gemma Bovery, Alex, and Rupert Bear. Not bad for a creative path so 'mindless and contemptible'.

The following essay attempts to highlight a selected number of those cartoonists, all of whom studied at the colleges. Most came up through the School of Graphics – though there's never been a degree on offer in cartooning *per se* – but a few have hailed from other schools, notably Fine Art. All of them diversified creatively into other areas as well – book illustration, advertising work, set designing, and so on. Some even ended up teaching back where they started (the fact that the miserable pay from lecturing often compares favourably to the pay for cartooning should tell us something about the fickle and sometimes exploitative world of the latter).

But what we should remember from the outset is that the relationship between a particular cartoonist's work and their time at college varies from individual to individual. Sometimes, they will have started cartooning before they got to college; sometimes they will have 'flowered' while they were there; sometimes, they became well known long after they had left. It is also true that different cartoonists have different opinions about the impact of their college years. For some they were pivotal, introducing them to new forms of art and providing a key inspiration. For others, college and work were two separate areas – some even confess that one hindered the other.

1 Alan Moore, Brian Bolland and John Higgins, cover for *Batman the killing joke*, 1988. Art: Brian Bolland. © Titan Books/DC Comics Inc.

For the sake of convenience, the world of cartooning can be divided into two broad spheres. The first consists of 'comic books'. These publications have tended to be defined as cheap, mass-produced literature containing as a significant proportion of their content 'comic strips' (stories told in sequential panels). Often, but not always, they will star a continuing character. In the UK, they are generally agreed to have originated at the end of the 1800s, and reached their peak sales at the end of the 1960s. Most people would associate the form with something like the *Beano*, or perhaps American comics like *Superman* and *Batman*.

The second sub-division consists of cartooning for press publications in a wider sense, typically in newspapers and magazines. This might include editorial cartooning – the production of one-shot cartoons to illustrate a topical or political story – and also 'gag' or adventure strips intended as light relief, usually published at the back of a paper. The first staff political cartoonist on a daily newspaper was hired in the 1880s, though today's crop of satirists often exhibit an attitude that hearkens back further, to the scatology of Gillray, Cruikshank and other pioneers. Importantly, this tradition also encompasses cartoon-orientated magazines like *Punch* and *Private Eye*.

Comic books started off in the UK as an adult medium. *Ally Sloper's half holiday* (1884) starred arguably the first superstar comics character (the eponymous Ally) and set the tone for a number of very popular adult 'funny papers' (*Comic Cuts*, *Illustrated Chips*, etc.). But by the First World War, this wave of comics was seen as old hat, and the form was being re-shaped for a much younger readership. Henceforward, comics would be stereotyped in the public imagination as a medium for the five-to-twelves: bright and harmless knockabout fun.

Yet, despite many people's (understandable) nostalgia for 'The Bash Street Kids', 'Desperate Dan', *et al.*, most of the great wave of kids' comics from the 1910s to the 1970s were not of good quality. Indeed, they consisted of lowest common denominator hackwork done for an audience that was perceived to be uncritical. More than this, because comics were imagined to be 'bad' for children – not least because they diverted them from such 'improving' pastimes as reading proper books – the cultural standing of the medium was extremely low. Dan Clowes' comment on its (perceived) 'contemptible' nature is perhaps fitting for this period in comics history.

Such attitudes had a knock-on effect for the circumstances of comic production. Creators worked for an often meagre per-page fee, with no royalties and no control over copyright. Their work was anonymous, and their status in the production process correspondingly low. Thus it is often very difficult to ascertain the contribution of graduates from Central and St Martin's to the industry at this time, though it is inconceivable that they were not playing a role (this was a big employer after all). Moreover, if individuals later went on to carve careers for themselves in other areas – graphic design, fine art or wherever – then their early years working for comics were not necessarily something they would include on a CV. It was simply not something thought to be worth owning up to.[2]

This attitude tended to change in the 1960s with the coming of so-called 'underground comics'. These were a new brand of comic orientated towards an adult readership (the first time this market had been seriously addressed since *Ally Sloper*, *et al.*), and are best described as an expression of the counter-culture. This was a movement which took off in the mid-late 1960s as aspects of the hippie subculture allied themselves with causes such as Anarchism, Socialism, Women's Liberation, Black Liberation, Gay Liberation, the Civil Rights movement in Northern Ireland, and protest against the Vietnam War. Add to this an interest in the spiritual value of mind-expanding drugs (marijuana and LSD being favourites) and of 'free love' (the pill had become widely available a few years earlier) and you had – simplistically speaking – a thriving anti-establishment movement. A counter-culture had always existed in British society, but at no point in history had it been so focused, or so large, as at this moment.

The art colleges played an important role in this utopian ferment. Famously, at Hornsey in 1968, in the wake of the near-revolutionary events in Paris, there was a full-scale rebellion and the college was occupied. St Martin's and the Central School saw their own sit-ins, strikes and protests. Meanwhile, outside the college gates, students were gravitating to the 'Arts Labs' – self-governing counter-cultural workshops that sprang up all over the country (the one in London was situated in Drury Lane). Here, and to a lesser extent in the college classrooms and studios themselves, the visual identity of 'the revolution' was established – often involving explosion-in-a-paintshop graphics best enjoyed when stoned.

The underground comics were part of the mix, and represented total aesthetic freedom. As the name suggests, they had nothing to do with mainstream comics, and were in many ways antithetical to them. Instead of pandering to the kids' market, these titles spoke to the counter-culture on its own terms, involving politics, sex, drugs, sex, rock and roll, and more sex. Writers and artists were not typically teamed up to work under the control of one editor. Instead, the underground creator controlled every facet of his or her individual creation. Also in tune with the hippie ethos, creators kept copyright over their work, and – in theory at least – received royalties.

So, for the first time, producing comics became the hip thing for students to do. The art colleges unofficially pumped out dozens of underground masterpieces from 1967 to 1977, typically in runs of a few dozen to the low hundreds, and commonly produced illicitly on college equipment. For our purposes, because it became *de rigueur* to sign work, until then a rarity in the mainstream, the identification of Central and St Martin's students has becomes easier. Indeed, it is interesting to note that at Central there even existed a semi-regular satirical magazine, definitely underground-influenced, which revelled in the name *The Galloping Maggot*. Not that these comics and magazines were necessarily condoned by the courses. On the contrary, there was a great deal of resistance to them among certain lecturers, who believed that comics were not art and should never be considered as such. But, alas for them, it was a (psychedelic) wave that couldn't be stopped.

Brian Bolland, who did a one-year postgraduate course in graphic design at Central from 1973 to 1974, was a minor star of the underground. He would go on to become one of the most bankable names in mainstream comics – more about which later – but already by 1973 his skill as a cartoonist was setting him apart. In terms of underground comics, which were often roughly produced and spontaneous, his fastidious line and anatomically believable figures were refreshingly different.

> I did contribute to *The galloping maggot*. But interestingly the course I was on didn't discourage me from comics. Indeed, I spent the whole year producing one comic book – a self-indulgent thing called *Suddenly at 2 o'clock in the morning*. Quite a lot of it got reprinted in the underground comics and magazines of the time such as *Cozmic Comics*, *Frendz* and *Oz*.

He admits that he was enriched by the wider knowledge of art history his college time gave him, but that it was rare to find a tutor interested in cartooning:

> When I went for my interview for a place at the Central there was one tutor there who was keen on some of the satirical magazines that contained cartoons, like *National Lampoon* in the US and *Hara Kiri* in France. I could tell that he was the one that got me accepted on the course. But then I don't think I saw him again for the course's duration.

One Bolland strip in particular became notorious, 'Little Nympho in Slumberland', a spoof of the classic

2 Brian Bolland, 'Little Nympho in slumberland', page from *Cosmic Comix*, 1974.
© Brian Bolland / H.Bunch Associates Ltd.

3 John Howard, Brian Bolland and Tom Frame, 'Judge Dredd: the judge child', double page spread from Part 18, *2000 AD*, prog 173, 16 August 1980.
Art: Brian Bolland.
© IPC Magazines Ltd.

American strip 'Little Nemo in Slumberland'.[2] It originated in *Suddenly at 2 o'clock in the morning*, and was widely reproduced elsewhere. Little Nympho's sexual adventures, including bondage and sex with aliens, were exquisitely drawn by the underground standards of the day, but were asking for trouble. Feminists objected, and for a while Bolland found himself under attack.

> Thirty years on (or even ten years on) that strip was still cringeingly embarrassing for me. But looking at issues of *Oz*, I can see that sex and nudity were common currency. That and the fact that at college we all spent many hours drawing nude life models, meant that 'Nympho' didn't seem that offensive at the time. I was just drawing what I knew.[3]

The underground comics revolutionised the whole way in which the wider industry operated – though the changes in attitudes to royalties, copyright, and of course content took a while to filter through. One particular mainstream comic, launched in 1977, came to embody the new approach. *2000AD* was a science fiction adventure title published by Fleetway, home of 'Roy of the Rovers' and others. But instead of focusing purely on a kids' audience, the comic took the risk of adding more adult subject matter, inspired in part by the underground. All the strips were credited, and in later years, there would also be moves towards offering royalties and some control over copyright.

Brian Bolland was one of the first artists to be hired. His amazing *2000AD* covers featuring the future lawman 'Judge Dredd' came to personify the comic.[3] Even the most surreal of science fiction scenarios could become believable under his pen: on one cover, the brutish cop looks on as a pair of floating lips tells him 'Help me, Judge Dredd! This planet's sending me to pieces!' Later, Bolland's previously proven penchant for drawing the female form came into good use as a woman counterpart for Dredd was added: 'Judge Anderson'.

2000AD became a seedbed for a new wave of British talent. The comic is still going strong today, despite having passed its once very futuristic-sounding title date, and despite not selling as well as it did in Bolland's day.

But one other Central Saint Martins graduate is worthy of note in *2000AD*'s more recent context. Laurence Campbell started contributing to the comic in the 1990s, and indeed has worked on Judge Dredd.[4] Campbell studied graphic design between 1993 and 1996, and was producing his own strips while still at college – though evidently this passion was not as indulged as in the case of Bolland.

> Comics weren't heavily encouraged, says Campbell. But by being a student I learned from being introduced to the styles of different graphic designers and fine artists, and I used that in my comics. Subsequently, a lot of people have labelled my work as being graphic design orientated, rather than illustrative, which I think is true in terms of my interest in composition, layout and so on.

> So, was he aware of Bolland?

> Of course! Every comics fan is. His Dredd is iconic, and so when I was asked to work on the character it was really a thrill. But I only found out fairly recently that [Bolland] had been to Central too.[4]

Campbell now splits his time between professional comics work and tutoring at the college – where he says he's sympathetic to aspiring cartoonists, but encourages them to look outside the comics world for inspiration.

Post-*2000AD*, the rest of the mainstream comics industry started to wake up. Over the Atlantic, the big American publishers began to see the value of adding more 'adult' content. The result was a new wave of superhero books in which moral ambiguity was the order of the day, as well as a more liberal attitude to sex and violence. Unsurprisingly, companies like DC Comics and Marvel began headhunting British talent from *2000AD*, and less surprisingly still, Brian Bolland was at the top of their list. From the 1980s to the present, Bolland has showcased his skills drawing world famous characters such as Batman, Superman and Wonder Woman. Today, pieces of his original artwork featuring the same fetch astronomic sums.

Bolland was not the only one to make it in the US, and the 'British invasion' has continued, more or less, to the present. Laurence Campbell, for example, has produced comics for Caliber Press and Image Comics.

4 Colin Clayton and Chris Downs, Laurence Campbell and Lee Townsend, Gary Caldwell, Ellie De Ville, 'Synnamon facing Mecha' part 3, page from *2000 AD*, prog 1364, 29 October 2003. Pencils: Laurence Campbell. © Rebellion.

The American market is attractive for lots of reasons. There's the money, of course, plus it puts the artist on a bigger stage. You're seen by more people over a longer period of time. In Britain, *2000AD* is a weekly, and it disappears from the shelves pretty quickly. But in the US, the titles are monthly and they stay there for much longer. It's a silly thing, but it counts.[5]

Yet not everybody was seduced by America and the appeal of the mainstream market. There remained a branch of cartooning that was resolutely anti-commercial, and which saw as its spiritual antecedent the 1960s underground. 'Alternative comics', as they became known, kept the underground's insistence on freedom of expression but jettisoned its more hippie underpinnings. The 1980s and 1990s were a kind of golden age for nonconformist comics, among them titles that tackled topics never or rarely covered before, and which pushed back artistic expectations. Small alternative publishers flourished, and autobiography became a major genre – a theme as far divorced from the (mainstream) superhero template as could be imagined. Dan Clowes' strip about his art school experiences fitted neatly into the new approach.

Punk, in particular, was an influence. This was a relatively short-lived phenomenon (its high point in the UK is generally recognised to have been between 1976 and 1979), but its impact was long-term and directed attention away from the old counter-culture obsessions. It led to new art styles and fresh ways of thinking about stories. In particular, punk fanzines offered a paradigm for a new comics 'small press', spurred on by the falling cost of photocopying. Such titles typically had minuscule print-runs (usually in the tens or low hundreds), nearly always lost money (just like the early undergrounds), and exhibited a rough-and-ready punkish vibe.

Students from Central and St Martin's took full advantage – sometimes using college equipment to produce their work – and the number of small pressers from the 1980s, 1990s and 2000s runs into dozens.[6] Rachael House, who studied fine art between 2001 and 2004, was already well known on the small press scene [**5, 6**] before she came to college:

> I love photocopying because it's so immediate. There are no commercial constraints and you have 100 per cent control. I also think that small press comics offer an important creative outlet for women, who may otherwise be put off comics by the over-emphasis on superheroes. A lot of friendship networks are created along the way.

House's comics are often autobiographical, and punk was clearly very important to her:

The whole DIY aspect to these comics is a statement in itself. If you want to make something happen, then make it happen! By using lo-tech means, a whole new world opens up.

Has her time at Central Saint Martins changed her comics?

The punk attitude is still there, I hope – but that kind of fits with the place, too. After all, the Sex Pistols played their first gig at the college. But my comics now include references to fine artists, which they never did before, so obviously that's a result of being immersed in the fine art world. In future, I want my comics to have a more 'art book' sensibility, but not to the point where you have to don white gloves and pay fifteen quid for them. They'll still be comics.[7]

5 Rachael House, cover of *Weedy and scrawny summer fun!*, self-published, July 2003.
© Rachael House.

6 Rachael House, 'Big Brother 2004', strip from *Weedy and Scrawny summer fun!*, self-published, July 2003.
© Rachael House.

Where next for the comics medium? Some commentators are pointing towards the internet. All the major comics companies have a website, often including on-line strips, and the indie and small press scene has adopted the technology with enthusiasm (from photocopiers to the web is perhaps not such a big step). But the rise of one communications medium does not necessarily entail the death of another – any more than the advent of cinema killed theatre – and we can expect traditional print comics to continue for a while yet. Potential cartoonists from Central Saint Martins thus have a range of options to choose from. Whether they can prove once and for all to the college establishment that cartooning is not a 'contemptible' creative choice remains to be seen. But the omens are good.

In newspaper cartooning, satire has always been the biggest genre. Most people associate the word with specifically political jokes. But the dictionary definition is much more broad: 'composition ridiculing vice or folly or lampooning individuals …'.[8] (And anyway, isn't all of life 'political'?) Our survey of press cartoonists who studied at Central/ St Martin's/ Central Saint Martins therefore includes content spanning everything from whimsical mockery to vicious scatology.

Alfred Bestall studied Illustration at Central between 1919 and 1922, and joined a growing throng of post-First World War satirists. His early style involved plenty of detail and cross-hatching – the kind of work in vogue at the time. At *Punch*, for example, a magazine which the young Bestall admitted was 'a fixation' for him, and where he became a regular contributor, the practice of 'illustrating the joke' was well established. He thus settled into a form of cartooning which was polished, if hardly distinctive from many other graphic satirists working contemporaneously. (Other Central and St Martin's students who would in time contribute to *Punch* were William Sillince, Michael ffolkes [sic] (real name Brian Davis) and Bruce Angrave.)

In terms of subject matter, Bestall's cartoons would encompass everything from the comedy of manners, especially the 'war between the sexes', to more politically-focused commentary – though this was a time when restraint was a watchword. The old viciousness of Gillray *et al.* had long since given way to a more deferential approach, especially with regard to the monarchy and politicians. As the great Sir David Low would later comment: [cartoonists were] 'dipping their rapiers in lemonade'.[9] For the mild-mannered Methodist Bestall, this was not an unacceptable state of affairs.

Rupert's Big Game Hunt

RUPERT CONTINUES THE SEARCH

"The wind blew me in there," he cries. / Then Rupert a queer trail espies.

The trail they follow with great care, / 'Til something flashes through the air.

"What's that!" cries Bill. Then down they run, / And find a sea lion having fun.

The sea lion says, "There's no fish here, / I'll have to go back now, I fear."

7 Alfred Bestall, 'Rupert continues the search', from *More Rupert adventures*, Daily Express Publications, 1943. Central Saint Martins Museum Collection.

Having attained a measure of success, he expressed mixed feelings about the impact of art school on his career. In 1925, he told a newspaper:

> Learn your technique at art school, but don't stay too long. If you do, you risk losing your most precious asset, individuality, and becoming a mere reproducer of other people's ideas.

He went on, in terms reminiscent of the tone of the Dan Clowes strip quoted at the beginning of this essay,

> Art schools turn out many admirable art teachers, but their tendency is, by immersion in technique, to overlay the individuality and power of self-expression of the student.[10]

But *Punch* wasn't the total of Bestall's career. He contributed to *Eve*, *Gaiety*, *Piccadilly* and *Tatler* (over 40 colour plates) among others, and in 1935 made a move away from satire that would occupy him for the next three decades. At the *Daily Express*, a cartoonist was desperately needed to take over 'Rupert Bear' (which had been created by Mary Tourtel in 1920).[7] Bestall rose to the challenge by modifying his old *Punch* style in favour of a lighter, more rounded technique (still illustrational, for all that), and by developing a writing style that could be both charming and surreal – the *Express's* dictum that 'evil characters' be avoided in the stories was adhered to, but Bestall delighted in introducing elves, a Chinese conjuror, and a variety of quirky new animal characters. He ended up producing over 300 stories, and establishing Rupert as an icon of English popular culture. He was awarded an MBE in 1965.

Mel Calman was a satirist who belonged in every sense to a more modern age than Bestall, but whose work shared

8 Mel Calman, pocket cartoon from the collection *Help!*, Methuen, 1982. © S. & C. Calman.

9 Mel Calman, pocket cartoon from the collection *It's only you that's incompatible*, Methuen, 1984. © S. & C. Calman.

many similarities with the latter's early career. He studied at St Martin's between 1951 and 1953, and thereafter made his name as a 'pocket' gag cartoonist for the national papers. His career, spanning the late 1950s to his death in 1994, took in the *Daily Express*, *Sunday Telegraph*, *Observer*, *The Sunday Times*, and *The Times*, as well as a great deal of auxiliary work (illustrating books, writing plays, etc.). During this time, his talent for minimalist laughs was clear: as his obituary in *The Times* put it:

> A pocket cartoon occupies only a square inch or so of the daily acres of newsprint. But these daily squiggles, scribbled under the shadow of a looming and unforgiving deadline, can pack more punch than the biggest headline.[11]

Like Bestall many years before, Calman's repertoire spanned both topical gags and satires of modern manners.[8] Although his humour has been described as 'gentle', there was often a darker undercurrent, especially when it came to quips about relationships (one of his books was entitled *How about a little quarrel before bed?*).[9] In this respect, his unmistakably 'Jewish humour' was of the black and self-deprecating variety, rather in the manner of his idols among the New York comedy set – James Thurber, S.J. Perelman and Woody Allen. Thus, the characters he created in his cartoons were anxious and neurotic, picking holes in their marriages and relationships with a sometimes masochistic vigour. Calman admitted that most of the laughs were in the text, but visually his small bumbling characters, big-nosed and depressed-looking – drawn with vivacious sweeps of the pencil – were also oddly endearing. When the cartoonist died, many readers felt they'd lost a friend.

By the early 1960s, it was time for a new wave of hard-hitting, and often outrageously crude, satirists. *Private Eye* was the focus; a new magazine (founded 1961) that had its origins in the British university system, and which prided itself on being anti-establishment for its own sake. This did not mean, however, that it had much in common with the hippie underground press. It never subscribed to the 'class-less society', far less to 'flower power', and indeed there were reports that *Eye* co-founder Peter Cook burned the first issue of *Oz* in a Soho pub. As historian David Huxley has argued 'if the hippies had come to power, *Private Eye* would have been as scathing about them (if not more so) as they were about Harold Macmillan and his government'.[12]

Without doubt the most distinctive of the early *Eye* cartoonists was Gerald Scarfe, who studied life drawing at St Martin's in the early 1960s. His 11 cover illustrations stamped a graphic identity on the magazine, and caused no small amount of controversy. He explains

10 Gerald Scarfe, cover for *Private Eye*, 23 August 1963. Central Saint Martins Museum Collection. © Gerald Scarfe.

11 Gerald Scarfe, caricature of Diana, Princess of Wales for the *Heroes and Villains* exhibition at the National Portrait Gallery, London, 2003. Central Saint Martins Museum Collection. © Gerald Scarfe.

Satire had been going through a dull phase. It had been very scurrilous back in the days of Gillray, Cruikshank and so on, but since the late 1800s the form had become bland, to the point where, in the Second World War, the cartoonists were supported by the country at large: David Low, for example, was drawing pictures of Hitler and so on, and people said 'right on!' – that's probably why they knighted him.

Private Eye, however, put an end to all that:

The magazine actually shocked the public, and I was encouraged by the editors, especially William Rushton and Peter Cook, to go as far as I could! So there I was, drawing shit, warts, pubic hair, anything you could think of … It caused quite a stir.

So much so that Scarfe's cover for the *Eye*'s 1963 annual caused it to be banned by the four largest book wholesalers (including W. H. Smith).[10]

Scarfe is convinced his time at St Martin's contributed significantly to his style:

I was very interested in life drawing, and particularly in anatomy – even to the point of buying medical books so I could study musculature, bone structure and so on. That influenced my cartoons quite considerably, and the attention to bodily detail got me a reputation as a 'grotesque' cartoonist.

12 Gerald Scarfe, caricature of Tony Blair and George Bush for the *Heroes and Villains* exhibition at the National Portrait Gallery, London, 2003. Central Saint Martins Museum Collection. © Gerald Scarfe.

13 Peter Brookes,
editorial cartoon for
The Times newspaper,
September 2003.
Central Saint Martins
Museum Collection.
© Peter Brookes.

14 Peter Brookes,
editorial cartoon for
The Times newspaper,
October 2003.
Central Saint Martins
Museum Collection.
© Peter Brookes.

He goes on to explain that, in terms of content:

I was aware of Gillray and so on before I went to college, but being a student helped me become much more familiar with the work of those first wave satirists.

Surprisingly perhaps, Scarfe himself was not hostile to the hippie underground:

There wasn't much rapport between *Eye* and the underground, it's true, but I did a cover for [underground newspaper] *International Times* which became quite a problem. It involved Mary Whitehouse, a famous anti-smut campaigner, having sex with Rupert Bear, who had become a symbol of the counter-culture [and who had previously been 'borrowed' for a famous strip in *Oz* which was duly busted] right in front of the Pope. This did not go down very well, and Whitehouse sued. The lawyers' letters were hilarious, but unfortunately *International Times* had to cough up.

Scarfe's subsequent career rarely inspired such censure. He went on to work for mainstream UK newspapers (notably *The Sunday Times*) and US magazines such as *Fortune*, *Time*, and the *New Yorker*, and found time to move into other areas.[11, 12] 'I've really been trying to push my craft of late. I've done opera, ballet, theatre design, animation, all sorts of things.'[13] Has he become so co-opted into the establishment that a knighthood is in the offing? Perish the thought.

With *Private Eye*'s success in the 1960s, mainstream newspapers rediscovered the value of political satirists. According to historian Mark Bryant, the period saw *The Times* and *Telegraph* employ cartoonists and caricaturists on a formal basis for the first time.[14] Peter Brookes, who studied graphic design at Central between 1966 and 1969, had been freelancing for political publications like *New Society* and *New Statesman* for some time before he became 'Political Cartoonist' for *The Times* in 1982.[13, 14] He explains:

Private Eye had certainly loosened things up. Political cartooning was something I got into over a long period, because in relation to *Eye*, which was definitely pretty savage with people like Scarfe and Steadman, and in relation to the underground press, the idea of working for mainstream newspapers was seen as being rather 'straight' and old-fashioned.

Brookes remembers his student days as being deeply influenced by the student upheavals around 1968 ('I recall a delegation from the LSE coming down to whip up support – without much luck, it has to be said – and various sit-ins and protests'), and upon leaving he ended up free-lancing for the underground, 'especially doing covers for things like *Oz* and *Frendz*'. His later political work was 'a natural interest', and he is perhaps best known for his satires of the Thatcher government. But he insists that even today his cartooning technique owes much to the methods he learned at Central: 'It's the same process – you're just applying it to a current situation'.[15]

It wasn't just the broadsheets that benefited from the post-*Private Eye* shift in attitudes. The period also saw the founding of specialist professional societies, such as The Cartoonists' Club of Great Britain and the British Cartoonists' Association, while in 1970 Mel Calman founded The Cartoon Gallery, a space devoted to cartoon art, which did a great deal in its own way to raise the stock of the profession.

Over at the liberal *Guardian*, the satire boom took on a particular complexion with the hiring of a young female cartoonist unafraid to lampoon the foibles of the middle class readers of the paper itself. Posy Simmonds studied graphic design at Central between 1964 and 1968, and like Peter Brookes (who studied in the previous year, and whom she knew) she vividly recalls the excitement of the times: 'It was 1968 and all that – and I remember these fabulous student parties and going to see "the Animals" play live in the college's underground car park.'[16] As for cartooning, she says she grew up in a house full of old *Punches*, but found that college wasn't necessarily an encouraging place. 'The course didn't really connect with cartooning: it just wasn't talked about. But I used to twist the projects to get my drawings in ....'

It was none other than Mel Calman who saw Simmonds' degree show and encouraged her to pitch work to the dailies. Once she'd made her professional break, the college became an inspiration for a number of strips: 'There was one tutor, up in 'Liberal Studies', as it was known then, who became the basis for my character 'George Weber, the Structuralist' – that was great fun.'[17] Unbeknownst to her, the staff at Central would buy the *Guardian* religiously to see if they could spot the references.[16]

Simmonds' satirical style was, and is, restrained, but with a waspish undercurrent based on recognition: no modern cartoonist better captures the minutiae of what people say and do. (Although her writing is sophisticated, the joy of her work has always been in the body language and facial expressions.) In the 1990s, her *Guardian* strips built on this. The serialised story 'Gemma Bovery' was an updating of Flaubert's classic, and involved a tragi-comic tale of personal politics versus lust.[16] It was collected into a graphic novel, and was nominated for a prize at the prestigious Angoulême comics festival in France. In so

15 Posy Simmonds, cover for *Gemma Bovery*, written and illustrated by Posy Simmonds, Cape, 2000.
© Posy Simmonds.

© Posy Simmonds 1993

16 Posy Simmonds,
'A lecture', cartoon for
The Guardian, 1993.
Central Saint Martins
Museum Collection.
© Posy Simmonds.

doing Simmonds became one of the few newspaper cartoonists to win respect among comics aficionados, and indeed, to make the crossover into the comics market.[17] Her latest work, 'Literary Life', a satire on the publishing business, while much more episodic, looks like repeating the trick. She was awarded an MBE in 2002.

There have been many more great cartoon satirists through the doors of the Central School, St Martin's and Central Saint Martins over the years. To end with just two of the more famous: Charles Peattie (Fine Art, St Martin's 1977–80) co-created 'Alex', a 20-something merchant banker(!), who first appeared in 1987 at the height of the yuppie phenomenon, and has been thriving ever since in the pages of the *Independent* and latterly the *Daily Telegraph*. His other co-creation, 'Celeb', an affectionate satire on the diminishing 'celebrity' status of a has-been rock star, debuted in *Private Eye* in 1987 and was later made into a TV series starring Harry Enfield.[18] Matthew Pritchett ('Matt') studied Graphics at St Martin's between 1983 and 1986, and has been the *Daily Telegraph*'s pocket cartoonist since 1988.[19, 20] His eye for the personal ramifications of political decisions, and his simple, direct drawing style have marked him out as the most amusing and talented cartoonist of his kind since Mel Calman. He, like Posy Simmonds, was awarded an MBE in 2002.

Is satire on the wane? Media commentators have been grimly shaking their heads and saying so for years. Some have argued that the form died the moment Henry Kissinger (or was that Yasser Arafat? or David Trimble?) won the Nobel Peace Prize; others that, in a post-9/11 world, there's a duty for cartoonists to be 'on side'. All nonsense, of course. Satire is still a massively valuable perspective, and one which continues to be feted by the UK's press. Indeed, it is probably in the rudest health it

17 Posy Simmonds, page from *'Fred'* written and illustrated by Posy Simmonds, Cape, 1987. Central Saint Martins Museum Collection. © Posy Simmonds.

18 Charles Peattie and Mark Warren, 'Celeb' from *Private Eye*, 28 May - 10 June, 2004. © Charles Peattie and Mark Warren.

has ever been – and 'rude' is the word, with younger cartoonists taking up where Gerald Scarfe left off (the Ian Hislop era *Private Eye* is arguably as controversial as it has ever been and still sells in numbers that shame most magazines). Can future graduates of Central Saint Martins find the energy to take up the torch? I for one will be scanning the degree shows, looking for signs.

Copyright © Roger Sabin 2005

19 & **20** 'Matt' (Matthew Pritchett), pocket cartoons for the *Daily Telegraph*, 2003/4. Central Saint Martins Museum Collection. © Matt.

Notes

1 *Eightball*, no. 7, 1991 (Fantagraphics Books). The strip is currently being adapted into a movie by the same team responsible for indie comics-based hits *Crumb* and *American Splendor*.
2 It has come to light during the writing of this book that Andrew Dodds, a student at Central and later a tutor at St Martin's, once contributed illustrations to the *Eagle*.
3 Brian Bolland, interview with the author, 12 November 2003.
4 Laurence Campbell, interview with the author, 28 February 2004.
5 *Ibid.*
6 To name just a handful: Michael Nicholson, who produced a series of much-loved comics starring a character called 'Ron'; Luella Jane Wright, who created a number of saltily subversive titles in the early 1990s (e.g. *Cunty*, a not-so-affectionate take on *Bunty*); and Ferry Gouw, who contributed to the award-winning small press anthology *Sturgeon White Moss*.
7 Rachael House, interview with the author, 24 March 2004.
8 *Oxford English dictionary, pocket edition*, Oxford University Press 2004.

9 Sir David Low, quoted in Mark Bryant, *Dictionary of 20th-century British cartoonists and caricaturists*, Ashgate, 2000, p.ix.
10 *Methodist Recorder*, 1925, quoted in Caroline G. Bott, *The life and works of Alfred Bestall*, Bloomsbury, 2003, p.53.
11 Obituary of Mel Calman, *The Times*, 12 February 1994, p.19.
12 David Huxley, *Nasty tales*, Critical Vision Press, 2001, p.48.
13 Gerald Scarfe, interview with the author, 5 March 2004. Side note: as a boy, Scarfe had several drawings published in the *Eagle*. One example won a prize (an Ingersoll watch), and the runner-up in that particular competition was none other than David Hockney.
14 Mark Bryant, *Dictionary of 20th-century British cartoonists and caricaturists*, Ashgate, 2000, p.ix.
15 Peter Brookes, interview with the author, 26 May 2004.
16 Simmonds met her future husband at Central, the graphic designer and typographer Richard Hollis. His contribution to the typesetting of *Gemma Bovery* would be much praised.
17 Posy Simmonds, interview with the author, 13 February 2004.

5 / Alan Powers
Book jackets

Dr Alan Powers is a Reader in Architectural History at the University of Greenwich, where he also lectures on Graphic Design. He is the author of *Front cover* (2001) and *Children's book covers* (2003), both published by Mitchell Beazley, and curated the exhibition 'Eric Ravilious: imagined realities' at the Imperial War Museum, 2003–4, and is author of the accompanying book.

Commissions

for book jackets have offered a steady income to artists and designers alike. For this reason, if for no other, they have a place in the story of art education and professional life which is neatly encapsulated in the years described by Eric Hobsbawm as 'the short 20th century', the period from the outbreak of the First World War to the fall of the Berlin Wall.[1] They were not unknown before this time, but they did not offer any artist a living. The growing popularity of jackets in the 1920s, at least in the English-speaking world, was a direct consequence of the social upheaval following the War, when the book trade began to shake off its snobbish anti-commercialism and attend to sales technique. The end date is more misleading, although if one is looking for the artist's hand transmitted directly by the print medium, that has become increasingly rare since 1990 and the full onset of computer design.

Jackets have usually been seen as ephemeral. The convention among book lovers was to discard them, on the basis that the binding was the part of the book intended to be seen. Collectors and publishers alike tended to deprecate illustrated jackets, since they were originally the distinguishing mark of cheap editions of 'popular' fiction. Even the publisher Richard de la Mare, the son of the poet, called the book jacket 'the wretched thing' as late as 1932,[2] which was particularly surprising coming from him, since it was de la Mare's firm, Faber and Faber, that had produced some of the best jackets during the 1930s. If this widespread attitude failed to dampen publishers' growing sense of the commercial value of book jackets, it did prevent institutional libraries from considering the book jacket as a significant part of the book. Those that have preserved book jackets at all have done so selectively, and in separate holdings to the books themselves. As a result, the history of the subject has largely to be reconstructed from examples in private collections and in the market place, where the rarity of good original jackets ensures that they now command premium prices.

1 Barnett Freedman, book jacket for Walter de la Mare (ed.), *Behold, this dreamer!*, Faber & Faber, 1939. Private collection.

BEHOLD, THIS DREAMER!

WALTER DE LA MARE

To write the history of book jackets in terms of the staff and alumni of two London art schools is necessarily a reductive exercise. Although both Central and St Martin's trained many fine practitioners, they have no unique claim to predominance in this field. What may be said, however, is that the founding ethos of both schools in the Arts & Crafts movement made them especially representative of the most interesting trends of cross-over between fine art and design during the 20th century, and that book jackets exemplify this as much as anything else. The origin of the Central at the Stationers' Hall in Bolt Court, Fleet Street, seems to have implanted a sense of priority towards printing which was consolidated when W.R. Lethaby appointed J.H. Mason, the designer of the popular 'Imprint' typeface, as teacher of printing, alongside Edward Johnston for calligraphy and his sometime student, Noel Rooke, for wood engraving. While it is customary to speak of the influence of the private press movement of the 1890s on the English printing renaissance of the 1920s, figures such as Mason and Rooke were essential in the transmission process.

Book jackets from before the Second World War can be classified partly in terms of the printing techniques for which they were designed, and it is particularly appropriate to the Central School's core beliefs to consider them this way. One can immediately see the difference between the artists discussed here and one of their contemporaries, Rex Whistler, also a prolific designer of book jackets in the 1930s, who had studied at the Slade School where the focus at the time was exclusively on painting and drawing. All Whistler's graphic work, without exception, was reproduced photographically, often imitating the effect of one medium through another, as when he made scraperboard engravings for Hans Andersen that in other hands might have been wood engravings. To the inexpert eye, the difference is not noticeable, but the attitude is still distinctly different.

By contrast, we might look at Barnett Freedman [1], an evening class student at St Martin's for five years up to 1922 before he went on to the Royal College, whose jackets appeared on Faber and Faber books alongside Whistler's in the 1930s. Freedman came from a family of Russian Jewish immigrants living in Whitechapel, and was one of many artists whose training became possible because of the London County Council scholarships. Freedman was in the Painting School at the Royal College, but had more in common with Design School student contemporaries such as Eric Ravilious and Edward Bawden. While his paintings are now somewhat forgotten, his highly distinctive lithographed book jackets have kept his name alive. In fact,

income from commissioned work was necessary to keep
Freedman and his wife, lacking other resources, alive in
the 1930s, proving the practical wisdom of Lethaby's learning programmes that encouraged adaptability of approach
and technique in students.

Freedman's work is also instructive as a demonstration
of the way that artists during the inter-war period, if they
were to achieve results to their satisfaction, needed to
understand the limitations and potential of printing
processes. Since the 1890s, colour printing had been
achievable through process-engraving a set of printing
plates with dot screens, which could be based on an artist's
full colour original. This is the printing technique used for
the colour illustrations of Beatrix Potter and Arthur
Rackham, and was a specialism at Bolt Court in the second
half of the decade. Even in the hands of the most skilful
printer and block maker, however, colour half-tone only
really worked when printed on heavily coated white paper,
which prevented the colours from sinking and reflected
them back. In book production terms, this paper was
unfriendly to the touch and for book jackets it seemed
even more destructive of the tactile experience expected of
a traditional book. The actual colour printing was often far
removed from the colours of the artist's original, and
because of its high cost, the process became associated
chiefly with long-run cheap fiction and crudely drawn

2 Joan Z. Atkinson,
book jacket for Stella
Gibbons, *Cold Comfort
Farm*, Longmans, 1932.
Private collection.

3 Robert Gibbings,
Book jacket for Robert
Gibbings, *Coming down
the Seine*, J.M.Dent,
1953.
Central Saint Martins
Museum Collection.

artwork, of a kind that, for completely different reasons of camp and nostalgia, we may rather enjoy today.

One alternative was to stick to relief printing from process line blocks without half-tone, a method adopted by many artists and naturally productive of an Art Deco geometric simplification that worked well in the 1920s. One almost-forgotten artist in this style was Joan Z. Atkinson, a student at St Martin's. She worked for a number of mainstream publishers, and her jackets include *Cold comfort farm* by Stella Gibbons (Longmans 1932).[2] Her line technique, slightly reminiscent of James Thurber, aims for immediate impact, with prominent lettering. Her work was never signed, and she is probably representative of a larger number of artists whose contribution to book jacket design can only be reconstructed when, as in Atkinson's case, a cache of proofs was kept together as a record.

Wood engravings brought the process closer to the artist's own hand, but these were seldom used for the whole jacket design, even by John Farleigh who became a strong advocate of the commercial use of the medium. Instead, a block from within the book was often reprinted on the cover, as seen even in the post-war period on book jackets by Robert Gibbings, himself both an engraver and author. As a Slade student before the First World War, Gibbings was given a commission for a bookplate, but was so disappointed with the printed result that he enrolled in evening classes at the Central to discover first etching, and then wood engraving under Rooke, which led him, after the war, to buy the Golden Cockerel Press and make a contribution, both as publisher and artist, to the development of wood engraving. The travel books which Gibbings wrote and illustrated came mostly after the Second World War, but have slightly disappointing jackets from a design point of view.[3]

Freedman was a pioneer in the use of hand-drawn lithography as a further alternative. While lithographic printing was used for a number of purposes where metal type and its cognate pictorial techniques were inadequate, it had an equivocal reputation. The trade was highly unionised, and the mysteries of the craft protected. An artist's original would disappear into the printer's hands, and re-emerge having been reinterpreted, perhaps with great skill, into the 'colour separations' necessary for building up layers of colour, but lacking the artist's authentic touch. Even so, it had the advantage over line-block and wood engraving in its ability to reproduce graduated tone, without the 'dot-infested' screen of the half-tone camera with its destructive effect on pure colour.

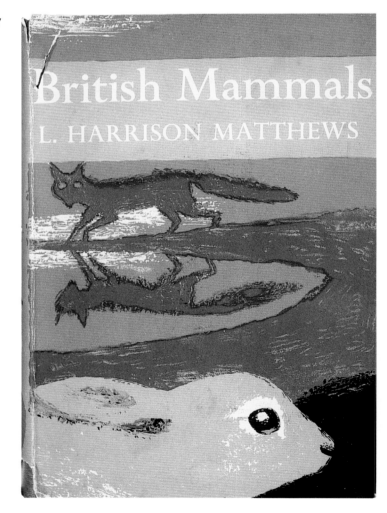

4 Clifford & Rosemary Ellis, book jacket for Leonard Harrison Matthews, *British mammals*, New Naturalist Series, Collins, 1952. Private collection.

The Arts and Crafts ethos that inspired the wood engraving revival had its counterpart in lithography, and Freedman succeeded in working in a 'hands-on' way on lithographic stone, at Curwen Press, Baynard Press and Chromoworks. This enabled him to manipulate the technique, particularly by scratching away highlights from darkly-drawn areas. He could design for two or three workings of colour only, thus economising on production but, with a coloured paper as a ground, achieving surprisingly rich effects. His work in this medium owed much of its success to his skill in drawing lettering (doubtless the result of studying under Edward Johnston) and inventing abstract background textures, which figure in nearly all his designs.

As Freedman wrote in 1936

The immense range and strength of tonality that can be obtained, the clarity and precision of delicate and fine work, and the delightful ease of manipulation by the artist directly onto the stone, plate or transfer-paper or celluloid, gives to autolithography a supreme advantage over other autographic methods.[5]

It is interesting that Freedman's book jacket work really began in the 1930s, when there was a reaction against the 'jazz modern' of the 1920s and a growing nostalgia for a neo-Victorian look. Although he illustrated several books, he more often designed jackets on their own, often interpreting the book title with a poetically selected image.

As a few printers became accustomed to the demands of artists, the necessity for the artist to draw directly onto stone or plate, with the requirement to spend a number of days at the printing works, was diminished. The jackets for the Collins New Naturalists series by Clifford and Rosemary Ellis [4] were prepared as full-colour artwork, but the colour separations (four, or sometimes three colours) could be clearly read from their poster-like clarity, even though they used textures like dry-brushed gouache as part of their repertory. Clifford Ellis studied at St Martin's in 1923–4, before going on to Regent Street Polytechnic where his wife, who was always jointly credited as a team effort, also studied. Their series of jackets ran from 1945 to 1985, totalling 70 designs.

With the introduction of transparent plastic lithographic plates from Germany before the Second World War, it became easier for artists to work directly in the medium. Although the plates were limited in the textures they permitted, the freedom they gave to see directly from one colour separation to another, enabled beginners to get started more quickly. After publishing the first of the Orlando books by Kathleen Hale (a Central

5 Kathleen Hale, book jacket for Kathleen Hale, *Orlando, the Marmalade Cat: his silver wedding*, Country Life, 1944. Private collection.

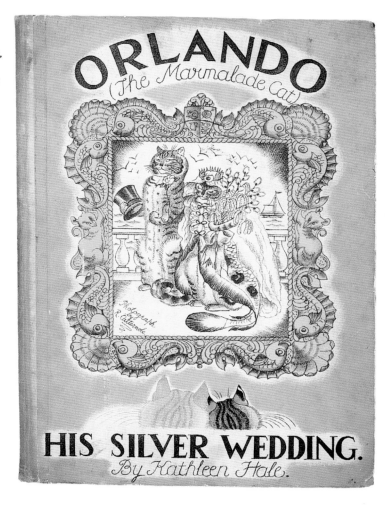

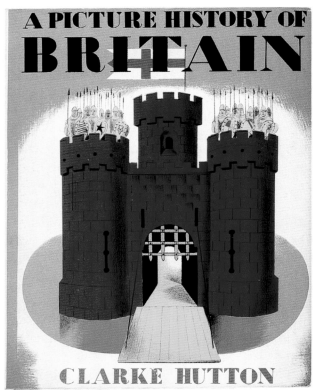

student from 1928 to 1930)[5] the publisher, Noel Carrington, explained that the intricate detail in the illustrations for the next book must be simplified, because of the cost of having it translated into colour separations at the press. Plastic plates (which had been patented in Britain as 'Plastocowell' by the printers W.S. Cowell of Ipswich), came to the rescue, as Hale was able to draw all the subsequent titles at home, taking four months over each, and rapidly becoming expert in judging the overlay of the four basic colours.

When Carrington went on in 1940 to set up Puffin Picture Books for Allen Lane, he was able to produce low-cost full-colour children's books by lithography, many of which were printed by Cowells. The artists included S.R. Badmin [6], a Central tutor in the 1950s, Enid Marx, and Clarke Hutton , both Central students in the 1920s. Hutton later taught lithography at the Central, and illustrated a series of books on the history of different countries for Oxford University Press in the 1960s, with strong colours and complex figure compositions.[7]

Freedman was closely associated with the Curwen Press, which contributed to the appearance of the exterior of books by commissioning a series of 'pattern papers' from artists. These were sheets with repeat unit patterns, originated by wood engraving, metal engraving, line block or lithography, but all printed on litho presses. They served the amateur bookbinding world, but were also frequently

THE
CATH-
EDRALS
OF
ENG-
LAND

BATS-
FORD
& FRY

THE CATHEDRALS OF ENGLAND

BATS-
FORD

6 S.R. Badmin,
book cover for S.R.
Badmin, *Trees in Britain*,
Penguin, 1943.
Central Saint Martins
Museum Collection.

7 Clarke Hutton,
book jacket for Clarke
Hutton, *A picture
history of Britain*,
Oxford University
Press, 1945.
Private collection.

8 Brian Cook,
book jacket for Harry
Batsford & Charles Fry,
*The cathedrals of
England:* illustrated
from drawings by Brian
Cook and from photo-
graphs, Batsford, 1934.
Central Saint Martins
Museum Collection.

chosen by publishers for binding trade editions. Artists
with Central and St Martin's connections who designed for
the range included Margaret Calkin James, Enid Marx [9],
and Diana Wilbraham who studied textile design at the
Central.

The most unusual method of colour printing in the
inter-war period was the Jean Berté process, of French
origin, as its name suggests. This is associated almost
entirely with the work of one artist, Brian Cook [8], working for the publishers B.T. Batsford (a family business),
from 1928, initially attending the Central School in the
afternoons and evenings, 're-drawing plaster casts under

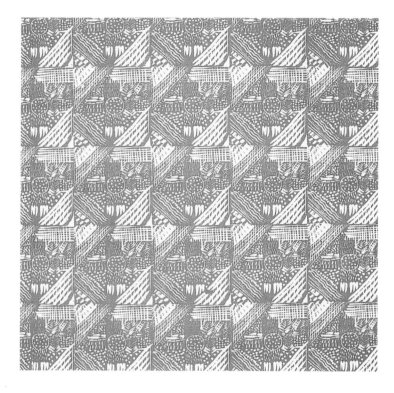

9 Enid Marx,
an example of a
pattern paper, repro-
duced in *Curwen Press
pattern papers*,
Whittington Press,
1993.
Private collection.

10 Lynton Lamb,
book jacket for Gilbert
White, *The natural
history of Selborne*,
Oxford University
Press, 1977.
Private collection.

John Farleigh; writing Gothic script under Noel Rooke; and
life drawing under somebody else'.[4]

The type of jacket that Cook began designing for the
English Life series after 1932 resembled the flat colour
work by poster artists such as Gregory Brown and Fred
Taylor, then considered suggestive of travel. From 1932,
Cook adopted the Jean Berté process in order to achieve
stronger colours which would print on a rougher paper. The
results were startling, as the process had been devised to
use water-based inks printed from rubber rollers which
could be more strongly pigmented in pink, purple and
green, creating an effect that Cook later described as
'blatant, bizarre, strident and unreal'.[5] Before the end of
the 1930s Cook decided that the style had run long enough,
but it was a prominent example of a publisher seizing the

marketing potential of book jackets in order to create a brand image.

The book jacket might not, therefore, be such a 'wretched thing' after all, since so much thought was given to its meaning and form. Indeed, it is often remarked that a lithographic jacket by Barnett Freedman is as much an original artist's print as a signed limited edition. The cost was seen by the publisher to be correspondingly high if unusual printing processes were being used, and the majority of jackets were usually attempts to create an effect of richness on a low budget.

Lynton Lamb [**10**] was a full-time painting student at the Central from 1924 to 1929, but on leaving went to work at Oxford University Press, with the job of redesigning standard bindings. He had no direct experience in this field, but, as George Mackie writes, 'the flavour of the bookwork which he had done, under Mason, obviously commended itself' to his boss, Gerard Hopkins.[6] In fact, after studying bookbinding at the Central with Douglas Cockerell, Lamb taught the subject himself. Commissioned to redesign the jackets for the Worlds Classics series just before the war, Lamb hit on a new way of drawing for line-block reproduction that allowed the blockmaker to achieve colour separation in solid tone. For economy the jackets only used black and one other colour (occasionally two) on white paper, but Lamb's development of the potential of these restrictions gave unity to the series. In addition, he developed a rough, almost pencilled quality of line when drawing with a broadnibbed fountain pen that went a long way to defeating the linear limitations of the blockmaking process.

Lamb's attention to the quality of line itself can be contrasted with that of Edward Ardizzone [**11**] who was trained by Bernard Meninsky at the the Westminster School of Art. Meninsky was also one of Central's great drawing teachers later on, and Ardizzone became one of his colleagues. Ardizzone's actual line is seldom remarkable, for he achieved tonal effects with multiple hatching, the shaping of which contributes to the life of the drawing. Like Lamb, Ardizzone divided his time largely between teaching and book work, in which latter category book jackets were demanded for the books he illustrated himself, as well as some which stand alone. Ardizzone nearly always worked over the whole front and spine of the book, incorporating his own lettering in an illustration. Although he was brilliant in black and white, most of his jacket work is in full colour.

By the time Ardizzone's career in book illustration was fully launched after the Second World War, process colour had made some advances. He made his own version of the technique, however, by drawing a black line plate

The
NATURAL HISTORY
OF SELBORNE
Gilbert White

The World's Classics

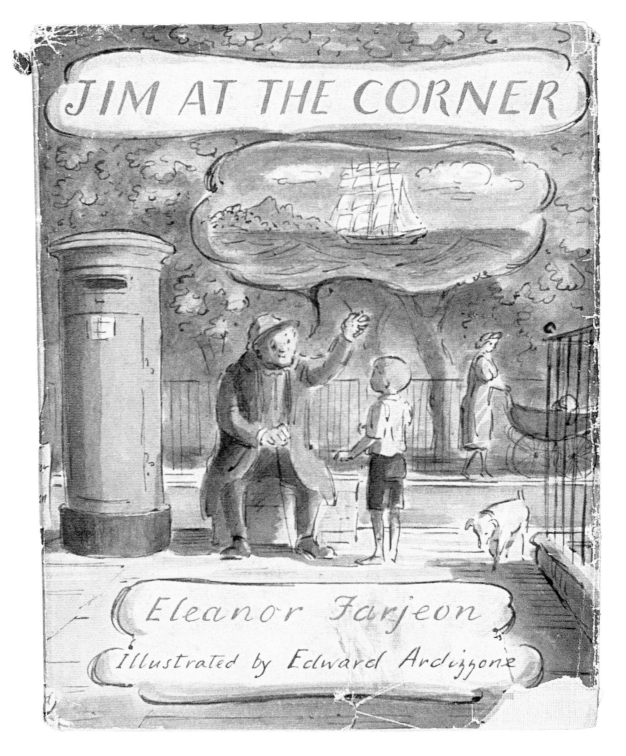

11 Edward Ardizzone, book jacket for Eleanor Farjeon, *Jim at the corner*, Oxford University Press, 1958. Private collection.

12 Harold Jones, book jacket for Kathleen Lines, *Lavender's blue: a book of nursery rhymes*, Oxford University Press, 1954. Central Saint Martins Museum Collection.

A BOOK OF NURSERY RHYMES

LAVENDER'S BLUE

Compiled by KATHLEEN LINES AND Pictured by HAROLD JONES

separately from the colour on a transparent overlay, with the result that while the colours were interpreted by dot screen, the line was printed solid and was better able to hold its strength against colours that had the delicacy of original watercolours.[7] Despite having one or two close imitators, Ardizzone's style was always immediately recognisable and still seems to confer an added quality to any book that has his work.

Harold Jones was a student at the Royal College alongside Barnett Freedman, who introduced him to book illustration in which he excelled as an English visionary artist. Later, Jones taught at Saint Martin's, and his children's books, including the frequently-reprinted *Lavender's blue* (OUP, 1954) [12], have been a lasting inspiration in their field. His skill in design and lettering make his jackets and his page layouts disciplined and composed.

A third artist who was a long-standing teacher (from 1947 to 1975) at the Central was Hans Tisdall [13]. Tisdall

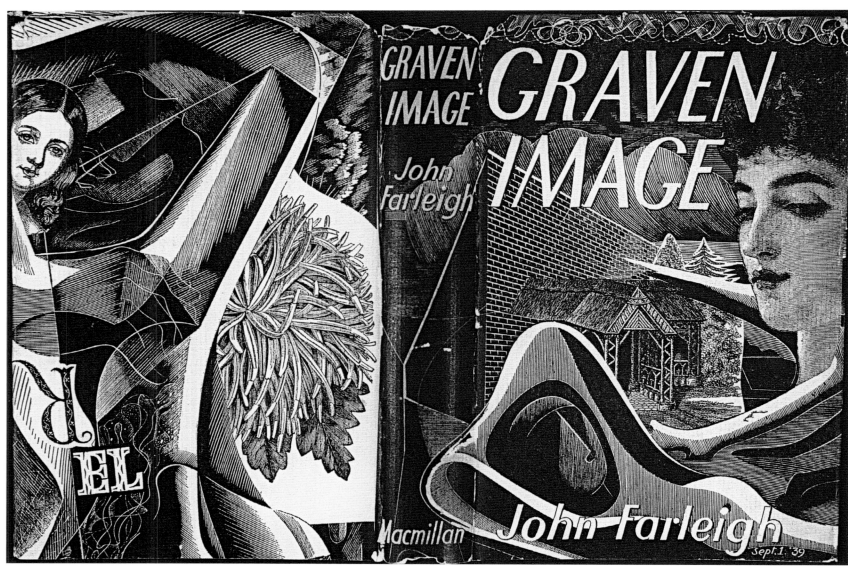

came to England from Germany in 1930 under his original name, Hans Aufseeser, and found work as a mural painter and textile designer, in addition to beginning his career in book jacket design for Cresset Press and Jonathan Cape. Tisdall's work is identifiable through his brush-drawn calligraphy, a skill he had learnt from Anna Simons, Edward Johnston's principal German pupil. In its freedom, it seldom resembled any known type-face, although Berthold Wolpe, a German émigré who created a house-style for Faber and Faber in the 1940s, sometimes worked with equal freedom. Both Tisdall and Wolpe showed a concern for the economics of production by limiting the range of colours. Tisdall from time to time enlarged his range from calligraphy to pictorial representation with a lively sense of hard-edge form.

John Farleigh was a student at the Central from 1917 to 1921, joining the staff in 1925 and becoming involved with the book production department, of which he became officially the head on the retirement of Noel Rooke in 1947. His illustrations for *The adventures of the black girl in her search for God* by George Bernard Shaw (Constable 1932), made him a well-known figure. The book itself, with its pictorial binding case covered in paper rather than cloth, was remarkably fresh and modern-looking for its time. Farleigh designed a number of book jackets during the 1930s, shifting from wood engraving to other media, including lithography for Sacheverell Sitwell's *Old fashioned flowers* (Country Life 1939). He wrote with insight on this aspect of his work in *Graven image* [14], (Macmillan 1940), a book with an engraved cover

13 Hans Tisdall, book jacket for Guiseppe di Lampedusa, *The Leopard*, ©Harvill Collins, 1960. Private collection.

14 John Farleigh, book jacket for John Farleigh, *Graven image*, Macmillan, 1940. Private collection.

15 Mervyn Peake, book jacket for Thelma Niklaus, *Harlequin Phoenix*, Bodley Head, 1956. Private collection.

16 John Craxton, book jacket for Patrick Leigh Fermor, *A time of gifts*, John Murray, 1977. Private collection.

17 John Minton,
book jacket for
Elizabeth David,
French country cooking,
Macdonald, London,
1958.
Private collection.

18 Val Biro,
book cover for
Theodora Fitzgibbon,
Making the most of it,
Hutchinson, 1978.
Artist's collection.

reproduced on the binding case, which appears to be a collage of his own engravings and historical images, slightly reminiscent of Max Ernst. For an artist of Farleigh's generation, it was a natural assumption that artistic beginners, to whom he mainly addressed the book, should expect to earn some quick cash with book jacket work, at least during their early years. He wrote:

> the dust wrapper has slowly become more important: the artist has discovered a new field for experiment, while the publisher has realised the display value of this new activity. So the glory that was once the binding is now the wrapper[8].

Their ability to diversify in this way was the direct result of their range of educational experience, and, as Farleigh said,

> the best wrappers have been made by illustrators who are designers in an even wider sphere than books: whose activities include painting, posters and several of the crafts such as etching, engraving and lithography.

During the first decade after the Second World War, the conditions in printing and publishing were difficult, but in spite of restrictions, publishers succeeded in bringing out some fine productions. Technically, little changed, although American book production showed levels of sophistication in design and production that were a challenge to complacency. The graphic style of the 1940s and 1950s reflected a temporary decline of interest in abstraction and the romantic impulse visible in the work of several Central tutors such as Cecil Collins and Mervyn Peake [15], who were recruited by the post-war Principal, William Johnstone, as well as the less well-known Laurence Scarfe, a teacher from 1945 to 1970, whose graphic work epitomises the Festival of Britain and the continuing influence of Eric Ravilious and Edward Bawden. John Minton, who taught at Central from 1946 to 1948, illustrated the first editions of several of Elizabeth David's cookery books [17] with wiry line drawings and coloured jackets, all densely worked with detail and redolent of northern longing for the Mediterranean.

The same artistic style resurfaced in the jackets designed by John Craxton (a student at Central in the 1940s) in the 1970s for two volumes of pre-war travel memoirs by Patrick Leigh Fermor, published by John Murray. Craxton, who moved to Crete in 1960, was a friend of the similarly expatriate author. These jackets [16] evoked a forgotten era, for the qualities that made illustration a strength in British art in the earlier part of the 20th century – naturalism, narrative, careful design, and respect for materials and process – were precisely those that, by the mid 1950s, many artists wished to distance themselves from most clearly. In book publishing, the freelance artist

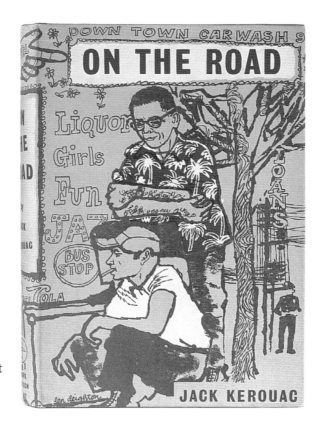

19 Len Deighton, book jacket for Jack Kerouac, *On the road*, Andre Deutsch, 1958.

was increasingly replaced as a jacket designer by the art director (Val Biro [18] filled this role at John Lehmann in the years before 1953 as well as designing his own jackets), photographer and typographer, working in various combinations. A jacket such as Len Deighton's for Jack Kerouac's *On the road* (André Deutsch 1958) [19], follows established precedent in its restricted colours and hand-drawn lettering, but for Deighton's own thrillers such as *Funeral in Berlin* (1964), his friend Raymond Hawkey created photographic jackets that jumped from the old world to the new. Although the hand-drawn image still had some distance to run, a turning point had come and the public were prepared for greater plainness or for more subtlety of graphic message on book covers.

The principal exception was in children's books, where hand-drawing has still not been displaced by other techniques, and where a rather nostalgic effect is often demanded. As already stated, since children's books are liable to be illustrated all the way through, the cover is less of a special event, apart from fiction for older readers

20 John Lawrence, book jacket for Adrian Mitchell & John Lawrence, *Nothingmas Day*, London: Allison & Busby, 1984. Artist's collection.

21 Glynn Boyd Harte, book jacket for Glynn Boyd Harte, *Murderers' cottages: a garden of residences of notorious criminals*, London: Warren Editions, 1976. Private collection.

where it may form the only illustration, or at least the only one in colour.

Susan Einzig (Central School from 1939 to 1941) for example, illustrated Philippa Pearce's classic children's novel, *Tom's midnight garden*, iin 1958 [23] for Oxford University Press, at the time one of the leading children's book publishing houses in Britain, with black and white pen drawings with a Mintonesque line and an atmospheric colour cover. The illustrations for Michael Bond's Paddington books, launched by Collins in 1958, by Peggy Fortnum, were the best ever made for these books, although the covers were a more throwaway affair. From 1936 onwards, Alfred Bestall's covers and end-papers for the Rupert annuals, collecting strips from the *Daily Express*, began to infiltrate themselves into the subculture of English childhood, with their clear line and colour drawing.

One of the finest children's book illustrators of the post-war period in Britain, Fritz Wegner [22], was a much-loved tutor in the Illustration department at St Martin's. His own work is distinguished by wit and craftsmanship, with a strong sense of the design of the printed page. As a young artist he designed covers for adult fiction, including the first English edition of *Catcher in the rye* (Hamish Hamilton 1951). Among his pupils in the late 1960s were Nicola Bayley and Glynn Boyd Harte, both of whom progressed to the Royal College to study under Quentin Blake and Brian Robb. They shared with these tutors a wide sense of inquiry into all aspects of the visual world, including nostalgic and obsolete things which were a rising component of the sixties counterculture. Unusually, Boyd Harte did not illustrate children's books, although *Murderers' cottages* [21], published by Jonathan Gili of Warren Editions in 1974, is in the form of a chap-book with 'adult' content. This book was the origin of Boyd Harte's revival of hand-drawn lithography in illustration, working with the Curwen Studio, which after 1984 was the surviving aspect of its parent company, the Curwen Press, dedicated to the production of artists' prints. The technique never returned in strength for trade books, partly for lack of artists wishing to use it, which meant that printers became unused to working in this way. On the other hand, an artist such as John Burningham, a Central student in the later 1950s, found the careful craft ethos constricting and was glad when technology made it easier to reproduce straight from artwork. The look of children's books is now dependent entirely on the nature of the artwork rather than the process, although the richness of effect that can be gained does not necessarily make for better book design. The anchorage of line is still found brilliantly displayed in the

22 Fritz Wegner, book jacket for Brian Alderson, *The tale of the turnip*, Walker Books 1999. Central Saint Martins Museum Collection.

23 Susan Einzig, book jacket for Philippa Pearce, *Tom's midnight garden*, Oxford University Press, 1958. Artist's collection.

work of Patrick Benson, a student at St Martin's in the 1960s and Posy Simmonds, a Central student in the late 1960s, among other illustrators of children's books.

Wood engraving has undoubtedly declined as a medium in mainstream illustration, despite enjoying a revival in the 1980s. It has nonetheless continued to be practised and taught by John Lawrence, who learnt it at Central with Gertrude Hermes in the 1950s. In, for example, *Nothingmas Day* (Allison & Busby, 1984) [20], with a text by Adrian Mitchell, Lawrence has found a new way to relate the cover to the illustrations within the book, for the former is composed of all the individual illustrations which interlock to form a complete picture, almost like a visual contents page.

I have not discussed paperbacks as yet as a distinct type of book production. As with book jackets themselves, the trade was initially sceptical about them. Sir Allen Lane launched the first Penguin Books in 1935, breaking most of the rules of publishing, although he initially preferred to leave the covers severely typographical, because he hated the idea that his products might be associated with the vulgarity of American pulp fiction.

There were a number of fruitful spells of illustration at Penguin between the 1950s and 1970s [24], although typographic designers like Derek Birdsall (Central School) offered strong competition. Unlike hardbacks, working in an increasingly competitive impulse-buying market, paperback publishers have often applied more professionalism and clear brand identity to their cover designs. Today, there is no real difference between the two types, except that paperbacks have come to dominate more sectors of publishing. At least they have the benefit for collectors of covers, that they are more likely to preserve their original visual style as they pass from hand to hand.

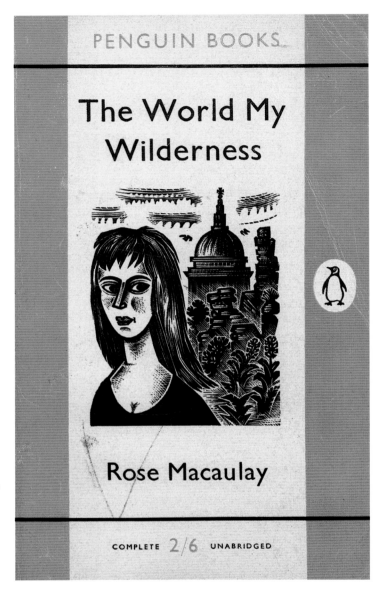

24 Derrick Harris, book cover for Rose Macaulay, *The world my wilderness*, Penguin, 1958.
Phil Baines' collection.

Copyright © Alan Powers 2005

1   Eric Hobsbawm, *The age of extremes: the short 20th century, 1914–1991*, Michael Joseph, 1994, *passim*.
2   Richard de la Mare, *A publisher on book production*, J M Dent 1936, p.41.
3   Barnett Freedman, 'Lithography, a painter's excursion', *Signature*, No.2, March 1936, p.11.
4   Brian Cook (ed.), *The Britain of Brian Cook*, B T Batsford 1987, p.13.
5   *ibid.*, p.15.
6   George Mackie (ed.), *Lynton Lamb, illustrator*, Scolar Press, 1978, p.xix.
7   This technique is described by Ardizzone in 'A simple technique in line and colour wash', in *Penrose Annual*, vol.46, 1952, pp.66–7.
8   John Farleigh, *Graven Image*, Macmillan, 1940, p.275.

6 / Paul W Nash
Central Saint Martins and The Folio Society

Paul W Nash is a freelance writer, bibliographer and book designer. He has written on private presses and printing history, completed the RIBA's Early Printed Books catalogue, and is co-editor of *The Private Library* and Honorary Librarian to the Folio Society.

The Folio Society

The Folio Society was founded in 1947 by Charles Ede in an attempt to bridge the gap between the expensive beauties of the private presses and the physically uninspiring post-war products of commercial publishers. He wanted to publish what he called the 'poor man's fine edition', well-designed and printed books with illustrations by contemporary artists that the general reader could, and would, buy. For nearly 60 years that has been the philosophy behind the Society's choice of texts, designers, illustrators and materials for printing and binding its editions.

The early years were difficult, and the Society had to cope with cautious printing firms, post-war paper shortages and rationing, and the generally depressed state of the economy.[1] But Ede was determined and, with the help of Christopher Sandford and Alan Bott (founder of the Book Society, the Reprint Society and Pan Books), he published his first book in late 1947 from premises shared with Sandford's Golden Cockerel Press in Poland Street.[2] It was, and is, in the choice of illustrators that the Society has often been at its most adventurous, and the concept of the illustrated book for the adult reader has been kept alive in Britain by Folio almost single-handedly. Apart from the Society, only the private presses and a few specialist publishers and societies have offered artists the chance to create new illustrations to substantial literary texts.

The first Folio book, Tolstoy's *Tales* (1947)[3] set the pattern by using paintings by a little-known artist (although this was partly an early attempt to keep costs down). Some 1,200 Folio editions have been published since then, the majority with new illustrations, often by young and up-coming artists. Between 1976 and 2003 the Society held an annual 'Illustration Award' in conjunction with the RCA, often employing the most talented among the winners to illustrate its books. It has also naturally employed some of the best established artists of the day. In 1948, for example, Edward Bawden drew a series of delightful colour illustrations for *Gulliver's travels*, although paper shortages meant that the Society could

Scandal

publish only the first two journeys at this time (a complete edition with new plates by the artist followed in 1965); Bawden went on to illustrate a range of books for the Society, from Beckford's *Vathek* in 1958 to the linocuts he made for *The hound of the Baskervilles* in 1987, towards the end of his life. Sandford introduced Ede to his wife Lettice and to John Buckland-Wright, both artists providing illustrations for early Folio titles. Buckland-Wright and Ede collaborated on some half dozen editions, most importantly the *Odyssey* (1948), *Iliad* (1950) and *Decameron* (1954–55), all illustrated with collotype reproductions of Buckland-Wright's sensual intaglio prints.

Another artist with a long association with Folio was Charles Keeping, whose lithographs appeared in a string of volumes beginning with *Wuthering Heights* in 1964. It is, however, his innumerable drawings for the works of Dickens, published between 1981 and 1988, which represent his most sustained contribution and, indeed, the only complete series of Dickens illustrations produced by a single artist. A similar fecundity and loyalty to the Society can be seen in the wood engraver Peter Reddick. In 1958 he provided his first frontispiece to a volume in the Society's octavo poetry series, John Donne's *Poems of love*, and went on to illustrate the complete novels of Hardy with his distinctive, woody wood engravings. Reddick is that relatively rare creature, the wood engraver who is equally skilled as a draughtsman, and has made drawings for seven of Trollope's novels. In all, his work has appeared in nearly 40 different Folio editions; most recently, in 2002, he provided more than 80 blocks for a substantial selection of Wordsworth's poems. The catalogue of illustrators associated with Folio is so comprehensive that it might almost be easier to list the important book artists of the past 60 years who have not worked for the Society.

Central Saint Martins and Folio

The relationship between the Central School of Arts and Crafts and Folio dates back to the Society's creation. In 1946, with Sandford's help, Charles Ede attended both the London School (later College) of Printing and the Central School, where he studied typography, printmaking techniques, drawing and painting, saying later

> I felt very strongly that if I was going to commission artists who worked in the auto-graphic media ... I must myself have engraved and cut wood, etched copper and drawn on the lithographic stone or plate.[4]

This practical approach served him well when choosing and communicating with artists, helping him to judge, for example, when to give a troubled mind space and time and

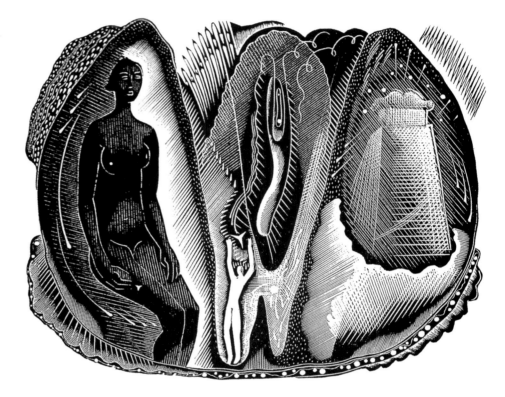

1 Dorothea Braby, two-colour wood engraving for Emily Eden, *The semi-attached couple*, Folio Society, 1955.

2 Blair Hughes-Stanton, wood-engraved head-piece for Thomas de Quincey, *The confessions of an English opium-eater*, Folio Society, 1948.

when to apply gentle pressure to a sluggard. Ede learned that the Central and St Martin's were greenhouses for young talent, and watched the shoots that sprang up there closely; also, to extend the metaphor, he watched the gardeners, picking illustrators carefully from among the students and tutors until he retired from Folio in 1971. Those that followed also commissioned many artists from the Central and St Martin's (and from Central Saint Martins after the two were merged in 1989), although often this was not done in the knowledge of the artists' background – they were simply chosen on merit, and the preponderance of Central students and teachers among them is testimony to the importance of the school as a training ground for book illustrators. In discussing the work of these artists I will take a media-based approach, although it will become clear that some worked in two or more media; nevertheless, such a division is perhaps less artificial than a purely chronological or stylistic approach might be.

Wood engraving and other relief techniques

The Society has done more than any other publisher to promote and sustain the art of wood engraving in Britain, and many of the finest artists in the medium have been trained at Central Saint Martins. Although he retired in the year the Society was founded, the influence of Noel Rooke can be seen in the work of many of the early wood engravers employed by Folio; Rooke taught at the Central between 1905 and 1947, and believed strongly that wood engraving should be a medium for artistic expression rather than merely a method of reproducing drawings or photographs for print; he also helped to promote the acceptance of wood engraving for the illustration of books through his teaching that creative art could combine with industrial processes to produce beautiful objects.[5] He was also instrumental in founding the Society of Wood Engravers in 1920, and when he retired from the post of Head of the Book Production Department in 1947, his colleague and former pupil John Farleigh took over (although he too retired shortly afterwards).

Dorothea Braby was the first Central-trained wood engraver to be commissioned by the Folio Society. She had studied under Farleigh in the 1920s, and Ede employed her for two books – *The poems of John Keats* (1950) and *The semi-attached couple* by Emily Eden (1955).[1] For the former she designed and cut a series of ornaments and a frontispiece, while the latter commission was more adventurous, demonstrating the Society's growing confidence and financial success: for Eden's book Braby prepared seven full-page designs, each printed from two separate

3 Derrick Harris, wood-engraved frontispiece for Henry Fielding, *The history of Tom Jones*, Folio Society, 1959.

blocks, in pink and black. The results, with the exception of the frontispiece, are extremely effective, and the artist designed the blocks in such a way that, in places, the pink overprints the black, giving effectively two tones or textures of shadow. This was typical of the experimental use of wood engraving, especially the use of two or more colours, which Folio fostered.

Braby's were not the first wood engravings made for Folio by someone associated with the Central School however, as in 1948 *The confessions of an English opium-eater* [2] had appeared with ten head-pieces by Blair Hughes-Stanton in his characteristic surreal style. He was not a student at the Central, but later taught there and had a profound influence on a generation of students until his retirement in 1979. His collaboration with Folio came about by a circuitous route, however, as the blocks had been commissioned and cut in 1930, but never used, for Jack Lindsay's Fanfrolico Press, and they came to Ede via Sandham when an edition of de Quincey's work was mooted in the early years of the Society.

Robert Gibbings had been a pupil of Rooke before the First World War, and by the 1950s was arguably the most famous wood engraver in Britain, known through his highly-successful series of travel books (which had begun with *Sweet Thames run softly* in 1940).[6] Again, Ede met him through Sandford, who had bought the Golden Cockerel Press from Gibbings in 1933, although his first Folio commission was not for wood engravings but for an introduction to an edition of Melville's *Typee* in 1950. It was a further three years before Ede was able to persuade Gibbings to illustrate a book for him, although he tried at least once in the interim, and it was only pressure of work that prevented Gibbings from acceding.[7] His 11 wood engravings for *An account of the discovery of Tahiti* (edited from the journal of George Robertson and published in early 1955) are typical of his late pastoral style and capture something of his love of the South Seas. Ede much admired Gibbings' work, and bought a painting from him in 1955;[8] it was probably only Gibbings' declining health before his death in 1958 that prevented further collaborations.[9]

Another wood engraver to learn the craft from Farleigh was Derrick Harris, who became in the 1950s one of the most prolific practitioners in the medium.[10] His illustrations for the *Radio Times* were so numerous that he was known for a while as 'Radio Times Harris'. He illustrated three books for Folio – Fielding's *Joseph Andrews* (1953) and *Tom Jones* (1959) [3], and Smollett's *Humphrey Clinker* (1955) – with brilliant cartoons, matching perfectly the masculine ribaldry of the texts chosen. He died by his

4 Frank Martin, two-colour wood engraving for Oscar Wilde, *Salomé*, Folio Society, 1957.

own hand in 1960 at the age of 40, afflicted with a depression and self-doubt which can hardly be detected in his exuberant art.

His natural heir is Frank Martin, who studied under Gertrude Hermes at St Martin's in the 1940s. He approaches the medium with the same energy and simplicity as Harris, although his imagery is more naturalistic and less mannered; he has excelled in other media too (notably intaglio printmaking and painting). For Folio he illustrated Thornton Wilder's *Bridge of San Luis Rey* (1956) and Wilde's *Salome* (1957) with two-colour wood engravings [4], and in 1958 provided images for two of the four volumes of *The book of a thousand nights and one night*. In 1961 he took over the illustration of Georgian literature from Harris, supplying blocks for Smollett's *Roderick Random* (1961), Hazlitt's *Essays* (1964) and Fielding's *Jonathan Wild* (1966), and went on to contribute to a range of Folio titles, including the Society's editions of Chaucer and Shakespeare, each illustrated by a team of wood engravers (Shakespeare's *Complete plays*, 1988, include his last work for Folio to date).

John Lawrence also trained with Hermes and there are similarities between his work and that of both Harris and Martin, with much the same vitality and sense of immediacy, although his blocks are more textured and sinewy. In 1967 he illustrated Defoe's *Colonel Jack* with 12 full-page images, each printed in two colours, and in 1970 tackled *Tristram Shandy*. There followed a long series of titles, often Victorian or older fiction. Most recently he prepared vinyl engravings for T. H. White's *The once and future king* (2003).[5] Each was printed within a border of a second colour, and then hand-coloured, the results being reproduced to delightful effect by the latest scanning and colour-printing techniques. Lawrence has also worked in linoleum (for *Robinson Crusoe* in 1972), in pen and ink – notably for *The diary of a nobody* (1969), which remains in print after 35 years – and in watercolour (for Waugh's *Sword of honour* trilogy), as well as designing several Folio bindings and supplying imagery for the Society's ephemera. His hand-coloured wood-engraved poster, made to mark the Society's 50th anniversary in 1996, is a particularly fine example of the last.

Sarah Van Niekerk's frontispieces for *The complete novels of Mrs Ann Radcliffe* (6 vols, 1987) are among my own favourites of Folio book illustration, with their delicate cutting and atmosphere of fairytale menace.[6] Van Niekerk's skill with the graver was also acquired under Hermes in the 1950s, and has been evident in her contributions to Folio's Chaucer and Shakespeare editions, as well as in Hector St John de Crèvecoeur's *The divided loyalist* (1978).

5 John Lawrence, hand-coloured vinyl engraving for T.H. White, *The once and future king*, Folio Society, 2003.

Simon Brett is, perhaps, the most important contemporary wood engraver to have been employed by the Society. His skill as a practitioner is matched by his creative imagination and facility, when necessary, to produce work in different styles and moods, mimicking Bewick or Derrick Harris. In 16 years he has contributed to fifteen different editions for the Society, also preparing binding designs for two others and selecting illustrations for *The Folio golden treasury* (1997). Among the highlights are Shakespeare's *Sonnets and a lover's complaint* (1989), another work illustrated by a team and one of the most harmonious Folio book designs; and some of the greats of English literature – *Clarissa* (1991), *Jane Eyre* (1991), *Middlemarch* (1999) and Keats' *Complete poems* (2001). The last is a real tour de force, including some 80 delicate and beautiful designs, many repeated in variant states.[7]

The Society also employs artists who work in other relief media, notably wood- and linocuts. The latter have been cut by John Lawrence for one title (see above), and by Clare Melinsky, one of the younger generation of artists to be trained at the Central, for *The witches of Salem* (1982). The Folio Society's commitment to wood engraving (and other relief techniques) remains strong, and is likely to continue for the foreseeable future,[11] as the medium is so very appropriate for book illustration, providing images that have a natural affinity with classical typography. This is partly because both arts are based upon the carved line: despite the rise of the computer, type design remains rooted in the ancient art of cutting relief punches to form the matrices from which metal type was cast, just as wood engraving relies on the cutting of a relief image in a block of boxwood.

Lithography

The medium of direct lithography has been confined, for technical reasons, chiefly to the earlier period of the Folio Society's activities. During the 1950s and 1960s, Folio artists were encouraged to work directly on a prepared surface (nearly always Plastocowell[12]) to create colour images which could be printed by a direct offset process. Usually the artist was limited to two colour separations, though the second series of Gulliver plates mentioned above was drawn in between four and six colours by Edward Bawden in 1965. Nigel Lambourne was the first Central-trained artist to be commissioned for such work (Lambourne was also a tutor at the Central), although his plates for Sterne's *Sentimental journey* (1949) were generally agreed to be less than a complete success.[13] He went on to develop a close working relationship with Ede, and to create some very effective lithographs for Folio (notably for O'Flaherty's *Informer*, 1961), as well as working for the

6 Sarah van Niekerk, wood engraving for Ann Radcliffe, *The castles of Athlin and Dunblane*, Folio Society, 1987.

7 Simon Brett, wood engraving for John Keats, *The complete poems*, Folio Society, 2001.

Society in several other media over the course of three decades.

Clarke Hutton was another early experimenter with the technique (like Lambourne, he was both a student and a teacher at the Central), creating passionate images for Thackeray's *Henry Esmond* (1950), Conrad's *Almayer's folly* (1962) and Charlotte Brontë's *Villette* (1967). Barnett Freedman's style was less explosive, more controlled and cerebral, and he took a keen interest in typography and design as well as in the fine arts. After training as a painter at St Martin's and the RCA he became a specialist in the one area of general book illustration open to artists in the 20th century – the dust jacket.[14] He was commissioned to supply a frontispiece and jacket for *Readings from Dickens* by Emlyn Williams (1953), and full-page lithographs, plus a title plate, endleaf design and decorative divisional titles, for each of seven *Ghost stories* by Walter de la Mare (1956). [8] Ede greatly admired Freedman's work, and would no doubt have commissioned further illustrations had the artist not died in 1958.[15]

Lynton Lamb trained as a wood engraver under Rooke, as well as studying typographical design and lithography at the Central School. It was as a lithographer that he made his greatest contribution to Folio books, providing plates for Wilkie Collins' *The woman in white* (1956) and James's *Washington Square* (1963), although he also supplied line drawings for several important titles, including Sassoon's Sherston novels. Among the other Central Saint Martins artists who contributed two-colour autolithographs to Folio books were Edwin La Dell (Wilkie Collins' *The moonstone*, 1951); Faith Jaques (Turgenev's *The torrents of spring*, 1967) [9]; and Walter Hoyle (Charlotte Brontë's *Shirley*, 1968) [10].

After 1970 there were occasional experiments with direct lithography. In 1984 Paul Hogarth prepared two-colour images for Conrad's *Nostromo*, and Anthony Gross, better known for his line drawings, made one interesting excursion into the medium for *The Forsyte saga* (1984), both using Plastocowell. The latter was a rare instance of Folio re-using illustrations which had appeared elsewhere, however; Gross's lithographs had originally been prepared for Heinemann in 1950. Existing prints have also been reprinted by offset lithography to good effect from time to time, as in 1998 when C.R.W. Nevinson's Great War lithographs were reprinted in Cecil Lewis's *Sagittarius rising*. As late as 1987 Plastocowell was used by Glynn Boyd Harte, who studied under Hogarth, for the plates in Fitzgerald's *Tender is the night*, and in 1996 (long after the closure of Cowell of Ipswich) the process was replicated using specially-prepared graphic film, onto which Boyd Harte

8 Barnett Freedman, autolithograph for Walter de la Mare, *Ghost stories*, Folio Society, 1956.

drew illustrations for the collected novels of E.M. Forster. The same artist's final work for Folio was a series of nine autolithographs for Arnold Bennett's *The old wives' tale* (2004) [11], published posthumously (he died in December 2003). Here again the artist drew his colour separations directly onto film, bringing the delicate tones of direct lithography gently into the 21st century.[16]

The medium was often chosen by Ede to illustrate 19th-century fiction. This seems a bold and curious decision, and one that paid off in a proportion of cases only. When examining the autolithographic illustrations published by Folio as a whole, one is struck by how dated many of them appear, by comparison to images produced in other media (Boyd Harte's more recent work is also 'dated' in a sense, since it attempts to capture something of the spirit of the period of Fitzgerald, Bennett and Forster; for *A room with a view* he cheekily adapted images of Julian Sands and Helena Bonham-Carter from the Merchant/Ivory film of 1985). Their curiously old-fashioned appearance is due in part, I think, to the fact that artists were encouraged to experiment in a young medium, producing work which was at the time innovative and largely without precedent for the illustration of books. The sad fate of such new stylistic ideas is to become fixed within a conceptual period, to represent a past era and an outmoded taste, while fashion moves on.[17] This is less true of relief and intaglio printmaking, painting and drawing, which exist within a

9 Faith Jaques, two-colour autolithograph for Ivan Turgenev, *The torrents of spring*, Folio Society, 1967.

10 Walter Hoyle, two-colour autolithograph for Charlotte Brontë, *Shirley*, Folio Society, 1968.

longer tradition that informs the artist, as well as the 'reader' of that art.

Intaglio prints

The Folio Society has twice done a very remarkable thing – illustrated books printed in large editions with prints taken directly from etched plates. This was possible because of Ede's discovery of Kultura of Budapest, a firm of security printers which possessed the machinery to make long print-runs from 'chromed' intaglio plates. The first such venture was a happy collaboration with Nigel Lambourne, who produced five full-page soft-ground etchings for a new translation of Virgil's *Georgics* (1969).[12][18] Ede described the plates as 'the peak of Nigel's achievements'.[19] It is thought-provoking to hold in one's hand a volume printed in an edition of more than 8,000 copies, with etchings pulled directly from plates made in a small studio by the artist's hands. The second such book, Pushkin's *Queen of spades*, was printed in the following year with eight etchings by Clarke Hutton. Again the edition was of more than 8,000 copies, and the results were similarly impressive.

Ede has said that engraving 'was my favourite medium because, more than any other, it actively encourages economy of line'.[20] However, the costs and complexities of the process, coupled with changes in the technology of security printing, meant that the two books mentioned above were rarities, and the difficulties of reproducing intaglio prints by planographic methods discouraged Ede and his successors from commissioning many such illustrations. The collotype process, however, when skilfully used, could produce satisfactory results, and a few books were illustrated in this way. Buckland-Wright's beautiful plates for Homer and *The Decameron* have already been mentioned, and collotype was sometimes used for drypoints, etchings, aquatints and engravings (as well as for drawings) until it became uneconomical in the 1970s. A particularly fine early example, by an artist trained at the Central (and later, briefly, a teacher at St Martin's), is the series of eight etchings prepared by Susan Einzig in 1954 for Daudet's *Sappho* and printed for Folio by the Chiswick Press.[13] The last book to have plates reproduced in this manner, Chekhov's *Short stories* (1974), was, fittingly, illustrated with aquatints by the stalwart Nigel Lambourne.

In later years lithographic printing, and now scanning and stochastic printing methods, have advanced to allow intaglio prints to be reproduced with more precision and 'depth' than ever before, although these techniques have rarely been employed by Folio for new art (though they have sometimes been used to reproduce historical prints).

11 Glynn Boyd Harte, lithographic design for the slip-case of Arnold Bennett, *The old wives' tale*, Folio Society, 2004.

ARNOLD BENNETT
THE
OLD WIVES' TALE

This is partly because of technical difficulties, and partly because the fashion in printmaking has been away from intaglio in recent years. Contemporary technology is so good, and growing better almost daily, however, that the use of intaglio plates for book illustration must be due for a revival. A few very recent Folio examples seem to point in this direction.

Pen and ink drawings and scraperboard

Line drawings have often been used to illustrate Folio Society books. The technique is relatively cheap because such pictures can be printed at the same time as the text, whether by letterpress or planographic printing, and this also allows the sort of integration between images and words which is much more difficult to achieve with other media. Given the joy that many artists take in making

12 Nigel Lambourne, soft-ground etching for Virgil, *The Georgics*, Folio Society, 1969.

13 Susan Einzig, etching for Alphonse Daudet, *Sappho*, Folio Society, 1954.

14 Edward Ardizzone, pen and ink drawing for G.K. Chesterton, *Father Brown stories*, Folio Society, 1959.

15 Val Biro, scraperboard for G.K. Chesterton, *The Father Brown stories*, second volume, Folio Society, 1996.

simple lines on paper, and the wide range of effects that can be produced even without colour, the dominance of line as a medium for book art is hardly surprising.

Numerous Central Saint Martins-trained artists have worked for Folio with pen and ink, and in related media, from Edward Ardizzone to Fritz Wegner (to take a purely alphabetical view). Ardizzone's drawings [14] for the *Father Brown stories* (1959) and *Travels with a donkey* (1967) show the artist at his very best, at least when working without colour; the latter volume (still in print) includes headpieces for the chapters which originally incorporated initials, although these were modestly removed by the artist after unfavourable comments were made.[21] Mervyn Peake (also a tutor at the Central) was one of the first artists to be commissioned by Ede, and drew 12 full-page images for *Dr Jekyll and Mr Hyde* (1948), to be printed in yellow and black. Ede was very pleased with the 'understatement' of the images, which 'contrast normality with the chill of horror faintly suggested; only one shows Hyde the monster in explicit detail, and this I found a caricature and would have preferred to omit'.[22] More than a decade later Peake was commissioned to illustrate Balzac's *Droll stories* (1961) with 24 drawings which, because of his failing health, he struggled hard to realise, ultimately succeeding with the assistance of his wife.

Lynton Lamb and Nigel Lambourne have already been mentioned as working in other media, but both were most prolific at Folio with pen and ink. Lambourne's drawings for *Moll Flanders* (1954) are particularly effective, and he had lost nothing of his power 30 years later when he illustrated Disraeli's *Sybil* (1983). Among the most productive of Folio artists is Val Biro, whose vignette drawings and scraperboard designs – from *The prisoner of Zenda* (1961) to Trollope's *Golden lion of Granpere* (1997) – betray his training as a wood engraver under Rooke, although he also studied other media at the Central during the War. Perhaps most satisfying are the full-page scraperboard designs he made for the two-volume edition of Father Brown stories (1996), in which he boldly took on Ardizzone (the illustrator of an earlier Folio Father Brown) and won by a short head [15]. Fritz Wegner also worked in scraperboard, producing some 30 vigorous designs for *Mother Courage* in 1965.

The hard labour of some artists, as well as their mastery of their medium, is sometimes quite astonishing. Charles Keeping's achievement in illustrating all the novels of Dickens has been noted already. Alexy Pendle has been very nearly as prolific. He too has specialised in Victorian fiction, the close shading and hatching of his scenery and architecture, the lines of his faces and creases of his

16 Leonard Rosoman, Drawing for Aldous Huxley, *Point count point*, Folio Society, 1958.

17 Michael Foreman, colour painting for Aldous Huxley, *After many a summer*, Folio Society, 1980.

costumes, being perfectly suited to the atmosphere of these books. To date he has illustrated four novels by Wilkie Collins, three by Elizabeth Gaskell and ten by Anthony Trollope.

Other Central artists who worked in line for Folio are too numerous and diverse to discuss in detail here, and there is space only for notes of a few more who made a special contribution. John Vernon Lord deserves honourable mention, as does Peter Brookes, whose work has ranged from Chaucer's *Troilus and Criseyde* (1990) to several novels in Folio's huge Trollope series. Leonard Rosoman has illustrated several important books, beginning with Huxley's *Point counter point* in 1958.[16] He succeeded, in *Brave new world* (1971), in matching the cold 'futuristic' design of the book with drawings of a similarly precise and disturbing quality. Michael ffolkes' sketches were just right for *Gentlemen prefer blondes* (1985),[18] and Paul Hogarth (already mentioned as a lithographer) has contributed drawings to a string of Folio's books, beginning with *The adventures of Sherlock Holmes* (1958). Charles Stewart drew some marvellously creepy images for Le Fanu's *Uncle Silas*, published in 1988, although many of the drawings had been prepared for an earlier abandoned edition; his work in colour has been equally exciting (see below).

Paintings and mixed media

In recent years it has become possible to reproduce paintings, collages and mixed-media artworks with remarkable accuracy, and the Society has experimented with the possibilities this offers. Among the work of Central and St Martin's-trained artists, Charles Stewart's paintings for *Mistress Masham's repose* (1989), and his own selection of *Ghost stories* (1997), are marvellously atmospheric and appropriate, in a traditional narrative style. Michael Foreman, on the other hand, was responsible for nine surreal images in full colour for Huxley's *After many a summer* [17] as early as 1980 (Huxley is an author who seems to have inspired Folio's designers to break out of their conventions, and the typography of the book is uncharacteristically asymmetrical). Foreman also used monochrome collage to good effect in his illustrations to McGonagall's *Poetic gems* (1985), capturing the crazy seriousness and accidental humour of the poet's failed brilliance. More recently, Posy Simmonds has drawn wonderfully witty cartoons for Belloc's *Cautionary tales* (1997) and *The Folio book of humorous verse* (2002) [19]. In the latter case, advances in printing meant that the artist's full-colour drawings could be integrated with the text in a way that would not previously have been economical.

18 Michael ffolkes, pen and ink drawing for Anita Loos, *Gentleman prefer blondes*, Folio Society, 1985.

19 Posy Simmonds, full colour drawing for *The Folio book of humorous verse*, Folio Society, 2002.

Speak Roughly to Your Little Boy

Speak roughly to your little boy,
   And beat him when he sneezes;
He only does it to annoy,
   Because he knows it teases.
      Chorus: Wow! Wow! Wow!

I speak severely to my boy,
   I beat him when he sneezes;
For he can thoroughly enjoy
   The pepper when he pleases!
      Chorus: Wow! Wow! Wow!

Lewis Carroll

It would be quite wrong, however, to give the impression that the reproduction of polychromatic art in Folio books was limited to the last two decades. Within the limitations of older printing technologies the Society has had considerable success at reproducing paintings by lithography, almost from the outset. This is best embodied in the first Shakespeare series, begun with *Romeo and Juliet* in 1950 and completed in 1976 with *Timon of Athens*. Here the opportunity was taken to reproduce, where possible, costume designs prepared for a particular 20th-century production of the play in question. Although the designs were not intended for publication, the results were often extremely satisfying. Ann Curtis, Ralph Koltai, John Minton, Tanya Moiseiwitsch, John Napier, Anthony Powell and Alix Stone [20] are among the costume-designers whose colourful work appeared in this way. All were either students or teachers (or both) at Central Saint Martins.[23]

Calligraphy, marbling, bindings and typography

Beyond the direct illustration of the Folio Society's books, other aspects of design have been affected by intelligences wrought at the Central. Calligraphic lettering has regularly been used for title pages and binding designs, drawn sometimes by the artist who illustrated the book, sometimes separately. Charles Stewart's hand-drawn title page for *Uncle Silas* is particularly effective, establishing the slightly camp penny-dreadful atmosphere of the book on its first page. He also designed the binding as a pastiche of a Victorian publisher's cloth binding with rich gold blocking.[21] Binding design is another aspect of Folio books where the artist's hand is felt. In the early days, Folio editions often had printed dust jackets and here too the artist could express his imagination; there are lovely early examples by Derrick Harris, Nigel Lambourne and others. But printed jackets were seldom used after 1955, when slip cases were generally introduced, and the focus of binding decoration moved from the jacket to the boards and spine. In the majority of cases the illustrator of a book was also asked to draw an image for the binding, something of a feat in those cases where the work required a completely different approach from that used elsewhere in the book. The technology of industrial bookbinding has advanced in parallel with improvements in printing, and these days it is possible to bind a book in cloth or paper decorated with a combination of printing in colour and traditional gold-blocking.

A good many books are bound in quarter cloth or leather with marbled papers on the boards, papers often manufactured by the Cockerell firm, founded by Sydney M. Cockerell, who taught bookbinding at the Central between

20 Alix Stone, costume design for Royal Shakespeare Company production of Shakespeare's *Measure for measure*. Folio Society, 1964.

21 Charles Stewart, gold-blocked design for the dark green cloth binding of Sheridan le Fanu, *Uncle Silas*, Folio Society, 1988.

22 Ian Mortimer, design for the title page of William McGonagall, *Poetic gems*, Folio Society, 1985.

1930 and 1940.[24] His uncle, Sir Sydney C. Cockerell, had been Secretary to William Morris; Ede became friendly with him in 1945, when they would discuss his memories of the Kelmscott Press, Morris, Burne-Jones and their circle.[25] Some Folio bindings are designed 'in house', and this is also true of general typographical design. But here too an outside typographer is sometimes commissioned, especially for an unusual or specialist job. The long tradition of the teaching of book design and typography at the Central School, originally under the control of J.H. Mason, means that many leading book designers have been trained there. Ian Mortimer is among them, and was employed to design the title page of McGonagall's *Poetic gems* [**22**], making use of his intimate knowledge of 19th-century typeforms. His exuberant display caught the outlandish tone of the verses, as well as the mood of the period.

Conclusion

Central Saint Martins has a place in the history of 20th-century book illustration that can only be called central. For its part, the Folio Society has striven to balance top-quality book production on an industrial scale with the creativity of the artist and designer. There has been a symbiosis, albeit at times an unconscious one, between the

POETIC

GEMS

SELECTED FROM THE WORKS OF

WILLIAM McGONAGALL

POET AND TRAGEDIAN

died in Edinburgh 29 September 1902

FOREWORD BY
SPIKE MILLIGAN

BRIEF BIOGRAPHY AND REMINISCENCES
BY

THE AUTHOR

TRIBUTE AND ODE
from three students at Glasgow University
and other
TRIBUTES AND TESTIMONIALS

DRAMATIC COLLAGES
BY
MICHAEL FOREMAN

LONDON
The Folio Society
1985

two establishments, and a glance at some of the names mentioned above will be sufficient to demonstrate the range of book artists who have emerged from the college and found in Folio a patron which has cradled them in youth and championed them in maturity.

Notes

1   See Charles Ede, 'Beginnings', in *Folio* magazine, Autumn 1987, pp.2–12, and Sue Bradbury, 'A brief history' in *Folio 50*, Folio Society and British Library, 1997, pp.[7]–16.

2   On the early relationship between Folio and Golden Cockerel see Ede, *op. cit.*, and Roderick Cave, 'Folio: a Cockerel's fledgling' in *Matrix* 17, 1997, pp.133–8. See also R. Cave, 'Fifty years of Folio books' in *Folio 50*, pp.[50]–6, notably pp.51, 53; and R. Cave and Sarah Manson, *A history of the Golden Cockerel Press 1920–1960*, British Library; New Castle, DE: Oak Knoll, 2002, pp.198–200.

3   For bibliographical details of the Society's output to 1996 see *Folio 50*.

4   Ede, *op. cit.*, p.10.

5   See Joanna Selbourne, 'The wood engraving revival' in Sylvia Backemeyer (ed.), *Object lessons: Central Saint Martins Art and Design Archive, a centenary publication*, Lund Humphries with the Lethaby Press, 1996, pp.[42]–6. See also Selborne, *British wood-engraved book illustration 1904–1940: a break with tradition*, Clarendon Press, 1998, notably pp.[51]–9, [171]–85.

6   See Martin Andrews, *The life and work of Robert Gibbings*, Primrose Hill Press, 2003.

7   Andrews, *op. cit.*, pp.318–19, 329, 337.

8   Andrews, *op. cit.*, pp.341–2.

9   Ede was involved in trying to arrange a memorial exhibition for Gibbings in 1959. See Andrews, *op. cit.*, p.377.

10 See Simon Brett, *Mr Derrick Harris 1919–1960*, Fleece Press, 1998.

11 It is to be regretted that the Society has taken to calling wood engravings 'engravings' on title pages and in advertising matter. This is really a misnomer, and the latter term should be reserved for engraved intaglio prints (see my comments under that heading).

12 Plastic plates patented in Britain by W.S. Cowell of Ipswich.

13 See *Folio 50*, pp.33, 76, the former including Douglas Martin's assessment of Lambourne's 1949 work as 'uncharacteristically tentative'.

14 See *Barnett Freedman: 1901–1958* (exhibition catalogue), Arts Council, 1958. On dust-jackets see Alan Powers, *Front cover: great book jacket and cover design*, Mitchell Beazley, 2001, and the same writer's chapter in the present book.

15 For a note on Ede's relations with Freedman see Ede's 'Some thoughts on book illustration', in *Folio 50*, pp.[40]–4, p.41.

16 On Boyd Harte see Alan Powers' obituary in *Folio* magazine, Summer 2004, pp.28–[32].

17 Alan Powers suggests that it was partly the use of two colours for autolithographs which gave them an 'old-fashioned look' (Powers, *op. cit.* (note 16), p.29).

18 See David Chambers' review of the book in *The Private Library*, 2nd series, vol. 2, no. 4, Winter 1969, p.190.

19 *Folio 50*, p.44.

20 *Folio 50*, p.42.

21 See *Folio 50*, p.131. See also Brian Alderson, *Edward Ardizzone: a bibliographical commentary*, Private Libraries Association, 2003, p.166.

22 *Folio 50*, p.[40].

23 See Anna Buruma, 'Half a century of theatre design', in Sylvia Backemeyer (ed.), *Making their mark: art, craft and design at the Central School, 1896–1966*, Herbert Press, 2000, pp.[91]–100.

24 Sydney M. Cockerell was trained by his father Douglas (Sydney C. Cockerell's younger brother), who founded the binding course at Central in 1897.

25 See Ede, *op. cit.* (note 1), p.7.

7 / Martin Baker
A long drawn-out affair:
Radio Times and illustrators

Martin Baker is a writer and illustrator of children's books and features on art and music for BBC Radio Three and Four and *The Times*. For many years he contributed drawings to *Radio Times* and in 2002 he curated an exhibition for the Ashmolean Museum, Oxford, of graphic work commissioned by *Radio Times*.

The deadlines that *Radio Times* allowed illustrators were impossibly short, often only two days: the

magazine commissioned work on Thursdays or Fridays and it had to be delivered first thing Monday morning. The assignment always disrupted weekends, and the families of illustrators often used subterfuge where commissions encroached upon domestic arrangements. Jim Russell was a tutor at St Martin's in the 1960s. His wife Rebecca resorted to hiding his artwork that, although finished, would have occupied the perfectionist artist, tinkering with details, until the deadline was reached.

Almost from its beginning in 1923, *Radio Times* offered artists phenomenal exposure. The weekly formatting of the magazine's comprehensive listing details demanded space fillers where text fell short and left gaps upon the page. Black line drawings, wood engravings, and scraperboard images reproduced well upon the cheap uncoated paper; halftones, derived either from photographic or painted images, seldom printed effectively. For the first few years, at least, commissions were rare and illustrations were most often selected from unsolicited submissions by artists, or by agents on their behalf. Fees varied with the status of the artist.

Maurice Gorham, who became the magazine's first titular art editor in 1927, had virtually no experience of art or of design but enthusiastically promoted work of the most modern schools that he formatted with more traditional styles. The magazine became an appetising visual buffet, with the futurist McKnight Kauffer complementing the orientalist Brangwyn as cover artists and, from the 1930s, there were Eric Fraser and Victor Reinganum jazzing with the more traditional Edward Ardizzone and Lynton Lamb, both Central School students; these four illustrators almost defined *Radio Times'* illustration styles for over four decades. The magazine became a resource for the finest black and white graphic work and was used by professionals in publishing and advertising alike. Fortunately Gorham did not suffer the bane of market research and so he possibly turned a Nelsonian eye to

1 John Farleigh, 'Holy Week Reading', *Radio Times*, 16 March 1951.

the fact that public regard for modernism was, at best, unenthusiastic.

From the start the BBC's general manager, John Reith, regarded *Radio Times* as a mere timetable, to guide the listener towards broadcasts that would contribute 'to the intellectual and moral happiness of the community'.[1] The puritanical Reith, who regarded his stewardship of the company – it became a corporation in 1927 – as a mission from God, could not have been aware that in the editorial offices below, Bacchus ruled, and a spirit (mostly whisky) of creative anarchy prevailed. The portentous editorial style of *Radio Times*, common in all publications of the period, was leavened by the drawings, and illustrators often succumbed to their own sense of humour. For example in the 1950s Laurence Scarfe, a tutor of illustration at the Central, included a television aerial in his drawing for 'Dido, Queen of Carthage', for which anachronism he was banned from the magazine for a year.

In 1929 the BBC published *The Listener*, a digest of current and forthcoming BBC programmes for which John Farleigh of the Central engraved covers, as did Edward Bawden. Farleigh also contributed occasional line drawings to *Radio Times*. Five vignettes he drew for the issue of Easter 1951, 'Holy Week Reading' [1], are powerfully expressionist images. During the 1930s other Central artists, including Margaret Calkin-James and Tirzah Garwood, contributed to BBC programmes and booklets. Garwood, who married Eric Ravilious in 1930, drew covers for *The Listener* and designed a new version of the BBC crest; she also produced engravings. Dorothea Braby, who had studied at the Central School from 1926 to 1931 contributed to *Radio Times* from the mid-1930s. Initially her work had an art deco gloss, however a drawing that she made later, 'Hedgerows' [2], is a finely-wrought synthesis of her observational and aesthetic skills. Clixby Watson, from St Martin's, produced work over two decades that is of outstanding quality. His 'Corn Dealer's Revenge' (*RT*, 17 September 1937) has the vivacity of contemporary children's illustration and, although it harks back stylistically to the early years of the 20th century, Watson kept abreast of the latest fads in illustration with consistent bravura. The nature of his chameleon ability, once regarded as 'slick', has meant that his stature as a great draughtsman has diminished, however the large body of work that he contributed to *Radio Times* deserves re-examination.

Another prolific illustrator, contributing at least 675 drawings to *Radio Times* from the 1930s to the 1960s, mostly for sports features, was Jack Dunkley who had studied at the Central in the early 1930s. Like Watson his repu-

2 Dorothea Braby, 'Hedgerows', *Radio Times*, date unknown.

3 Jack Dunkley, 'The offer', *Radio Times*, 27 December 1961.

Radio Times (Incorporating World-Radio) May 14, 1948.
Vol. 99. No. 1283. Registered at the G.P.O. as a Newspaper

SCOTTISH EDITION

RADIO TIMES

JOURNAL OF THE BBC

PRICE TWOPENCE

PROGRAMMES FOR
MAY 16—22

'A Whit Monday Picnic,' by Edward Ardizzone

THE GENERAL ASSEMBLY
of the Church of Scotland
A recorded report of the opening ceremonies
in the Home Service on Tuesday at 7.30 p.m.
Impressions in 'Seen from Scotland' on Saturday

Bernard Shaw's
'ARMS AND THE MAN'
on Monday evening in the Home Service

TRIP TO THE SEASIDE
Down London River on the 'Royal Eagle,' and
a tour of Margate's holiday entertainment
Whit Monday in the Light Programme

Wilfred Pickles's
CHILDREN'S TREAT
Whit Monday at 6.15 p.m. : Light Programme

LORD SAMUEL
on Gladstone
Wednesday in the Third Programme

VICTOR DE SABATA
conducts the Wednesday concert, which includes
the Symphonie fantastique by Berlioz

BACKHAUS
the distinguished pianist broadcasts on
Tuesday (Third) and Friday (Home Service)

THE MARSHALL PLAN
Tuesday's Focus in the Light Programme

'MY BROTHER JONATHAN'
Radio version of the British film in
Friday's Picture Parade

THE Light Programme is offering something novel in the way of Whitsun radio entertainment this year. Wynford Vaughan Thomas will make a trip down London River from Tower Bridge to Margate on board the *Royal Eagle* and listeners will be invited to join him for a day at the seaside. When he goes ashore at Margate he will hand over to John Ellison, who will conduct a tour of the sands and introduce broadcasts from pier and pavilion. The five-part programme begins at 9.10 a.m. with a description of the departure of the *Royal Eagle* from Tower Pier and ends at 10.35 with the return of Wynford Vaughan Thomas and his fellow-holidaymakers to Victoria station. The first part will include a special edition of *Down Your Way*.

There will be the usual Light Programme round-up of Whit-Monday sport—two cricket matches, racing at Hurst Park, athletics at the White City—and in the evening a broadcast of Variety from the British Legion Rally at the Royal Albert Hall.

Some of the broadcasts in the Light Programme will come from far afield. The Forces Networks in Frankfurt, Hamburg, and Berlin are combining with the BBC in the Continental round-up of entertainment and holiday greetings, with which the day will open, and later there will be contributions from Colombo, Ceylon, and Hilversum, Holland.

ON Friday afternoon, in the cloisters of Westminster Abbey, Mr. Churchill will unveil a Memorial to the fallen of the Commandos and Airborne Forces of the second world war and to the men of the Submarine Service of both world wars. Before the unveiling there will be a service in the Abbey and the congregation will include many senior officers of the Royal Navy, the Army, and the R.A.F. About a dozen V.C.s will be present and the next of kin of several V.C.s who fell during the late war will have places of honour in the Choir. There will be a broadcast from the Abbey in the Home Service between 3.25 and 4.20 p.m.

The Memorial, which is in three parts, shows bronze figures of a sailor in the Submarine Service, a private in the Commandos and an airborne parachutist. It is the work of Gilbert Ledward.

THE fiftieth anniversary of the death of Gladstone falls on Wednesday, and that evening Lord Samuel, one of the few men now alive who heard him speak in the House of Commons, will broadcast a tribute in the Third Programme. Lord Samuel had already fought his first parliamentary election when Gladstone died at Hawarden in his ninetieth year.

SIR CHARLES WEBSTER, who will speak on Fundamentals of British Foreign Policy in the Third Programme on Monday, is a distinguished scholar who has not only written history but helped to make it. He attended the Paris Peace Conference of 1919, was a member of the British Delegation to the Dumbarton Oaks Conference, and took part in the San Francisco Conference of 1945.

LORD FORRESTER, who will broadcast after the nine o'clock News on Sunday, is managing director of a large industrial firm with branches all over the world. He was trained as a biologist and has many interests outside industry. A number of the ideas he put forward in a Third Programme broadcast last year on the implications of full employment attracted widespread attention abroad. On Sunday he will look at the social and industrial life of Britain and advocate the need for bolder thinking and planning.

THE main dramatic production in the Third Programme this week is an English version of Jean Anouilh's play *Medea* (Tuesday and Saturday). Anouilh follows a current fashion in taking themes from the classical Greek drama, and his plays are highly esteemed in his own country. The radio *Medea* will be discussed in *The Critic on the Air* by Merlin Thomas, Tutor in French Literature at New College, Oxford, who has made a special study of Anouilh.

WORLD THEATRE PRESENTS

Donald Wolfit and Miles Malleson in

'TARTUFFE'

BY MOLIERE

Freely adapted into English by
MILES MALLESON

★

MONSIEUR ORGON, *a rich merchant*	Miles Malleson
DAMIS, *his son*	Desmond Carrington
MARIANE, *his daughter*	Violet Loxley
MADAME PERNELLE, *his mother*	May Agate
ELMIRE, *his second wife*	Frances Rowe
CLEANTE, *Elmire's brother*	David King-Wood
VALERE, *betrothed to Mariane*	Robert Rietty
DORINE, *maid to Elmire*	Jessie Evans
LOYALE, *a bailiff*	John Moffatt
A POLICE OFFICER	Hamilton Dyce
TARTUFFE	Donald Wolfit

SCENE
Paris 1660. The house of Monsieur Orgon, a rich merchant
Rhymed couplets by Sagittarius
Music adapted by Leslie Bridgewater from Rameau, Lully, and Campra

PRODUCED BY WILFRID GRANTHAM

at 9.15

---

tation has suffered, possibly because of his artistic fecundity. One of his last commissions, in 1961, was for a quietly announced *Comedy Playhouse* introducing two rag and bone men, 'The Offer' [3], that became one of the BBC's most popular series, 'Steptoe and Son'.

In 1932 Edward Ardizzone, who had as a child known Maurice Gorham, began his long association with the magazine. Ardizzone had been an evening student of James Fitton at the Central. His style reflects the vignettes by the great Dickens illustrators, and his cross-hatched pen lines emulate the pattern achieved by the process engraver's intermediary burin. A cover vignette he drew for Whit Monday [4] is a post-war ideal of family life and is, perhaps, a scene memorised from a family outing. His daughter, interviewed in 2000, says that her father rarely drew from life for his illustration work, 'except in formal life classes: he did all his drawing from memory, drawing what he'd seen half-an-hour before'.[2]

Another *Radio Times* stalwart was Lynton Lamb. From 1928 until 1930 he studied at the Central School of Art under Noel Rooke, Bernard Meninsky and A.S. Hartrick. Lamb believed that literature did not need illustration to explain it; however that if drawings were to

4 Edward Ardizzone, 'A Whit Monday picnic', *Radio Times*, 14 May 1948.

5 Lynton Lamb, 'Tartuffe', *Radio Times*, 9 August 1951.

accompany the text then they should be well drawn, from life, and accurate.

Lynton Lamb and Edward Ardizzone worked from opposite ends of the creative process, Ardizzone drawing from memory, while Lamb insisted on drawing from life, using as much research as possible. Stylistically their work differs in that Ardizzone's drawings have the appearance of etchings while Lamb made drawings that resemble lithographic prints; and, whereas Ardizzone's work has the vivacity of a Rowlandson sketch, Lamb's earnest, lugubrious approach, for example 'Tartuffe' [5], reveals a more cerebral personality.

Mona Moore was a student at both the Central and St Martin's before the war, during which Kenneth Clark appointed her as a war artist to record the storage of the National Gallery's art treasures in a Welsh tin mine. Of her *Radio Times* illustrations, 'Judgement Rock' [6] is a fine example, and possesses real passion and creative freedom.

Dispatched by his parents, alone at the age of 14, Fritz Wegner endured a perilous train journey in July 1938 from Vienna to London in order to escape the Nazis. After his arrival in England he was found a place at St Martin's by a refugee committee who recognised his artistic abilities. He remembers that there were few teachers left at the college and that students were instructed to draw from plaster casts, models and skeletons. One tutor, George Mansell, a scholar known for his lettering, design and calligraphy, sensitive to Wegner's homesickness and youth suggested that he should come and live with him and his French wife and be apprenticed to him in his design practice.

Similarly, at the age of 17, Susan Einzig left Berlin in 1939 as one of the last young people to escape from Germany. She enrolled at the Central School and studied first in London and then in Northampton where the school had been evacuated during part of the war. For these artists, some unused to the sly deceptions of the English language, ambiguity in communication was avoided in favour of ideas of simplicity and directness, echoing Alberti's dictum of the subtraction of unnecessary detail to illuminate meaning. They created a new graphic syntax that led to what became a golden age for graphic art and design in the post-war years, bringing conceptual semiology to the graphics industry long before it became devalued by the commercialisation of today's 'fine' arts cartel.

One of the most formidable, and unsung, promoters of this talent was Eucharis (Cara) Strong. She had studied art at the Central in the mid-1930s and developed an acute understanding of fine draughtsmanship and good illustration. By the 1950s she had established Saxon Artists, which became one of the most respected illustrators' agencies in

6 Mona Moore, 'Judgement Rock', *Radio Times*, 12 December 1947.

7 Terry Greer, title unknown, *Radio Times*, date unknown.

London. Fritz Wegner was the first artist that she represented and he was soon joined by other Central and St Martin's progeny and tutors: Stanley Badmin, Andrew Dodds, Terry Greer, Derrick Harris, Faith Jaques, Ivan Lapper, and Jim Russell. When a new art editor, Ralph Usherwood, was appointed at *Radio Times* in 1950 it was most often Cara Strong's team of artists that were his first choice for commissions.

An intriguing and elusive figure in British illustration is Terry Greer. His drawings for *Radio Times* were made by creating the image in reverse and transferring it in a monoprint style to blotting paper. The arbitrary nature of the process achieved a dramatic spontaneity that always created an arresting image on the page [7]. Greer had studied illustration at St Martin's from 1947 and became one of Saxon Artists' most highly-successful illustrators. In the 1970s he chose to become a writer, and a script for *Doctor Who* is referenced, and four plays produced between 1973 and 1978 are credited, but his subsequent career, sadly, is unknown.

Two totally disparate artists, Paul Hogarth and Mervyn Peake, demonstrate the variety of interpretative volition. For Hogarth, like Lynton Lamb, the eye is the primary instrument, selectively choosing features from life that harmonise with his own unique view. 'Ham House Richmond' [8] gives a tantalising indication of his later celebrated style, the journalistic drawings made from life with an oblique impetuosity. He had studied at St Martin's from 1938 to 1939 and later became a tutor of illustration at the Central from 1951 to 1956. By contrast, Mervyn Peake's gothic imagination in both his drawing and writing was probably intensified by an assignment to Belsen in 1945. The experience certainly affected his health. He conjoined the duties of writer and illustrator: the texture of his writing in the Gormenghast trilogy has the same obsessive denseness as his cross-hatched drawings. For Peake, described as the greatest illustrator of his time, memory was arguably the primary source. In 1946 he described the duty of the illustrator: 'It is for you to leave the spectator with no option but to see what you liked.'[3] From the mid-1950s, already suffering from Parkinson's disease, he tutored at the Central School where, during 1960–1, John Lord remembers that he 'was in a very bad way, and he seemed to be abstracted when he talked to you, and he had a tremor'.[4] Of the few works that Peake contributed to *Radio Times*, 'Malone dies' (*RT*, 13 June 1958), is a bleak intimation of mortality.

John O'Connor had trained with Eric Ravilious and John Nash. He tutored at St Martin's from 1964 until 1975. His familiarity with the Suffolk countryside is reflected in

'Danger, Men Working'

Adapted for broadcasting by the author, J. D. STEWART

Mary Reilly, *a shorthand typist*...........................Patricia Stewart
Desmond Doherty, *general foreman*...................Joseph Tomelty
Erskine Craig, *a civil engineer*.........................Allan McClelland
Paddy Hoy, *a disabled craftsman*.............................J. G. Devlin
Gerry McMahon, *a navvy*..............................Patrick McAlinney
Charlie Quinn, *a foreman*.......................................John McBride
Sam Toler, *a ganger*..Noel French
John Peoples, *a foreman*.......................................Will Leighton
Fred Scanling, *a chief ganger*...Pat Magee
Major Trumbull, *Engineer in Charge*...................Michael Kelly

The play is set in Northern Ireland, on a site where a hospital is under construction, and it examines the impact of mass-production methods and mass-production mentality on a community of workmen accustomed to other, more personal methods

PRODUCED BY TYRONE GUTHRIE
at 9.15

8 Paul Hogarth, 'Ham House, Richmond', *Radio Times*, 23 October 1953.

9 John O'Connor, 'Curlew River', *Radio Times*, 18 June 1964.

10 Faith Jaques, title unknown, *Radio Times*, date unknown.

11 Leonard Rosoman, 'Danger, men working', *Radio Times*, 6 July 1951.

12 John Minton, 'The lady from the sea', *Radio Times*, 19 September 1952.

AT 9.15 WORLD THEATRE PRESENTS
'The Lady from the Sea'
BY HENRIK IBSEN
IN A NEW TRANSLATION BY PETER WATTS

'Now we shall both be married to the sea—and to each other'

Dr. Wangel...William Fox
Ellida Wangel, his wife.....................................Marie Ney
His daughters: Boletta.................................Nancy Nevinson
　　　　　　Hilda.................................Margaret Barton
Arnholm, a tutor...Heron Carvic
Lyngstrand..Ronald Sidney
Ballested...John Turnbull
A Stranger..Valentine Dyall

SCENE: *a small town at the head of a landlocked fjörd in Northern Norway, 1888*
PRODUCED BY PETER WATTS

13 Derrick Harris, 'Shepherd Market', *Radio Times*, 4 May 1956.

'Curlew River' [**9**], a powerful and free-ink drawing that matches the sombre mood of Britten's Nōh-inflected church parable.

One of the most popular of British illustrators, Faith Jaques, began illustrating for *Radio Times* in 1948. She had studied at the Central from 1946 and began receiving commissions while still at college. For over 20 years the quiet Chekovian wit of her drawings, for example the girl with guitar [**10**], elevated the pages of the magazine. Her career highlights one of the sad facts of the illustrator's life, that the work occupies a transient and undervalued place in our culture. Jaques had fought unselfishly for the rights of fellow illustrators. She hoarded her own work, as she said, 'for a rainy day'. On her death in 1997 this treasure was unceremoniously thrown into a refuse skip. Fortunately some of it was rescued, thanks to the sensitivity of a waste removal man, and is now stored at the European Illustration Collection in Hull. Unfortunately the issue of copyright remains and illustrators are still offered the kind of draconian contractual conditions (and fees) that Julius II, if not the artist, would have been quite happy to sign.

The unifying quality of the illustrations in *Radio Times* throughout the 1950s was draughtsmanship based upon observation, always subservient to the subject and allied to an appreciation that an economy of detail and use of areas of black and white added a powerful dynamic to the draw-ing. In keeping with the new expressive freedoms of the times, especially towards the end of the decade, the styles became colloquial, the drawings lost the gratuitous decora-tion of previous years and achieved an almost forensic clar-ity. Leonard Rosoman, a student at the Central School from 1938 to 1939, was greatly influential in redefining this new way of drawing, and he's recalled by those he taught as showing how the use of white space in a composition could augment the inherent drama of the subject. His stature as one of Britain's leading fine artists, equally at home work-ing at the miniature scale of *Radio Times* commissions [11] or as a muralist for the Royal Academy, has been widely recognised and admired by his peers. He has been a Royal Academician since 1970, and was awarded the OBE in 1981. Behind the panoply, however, Rosoman possesses great modesty and a wicked sense of humour.

One illustrator almost defines the age. John Minton produced outstanding work for *Radio Times*. This is distin-guished by a graphic rhetoric that defies the limited size of the published drawings. These have a ferocious, brooding poetry that is as uncompromisingly romantic as the land-scapes of Samuel Palmer. Minton's influence in his work and his subsequent teaching – he taught at the Central School of Arts and Crafts during 1947 – was enormous. Margaret Levetus, a student at the Central from 1936 to 1939, recalls a tutorial visit by Minton to Sir John Cass College, where she was teaching around 1950.

> With simply a blackboard and a piece of chalk for visual aids, he talked about drawing, occasionally demonstrating with a few lines, and kept his audience enthralled. He shimmered with vitality and looked like an extremely animated El Greco character – dark, thin and elongated, but full of fun. He must have been a most inspiring teacher, and he was a superb illustrator.[5]

Veronica Hitchcock, working at *Radio Times* in 1952, remembers 'Johnny Minton sweeping into the offices wear-ing a long black coat with an astrakhan collar looking very Russian to deliver his drawings for the week'.[6] His drawing for Ibsen's 'Lady from the Sea' [12] is a characteristic piece that Minton responds to with empathy for the stranger in the play.

The expense of box, the close-grained wood traditionally used for engravings, made it too costly a material to use for the minimally paid *Radio Times* commissions – scraper-board and, latterly, vinyl were used as an economical alter-native. A rare exception was some of the work commissioned from Derrick Harris, for which he was given complete freedom. The majority of this was drawn rather

14 Val Biro, 'Falstaff',
Radio Times, c.1970.

than engraved, although Harris replicated the precise quality of engraved wood in his drawings, as in 'Shepherd Market' [13].

The work of Val Biro also draws from engraving sources though using the medium of scraperboard. Biro was born in Budapest and, at the age of 18, in 1939, he was sent by his father to train as an illustrator at the Central School of Art in London, where he remembers tutorials from Noel Rooke,

> a neatly dressed figure with a goatee beard who would sit down at my board and draw in the margin of my cartridge paper an exquisite detail with the utmost precision.[7]

On leaving college he worked for a variety of publishers before Ralph Usherwood commissioned his first illustration for Radio Times, a little decorative angel, in 1950. Influenced by Rex Whistler, he developed a style where baroque and rococo originals were given revivified potency. Of all the illustrators commissioned by Radio Times, Val Biro refined the ornamentation of the 18th century cartouche to perfection with wit and without slavish pastiche as in 'Falstaff' [14].

European influences are certainly present in the work of Anthony Gross. He was born in Dulwich to a Hungarian father and an Italian/Irish mother. For a short time he became a student in Paris at the Académie Julian, and at

15 Anthony Gross, 'Point of departure', *Radio Times*, 2 February 1951.

the Ecole des Beaux Arts. Working in France as a painter and film animator and producing etchings he developed a free graphic style. In 1936 he illustrated Jean Cocteau's *Les enfants terribles*, intriguingly mimicking the author's own poetically simple linear technique. He first worked for *Radio Times* in 1951, a commission for Jean Anouilh's 'Point of Departure' [**15**]. This drawing, now in the Victoria and Albert Museum, is cited by Usherwood as one of the most distinguished ever done for the magazine. It imbues the subject with a dreamlike quality and has the character of an etching; the Cocteau style is present and the radial lines invoke something of the Swiss painter Hans Erni who coincidentally had also studied at the Académie Julian. For about five years, from 1946, Anthony Gross taught at the Central School where Harold Cohen remembers him as a strict tutor. 'He would plumb-line your drawing and if it was out of true you would be ordered in no uncertain terms to start all over again.'[8] Peter Harle, another of his Central School students, who became art editor of *Radio Times* in 1960, asked Gross about his use of the plumb-line. Gross's answer, in the light of his apparent loose style of drawing, that preliminary drawings required a vertical reference against which other lines can be measured,[9] reveals something of his disciplined methodology.

In the immediate post-war years BBC's Children's Hour broadcasts still held a powerful nostalgia. Margaret Levetus made a seminal drawing in 1950 that comprehensively evokes children's fictional heroes of the time. Her panorama, 'The chain' [**16**] is a time capsule of the classic literature that the Home Service broadcast for children. Contemporary children's fiction was also adapted, amongst which the Jennings books were most popular. Geoffrey Whittam, who had also studied at the Central (1946-9), enjoyed great popularity as a children's book illustrator and was an obvious choice when it came to commissioning drawings for the many excursions to Linbury Court Boarding School that were broadcast from 1948 [**17**]. Another Central School student, Peter Firmin, created one

16 Margaret Levetus, 'The chain', *Radio Times*, 22 December 1950.

17 Geoffrey Whittam, 'Jennings and the festive spirit', *Radio Times*, 24 February 1954.

18 Peter Firmin, 'Noggin and the flying machine', *Radio Times*, 1 August 1968.

19 Susan Einzig, 'The trial of Madame Lafarge', *Radio Times*. 13 December 1957

20 James Boswell, 'Look back in anger', *Radio Times*, February 1967.

of the iconic children's television cartoon series, 'Noggin the Nog', of which 'Noggin and the Flying Machine' [18] is a vivacious memento, beautifully drawn with liberal use of the artist's finger prints for texture.

After the war, artists such as James Boswell, Pearl Binder, Susan Einzig and Fritz Wegner made powerful arguments in their illustrations for tolerance, humanism and social equality. James Boswell, for example, was a leading figure of the nation's socialist drive and his work was uncompromisingly committed to left-wing causes. In 'Look Back in Anger' [20] he imprisons the figure of Jimmy Porter behind the bars of the iron frame of the bed – an image that sums up the character's social alienation in this seminal play.

The work of Susan Einzig exemplifies the intellectual integrity of these artists. Einzig's profound love and knowledge of literature was shared by editor Ralph Usherwood and he was able to brief the chosen illustrator with a succinct precis of the work to be illustrated. Susan Einzig's careful and diligent research resulted in many outstanding drawings, each imbued with an authority that added verisimilitude to the broadcast feature. The artwork of her commissions bears witness to her scrupulous attention to the subject, with tireless alterations, corrections and redrawing that would have been deemed unnecessary by an inferior artist. 'The trial of Madame Lafarge' [19] is a study with all the power of Daumier.

Photographs of the actors in radio dramas seldom match the image of their characters created in the mind of the listener. Andrew Dodds was fortunate in being asked to draw the characters for a serial before it was broadcast. His farming background influenced Ralph Usherwood who asked him for a drawing in 1951 to highlight a new Light Programme series, 'The Archers'. Dodds used his own family as models for farmer Archer and his wife. For another radio play his drawing of old Jacob lighting his pipe with five pound notes ('Money isn't everything' *RT*, 1953) [21] is a bucolic character study that could only have been drawn by an artist skilled in drawing from life. Dodds was a student at the Central School in 1947 and taught illustration at St Martin's from 1951 to 1972.

Laurence Scarfe, a tutor at the Central from 1945 until 1970, where he taught the graphic design aspects of illustration, was a frequent choice for *Radio Times* when it came to illustrations of dramas from the classical repertoire. Scarfe drew upon his love of Italian architecture for the drawings, for example 'Romeo and Juliet' [22] and these, while stylish and contemporary, reflected careful study of renaissance originals.

Old Jacob, the pigman, never forgave his brother Frank for stealing his fiancée, and when the brother died and left him three thousand pounds he saw no reason to change his sentiments
'MONEY ISN'T EVERYTHING'

JIM DALE IN
'Celery Quarter Blues'
The story of a greengrocer's son who leaps to fame as a singer—and looks after he leaps
at 9.15

21 Andrew Dodds, 'Money isn't everything', *Radio Times*, 1953.

22 Laurence Scarfe, 'Romeo and Juliet', *Radio Times*, 8 October 1954.

23 Len Deighton, 'Celery Quarter Blues', *Radio Times*, 13 December 1957.

Before the success of *The Ipcress File*, Len Deighton, a student at St Martin's in 1949 following service in the RAF, contributed illustrations for an *Observer* cookery strip that became a model of graphic communication. He was also commissioned by publishers and by London Transport for a poster depicting English village life. He did many drawings for *Radio Times*. 'Celery Quarter Blues' [**23**], for example, is experimentally drawn with the dropper from an india ink bottle and has an improvisatory quality that absorbs the dynamic influences of American illustration of the time.

Ian Ribbons, a tutor at St Martin's from 1976, possesses a style that is so skilful, fluid and impromptu that it all but hides his very careful research and astute observation. For *Radio Times* he contributed many truly distinguished drawings and 'The flight to Varennes' [**24**] is a playful and consummate take on 18th-century French sources.

Bruce Angrave had studied at the Central School of Art and, after the Second World War, during which he worked for the Ministry of Information, he became a multi-talented freelance designer and illustrator. Angrave's cheerful drawings have something of a dated appeal, however 'Apple v. the rest' [**25**] has a nostalgia and shows his ability to caricature without obsequious reverence.

24 Ian Ribbons, 'The flight to Varennes', *Radio Times*, 13 June 1958.

25 Bruce Angrave, 'Apple v. the rest', *Radio Times*, 31 July 1969.

26 Jim Russell, 'My friend Charles', *Radio Times*, 8 August 1963.

27 Fritz Wegner, 'Unmarried mothers', *Radio Times*, 14 February 1963.

28 John Lord, 'Ars
longa, vita brevis',
Radio Times, 1960s.

Angrave came into his own as a paper sculptor bringing an iconoclastic *joie de vivre* to the elaborate technique.

By the end of the 1950s St Martin's had an enviable reputation among art colleges in Britain. The Central was where one went to acquire craft skills, the Slade for fine art, and the Royal College of Art to receive the imprimatur of the great and the good, but St Martin's was where you went for drawing, the basis of all disciplines in art. Tutors included Ivan Lapper, Jim Russell and Fritz Wegner, all of them contributing to *Radio Times*. Lapper produced drawings that emulate film poster art of the time. His ability to montage faces and historical detail was remarkable. Also remarkable is the size of his originals, often working up to A3; the drawings when reduced have the impact of a seamless image, for example 'The scandalous death of Adolf Hitler' [**33**]. Jim Russell on the other hand contributed drawings that veer towards abstract expressionism. 'My friend Charles' [**26**] has the appearance of a lithograph, yet is an ink drawing in which the explosive textures almost hide the very fine draughtsmanship. Fritz Wegner's illustrative genius – not hyperbole in this artist's case – was his ability to illuminate the subtleties of character of the people he depicted, with humanity and entirely without exaggeration. In 'Unmarried mothers'[**27**] Wegner's quiet humanism transformed a subject that once caused scandal into a positive celebration of motherhood.

In the 1970s Peter Brookes, who would later refashion political graphic aphorism for *The Times*, began drawing for *Radio Times* and *The Listener*. He had freelanced from 1966 after studying at the Central School and teaching there from 1976 to 1978. His disingenuous and attractive style conceals a surreal ability to turn the earth upside down. Brookes' covers for *Radio Times* are amongst the greatest that the magazine published [**30, 31**].

Possibly the artist who took the line for a walk to its ultimate microcosmic destination is John Lord. His use of the Rapidograph – a notoriously temperamental capillary drawing pen whose tubular nib clogged at every opportunity, requiring vigorous shaking to clear congealing ink from its barrel (he says that his family became quite used to being spattered with the fallout!) – allowed him to pursue linear detail that had seldom been achieved before, for which he remembers being frowned upon by his tutors at the Central. His drawing for John Arden's play, 'Ars longa vita brevis' [**28**], is an obsessive, unsettling image in accord with its subject.

With the publication of ITV's *TV Times* in 1955, printed by photogravure and with the occasional advantage of full colour, *Radio Times* appeared dated. In the following decade it was redesigned countless times and in 1968 a

29 Glynn Boyd Harte, cover for the Proms issue, *Radio Times*, 11 July 1981.

RadioTimes

Remember Hiroshima . . .
On 6 August 1945
the first atom bomb
was dropped on
the Japanese city.
This week BBC2 looks
back on 30 years
of living in the
shadow of the bomb.
Inside: the impact of the bomb

広島を憶えていますか

30 Peter Brookes, 'The Proms', *Radio Times*, 15 August 1978.

31 Peter Brookes, 'Remember Hiroshima', *Radio Times*, 2 August 1975.

new art editor was appointed, David Driver, who initiated changes that produced a design classic. Driver's use of typography and dramatic cropping of photographs created a mass-market magazine that equalled the best editorial design of the time. The cover and some inside sections were printed in gravure, allowing full-colour illustrations and, for the first time, photographs that reproduced well. As a result the use of black and white line drawings was curtailed and confined to the letterpress sections. Illustrations were commissioned from a new generation of artists who used airbrush, watercolours, coloured pencil and other techniques exploiting the tonal delicacy that gravure printing in colour allowed.

Among those from the Central and St Martin's were Glynn Boyd Harte, a student at St Martin's in the 1960s, who brought a sophisticated gloss to representational illustration as in his cover, 'The Proms' [29]; Janet Woolley who drew images in a flattened perspective that gave her work a timeless quality; and Sara Midda who cast magic upon everything she drew. Midda had studied at St Martin's in the 1970s and is remembered as highly sensitive and easy to tease, serious, and always accompanied by her small dog. Her work first appeared in *Radio Times* at the beginning of the 1970s and exhibited great poetry and finesse. Her sensuous drawing for 'Chéri' [32] perfectly evokes the intensity of Colette's 1930s Paris. The originality of her style (it has been much copied by inferior hands since) is unanimously admired here and throughout the world, and she holds a special place of affection amongst her peers.

Brian Thomas studied first at Goldsmiths' College where lithography lecturer, Bernard Cheese, arranged for him to have an interview with Eric Thomas, the Head of Illustration at St Martin's.

> I was successful and began to study illustration for the National Diploma in Design. I was the last of the 'old guard' as the following year saw the start of the new Diploma in Design. It was a marvellous time in the early sixties to be in the heart of London. I was very fortunate to have Ivan Lapper, Jim Russell, Fritz Wegner and Andrew Dodds as tutors.[10]

In 1967 Thomas joined *Radio Times* as a designer where he remembers having 'the strange experience of commissioning my former tutors!'[11] Thomas became a linchpin of the magazine, becoming managing editor in 1988 and production editor in 1996. His positive attitude towards the benefits of computer technology gave direction to BBC Worldwide's utilisation of the electronic medium and greatly assisted the economic future for *Radio Times*.

Wednesday *Radio*

12.27
Just a Minute
(Monday's broadcast) ‡
12.55 medium wave only
Weather, programme news

1.0
The World at One:
News
William Hardcastle

1.30
The Archers
(Tuesday's broadcast) ‡

1.45
Woman's Hour
medium wave only from 2.0
Presenter Sue MacGregor
Guest of the Week:
Artur Rubinstein
2.0-2.2 News
Reading your letters.
If I Were Editor: a Woman's Hour listener exchanges her views about the programme with editor WYN KNOWLES.
Wanted – Happy Christmas Volunteers! ‡: DOROTHY GRACE ELDER discovers how the Christmas spirit crosses the Borstal walls of Scotland.
Duck with a Difference: BERNARD JACKSON takes a Chinese dinner with IRENE HUANG.
DAVID BUCK reads
The Castle Inn
by STANLEY J. WEYMAN (3)

2.45
Listen with Mother
medium wave only
Story: The Little Red Motor Car by HILARY HASHGEN

3.0 News

3.5 *Stereo*
Afternoon Theatre
Jigsaw
A psychological thriller by DEREK HOODINOTT
The story of a young man, Bob, who plays on the mental instability of his former schoolfriend, Graham, with terrifying and disastrous results.
Bob...............NOEL JOHNSON
Graham............JOHN CARSON
Val...............NORMA RONALD
Jean..............JANE THOMPSON
Det-Sgt Cooper
        JOHN FRANKLYN-ROBBINS
Producer DAVID H. GODFREY

4.0 News

6.45
The Archers
(Repeated: Thursday, 1.30 pm)

7.0
News Desk
John Tidmarsh

7.30
Celebration
J.B.
He was officially Sir John Barbirolli, but to music lovers everywhere, from Berlin to Houston, Texas, and above all in Manchester, he was just ' J.B.'
Michael Kennedy, his friend and biographer, presents a portrait of him in words and — mostly — music.
Producer STANLEY WILLIAMSON

8.15
Midweek Theatre
An Aspidistra called Edward
(For details see Thurs, 3.5 pm)

9.0
Reith Lectures 1974
The New Liberty

lover of the famous courtesan, Léa de Lonval. Now he must marry and leave his 49-year-old mistress. But Léa has made the mistake of falling in love with this last of her young lovers and without her he is lost. Producer JOHN CARDY

11.0
The Financial World
Tonight
Radio 4's International Business Report: Market Trends

11.15
Today in Parliament

11.30 News
preceded by Weather
11.51 Inshore forecast
11.54* Closedown

Regional News
VHF only
and weather throughout the day: 6.50-6.55 and 7.50-7.55 am; 12.55-1.0 (except London and South East) and 5.50-5.55 pm

Young and old alike envied her the possession of Chéri. 'Though, good heavens!' Léa would say, 'there's no reason why they should. They're welcome to him!' 10.45 pm

32 Sara Midda, 'Chéri', *Radio Times*, 28 Nov 1974.

33 Ivan Lapper, 'The scandalous death of Adolf Hitler', *Radio Times*, 1 May 1975.

34 Janet Woolley, vignette for Soap & Flannel, *Radio Times*, 2003.

Hitler: ' In the future, anyone who tells anyone else that the war is lost will be treated as a traitor . . .'

The war is lost and many of the faithful desert the   *Führer's bunker. Claustrophobic madness sets in: 8.0 pm*

GARGRAVARR · CUSTODIAN OF THE TOTAL PERSPECTIVE VORTEX · · · KNOWS WHERE HIS TOWEL IS

THE GHOST OF ZAPHOD BEEBLEBROX THE 4TH GIVES HIMSELF A NASTY SHOCK

THE ENORMOUS TERRIBLY WISE OLD BIRD · · · IN A FLAP

MARVIN THE PARANOID ANDROID AT THE END OF A HARD DAYS CRYING

ARTHUR DENT EARTHMAN RESTS AFTER A PAN GALACTIC GARGLE BLASTER

35 George Hardie, 'The Hitchhiker's Guide to the Galaxy', *Radio Times, c.*1978.

Those who still contribute to the magazine include George Hardie, Clare Melinsky and Janet Woolley. Hardie had studied graphic design at St Martin's from 1965 to 1967 with Ron Sandford, Mike Foreman, Fritz Wegner and Harry Sida, and then at the RCA where he says that he became more of a designer/illustrator. Subsequently Hardie has had a distinguished academic career – teaching at St Martin's and at colleges of art throughout the UK, Europe, the USA and Japan. Hardie began illustrating for *Radio Times* in the early 1970s and his work presents elegantly witty graphic solutions to often difficult briefs such as *The Hitchhiker's Guide to the Galaxy* [**35**].

Clare Melinsky's consistent mastery of the linocut maintains the tradition for printmaking that *Radio Times* made popular from its beginning. In 'At the Boar's Head' (*RT*, 3 August 1983) she wittily counterpoints Falstaff's corpulence with the barrel, in a skilful pastiche of an early chap-book woodcut. Melinsky remembers her time at the Central, initially a foundation year in 1972, as 'lots of drawing and mark-making with Jeff Hoare, Ann Martin and Derek Boshier'.[12] In this year she was introduced to linocut printmaking by Moy Keightley during a one-week course that she says was seminal.

Janet Woolley, Visiting Tutor – later Professor – in postgraduate illustration at Central Saint Martins (1985–99), produced a weekly illustration in *Radio Times* for 'Soap & Flannel' for many years until August 2003 [**34**]. She had invented the style, a hybrid of drawn illustration and photomontage, for a New York trip. Later, with the introduction of computer imaging – a technology that Woolley has embraced and mastered with consummate originality – she developed the new technique digitally, adding finishing touches by hand to the print.

The work of the illustrators who now contribute to *Radio Times*, in its new, populist incarnation, is mostly confined to small decorative flourishes at the periphery of the radio listings pages. The art editorial department of the magazine still struggles valiantly to maintain the

aesthetic of earlier years and there are occasional flashes of brilliance by artists who learned their craft in the precomputer age, but on the whole the standard does represent a diminished future for editorial illustration.

Copyright © Martin Baker 2005

Notes
1   Quoted in 'Yesterday's Britain', *Reader's Digest* 1998.
2   Joanna Carey in the *Guardian*, 4.1.2001.
3   Mervyn Peake, *The craft of the lead pencil*, Wingate 1946.
4   John Vernon Lord, 'Student at the Central School of Arts and Crafts, 1960-61', unpublished memoir.
5   Margaret Levetus, to the author, 2001.
6   Veronica Hitchcock, to the author, 2001.
7   Val Biro, *Autobiographical sketch*, Gale Research Inc., 1992.
8   Harold Cohen, to the author, 2001.
9   David Driver, *The art of Radio Times*, BBC, 1981.
10 Brian Thomas, to the author, 2004.
11 *Ibid.*
12 Clare Melinsky, to the author, 2004.

8/ Paul Rennie
Modern publicity: advertising and illustration 1920–70

Dr Paul Rennie is a print and design historian. He is Eckersley Archivist at the London College of Communication and has contributed to many design publications. Together with his wife he runs a gallery specialising in the work of artist designers in Britain.

Commercial art is a

term used to denote the visual material associated with the developing industrial and commercial economies of the 19th and 20th centuries. Usually, it is used to refer to images reproduced in very large numbers and associated with the advertising, packaging and point-of-sale material of various products and services. It is not usually associated with the original design, or artwork, from which these are derived. The term is therefore linked with the commercial, mass-produced and ephemeral by-products of modern society. All of this has tended, whatever the cultural significance of the material, to contribute to its being overlooked by historians.

The characteristics, itemised above, are precisely those that make this material significant in relation to the history of both the Central School and St Martin's in London. Indeed, the illustrated posters, packaging, and magazine design by tutors, students and artists associated with the schools, provide an opportunity to examine the developing and inter-related worlds of commerce, print culture and education. The connections between the worlds of commerce and art have usually been explored in relation to the avant-garde interest in the symbolic potential of the visual language of modern art as applied to the world beyond the gallery. The tradition of illustration in commercial art had tended to be dismissed as 'literal and banal'.[1]

These notes attempt to describe the engagement of the two schools with their surrounding environments through the emergence of the specific skills of commercial illustration. This engagement is traced through the developing print technologies of reproduction and the personalities of the staff and students at the schools.[2] The British social and political context of the mid-20th century allowed illustration to flourish within both the commercial and political spheres. The radical potential of this work, exemplified in the use of illustration to project the social-democratic landscapes of post-war reconstruction, and the Festival

1 Freda Lingstrom, 'Cheap fares', poster for London Transport, 1929.
© London's Transport Museum.

of Britain in 1951, is therefore greater than we might have expected.

I have chosen to divide this essay into two parts. The first tells of the craft traditions of lithography that dominated commercial art before 1939. The second maps the post-war development of mechanical reproduction and the concomitant development of a technocratic design community as part of consumer capitalism.

Lithography, advertising and illustration

The technical determinants of commercial art are described entirely by reference to lithographic printing. Aloys Senefelder invented lithography in 1796. The processes are based on the fact that oil and water do not mix, which allows a print to be made from drawn marks. The invention marked a considerable technical advance on the existing intaglio and relief processes in printmaking, since a print could now be made without the costs of engraving a metal plate or cutting a wood block. Lithography was first used for printing sheet music, which became widely and cheaply available for the first time. Implicit within the visual characteristics of musical notation was the potential for combining image and text that came to define the development of poster art by the end of the 19th century. Lithography also made the printing of technical data, such as railway timetables and statistical information, much cheaper. Furthermore, the absence of any need for excessive pressure enabled much larger areas to be printed.[3]

The impact of scale had several important consequences in the development of lithography during the 19th century. The large printing surface of lithographic stones enabled several images to be printed in a single pass through the machine and made the process ideally suited to the emerging demands of manufacturers for labels and packaging from the mid-19th century onwards.

By the end of the century the artisan skills and plant engineering of lithography had been established so as to support a rapidly expanding market in commercial art associated with the developing advertising industry. From the 1890s poster design became the most obviously visible form of advertising as metropolitan London was transformed by the expansion of the railway network and the rapid increase in population.

It was against this background of rapid growth and transformation that the two schools were established,[4] St Martin's School of Art in 1854 and the Central School of Arts and Crafts in 1896. The origins of the schools are contemporary with the technical developments described above and with an emerging sense of unease, within Victorian society, of consumer capitalism.

The objectives of 19th-century design reform were to foster an awareness of good design amongst the educated classes. It was also hoped that the utility of properly designed objects would benefit consumers and add a redeeming aesthetic dimension to modern life. In its extreme form the design reform movement aimed to define a utilitarian functionalism in design as 'good' and to connect these characteristics with the emerging emancipatory politics of socialism.

The schools pioneered a form of egalitarian co-education with classes in which young men and women mixed. The bohemian temper of the schools was further enlivened by the low fees payable by students. The fee structure made the schools especially attractive to female students and to students from East London. It would be fair to characterise the schools' demographic as projecting a popular bohemianism that anticipated the youth culture of the 1960s. The schools nurtured the first cohort of female artist designers that included Enid Marx, Margaret Calkin James, Pearl Binder, Freda Lingstrom [1], Betty Swanwick and Pearl Falconer. In addition, the radical potential implicit within the schools' structure created a natural alignment between its students and the radical left of the 1930s. It is not an accident that the founder in 1933 of the social-realist Artists International Association (AIA), James Fitton, should have been a student at the Central School and would eventually become a teacher of lithography there. The resulting bohemianism was, appropriately, less elevated than its Hampstead predecessor and centred on the now chic areas of Hoxton, Shoreditch and Brick Lane.

By the beginning of the 1920s it had become clear that the philosophical ambitions of design reform could not be met without an engagement with the mass market which itself required processes of industrial production and mechanical reproduction. Within the context of advertising this required the specialised teaching of drawing and illustration for lithographic reproduction. The lithography classes at the Central School were part of the School of Book Production under Noel Rooke. The craft-based origins of the class manifest themselves in the inclusion, within the weekly schedule, of illustration and life-drawing classes. The result was a generation of students who perceived themselves as artist designers who worked across a wide range of media and projects. This approach was exemplified by the career of Enid Marx who was successful as artist, illustrator, textile designer and writer. [2]

2 Enid Marx, wood engraving from *A childhood* by Frances Allinson, Hogarth Press, 1937. Central Saint Martins Museum Collection.

3 Clifford & Rosemary Ellis, 'Third test match, the Oval', poster for London Transport, 1939. © London's Transport Museum.

The Central School's role in the promotion of wood engraving and the revival of wood-engraved decorations in progressive publishing during the 1920s and 1930s is well known. The impact of lithography is similarly significant and manifests itself through a golden age of poster design before developing into lithographic picture making and book illustration. At the same time lithographic illustration dominated the commercial environment in magazine publishing, point-of-sale and packaging. These concerns were reflected more straightforwardly in the commercial art and illustration classes at St Martin's. Before looking in more detail at the personalities involved in these classes we should briefly describe the advertising environment in London.

The most significant patron of the advertising arts in London between the wars was Frank Pick of London Transport.[5] Pick's relations with the world of art education had begun through his membership of the Design and Industries Association (DIA). This had been established in 1915 to promote a model of design awareness and education based on the German model of the 'Werkbund' which proposed closer links between manufacturers and craftsmen. The founder members of the Association included Lethaby and Rooke from the Central School, along with Pick and Ambrose Heal of the eponymous furniture store. The network of relations established through the DIA was to support the development of commercial art and design in London.

Frank Pick had conceived of a regulated and coherent advertising environment throughout London Transport that was part of an integrated architecture of mass transit. The poster sites became, in consequence, part of an ordered and systematic approach to visual communication expressed throughout the organisation. Pick realised that there was not sufficient commercial advertising to fill all the spaces on his platforms and so he undertook to commission poster designs on behalf of his organisation. The purpose of these advertisements was primarily to encourage passengers to use the network during off-peak hours and at weekends. Accordingly there were posters for destinations outside town and for events within. The display of poster images became, in effect, a *de facto* art gallery.

The full list of staff and students from the two schools' personnel associated with London Transport publicity is beyond the scope of these brief notes although we should mention Bruce Angrave, John Farleigh, Laurence Scarfe, John Minton and Alan Fletcher from the Central, a list that represents a commercial and creative relationship extending over 70 years. A similar list for St Martin's would

include Mabel Lucie Attwell, Barnett Freedman, Len Deighton, Clifford and Rosemary Ellis [3] and, more recently, Bruce McLean and Jennie Tuffs.

Pick's role in the promotion of commercial art as a defining characteristic of 'commercial identity' also brought him into contact with the key figures of the printing industry in London. The most significant of these were Gerald Meynell and Harold Curwen. Meynell was an energetic promoter of 'beauty in advertising' and 'printing of distinction' as a means of advertising his Westminster Press. The Press was a large general printing works with facilities for magazine, book and pamphlet production as well as a specialised poster design and printing department. The Curwen Press was not such a large organisation but was equally significant. Harold Curwen was an enthusiastic supporter of illustration and design as a means of distinguishing the ordinary letterpress jobs that make up the bulk of a 'jobbing' printer. [4, 5] He aimed to add 'a spirit of joy' to the work from his press. Both Harold Curwen and Gerald Meynell were extraordinary in their willingness to include artists and designers as part of the team at their works.[6]

Fitzgerald Spencer Pryse was one of the great lithographers of the 20th century.[7] He taught lithography at the Central School from 1922 to 1932. He first came to attention in 1910 when he began to design Labour Party propaganda. His work, drawn direct onto the stone, began to explore the expressive potential of lithography. His contemporary Frank Brangwyn was a similarly skilful lithographer. Both artists produced propaganda posters during the Second World War and Pryse was amongst the first artists to be commissioned by Frank Pick as publicity

4 Barnett Freedman, Calendar for the Curwen Press 1937. Central Saint Martins Museum Collection.

5 Lynton Lamb, 'Brighton, the Lanes', wood engraving commissioned by the Curwen Press for Kemp Town Brewery, Brighton, 1930s. Central Saint Martins Museum Collection.

manager of the Underground Electric Railway (later London Transport).

Pryse developed a dramatic and expressive style that made use of the possibility, implicit within lithography, for the artist to work direct on the printing plate. The result was a design made up of marks, drawn by the artist, and highlighted with a second and third coloured printing to add both colour and a powerful perspective effect. The new style was easily distinguished from the prevailing taste of most commercial lithography that aimed, through a sense of artisan pride, to produce an accurate facsimile of the original design.

Pryse was commissioned to produce posters for the Empire Exhibition at Wembley during 1924.[6] The exhibition sought to recast imperial relations and to create a sense of community and shared interest between the peoples of Britain and Empire. Accordingly, the posters were conceived as a frieze that showed the peoples of the Empire gathering crops and materials. The posters were printed quad royal size (50 inches wide by 40 inches high) so as to be displayed on railway platforms and other suitable sites. The exhibition itself was not entirely successful and was extended into a second season in an effort to recoup some of the costs. The propaganda efforts of the exhibition were partly continued through the creation of the Empire Marketing Board and the Empire Film Unit.

Pryse's efforts in promoting a more direct and expressive form of lithography should not go unrecognised. Indeed, the emphasis on expressive lithography was a characteristic of the Central classes. Pryse taught the class with A.S.Hartrick who taught lithography at Central from 1914 to 1929. He had been a professional illustrator in the 1890s, a founder member of the famous Senefelder Club, and published *Lithography as a fine art* in 1932. The idea that lithography offered the potential for original and artistic work had been implicit in Pick's gallery project at London Transport. Harold Curwen promoted this idea through the practice of 'autolithography' where artists were encouraged to work, in person, at the litho press. In consequence, he was able to identify lithography as a progressive and original form of printmaking which has been acknowledged through its legacy in artistic printmaking and the post-war development of the limited edition print market. Barnett Freedman was, as the most talented lithographic artist of his generation, the most vocal supporter of the 'autolitho' project.[8]

Barnett Freedman was a remarkable artist who had taught himself to draw during a long period of childhood illness. His professional life had begun in 1916 as a draughtsman for a firm of monumental masons. For five

BRITISH EMPIRE EXHIBITION 1924
SCENES OF EMPIRE SERIES · · No.P22   APRIL — OCTOBER   SCENES OF EMPIRE SERIES · · No.P22

6 Gerald Spencer Pryse, 'British Empire Exhibition, April–October 1924', poster for the Empire Marketing Board. Courtesy of Paul & Karen Rennie.

7 Barnett Freedman, 'For reliability, Shell lubricating oil', advertisement for Shell, 1932. © Shell Art Collection at the National Motor Museum Beaulieu, Hampshire.

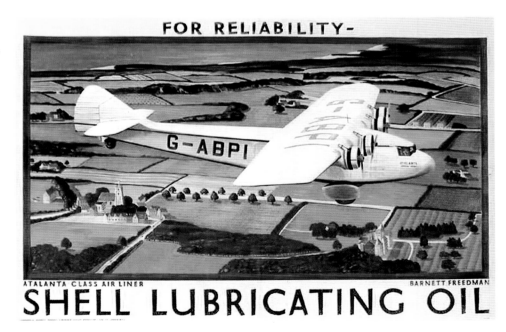

FOR RELIABILITY-
G-ABPI
ATALANTA CLASS AIR LINER   BARNETT FREEDMAN
SHELL LUBRICATING OIL

years he attended evening classes at St Martin's before being accepted, in 1922, by the RCA where he was introduced to the Curwen Press by Paul Nash.

His work in lithography included books and illustrated ephemera and posters for Shell and London Transport and for Ealing Films.[7, 8] Freedman had, through his interest in the technique of lithography, become friends with Curwen and also with Thomas Griffits of the Baynard Press. Griffits had been apprenticed into the lithographic trade in the 19th century and had become, by the 1930s, the most technically expert craftsman in the industry. Freedman and he exchanged tips and tricks in a spirit of friendly rivalry. Griffits also published two books on the techniques of lithographic printing that stand as testimonials to the artisan skills of the industry.

The access of artists to lithographic workshops, exemplified by Freedman's experience, transformed the style and subject matter of lithography. The drawn marks from which lithography is made allowed a style of graphic reportage to emerge that was able to sustain the radical images of the Artists International Association. The radical platform offered to artists was further extended by the development of lithographic images as inexpensive, popular and original prints. The development of the popular press, especially in its illustrated forms of address to children, offered further opportunities from the 1940s onwards.

James Fitton joined the teaching staff as lithography tutor at the Central School, and succeeded Hartrick in 1938. Fitton had been a student under Hartrick in the late 1920s along with James Boswell, James Holland and Pearl Binder. The four, drawing inspiration from the visual satire of Hogarth and Grosz, resolved to promote a visual culture of Left ideology as a counter to the rise of fascism. Fitton was a founder member of the AIA as were James Holland and James Boswell. The AIA developed into an organisation supported by many artists working in different styles.[9] The combination of anti-fascism and bohemian culture made the organisation resistant to the more doctrinaire elements of Left political management.

Fitton, Holland and Boswell produced many fine images for the *Left Review* and, during the Second World War, a series of lithographic images of the Home Front, celebrating the stoicism, heroism and contribution of ordinary people.[9] Fitton also designed many posters for London Transport.

Fitton's friend and colleague Pearl Binder produced political images of London's East End communities. Binder had visited the Soviet Union several times during the 1930s and used her experience as a source of material.

8 Barnett Freedman, 'Circus', poster for London Transport, 1936. © London's Transport Museum.

9 James Fitton, 'A clear plate means a clear conscience', Second World War poster for the Ministry of Food, 1941. Courtesy Paul & Karen Rennie.

her own letters, was trying to teach Grandma. They used to study together, Polya curled on Grandma's lap and both their heads bent over the alphabet book. But Misha preferred to roll over and over on the grass with Pavel and toss him up in the air.

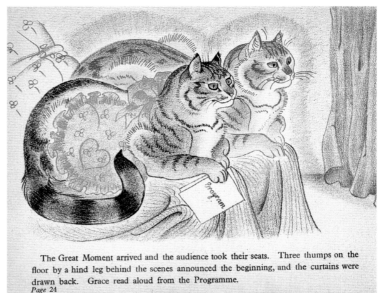

The Great Moment arrived and the audience took their seats. Three thumps on the floor by a hind leg behind the scenes announced the beginning, and the curtains were drawn back. Grace read aloud from the Programme.
Page 24

Her *Misha learns English* was Anglo-Soviet propaganda published by Picture Puffins in 1942.[10]

Jesse Collins had exhibited at the famous Whitechapel exhibitions organised by the AIA at the end of the 1930s. He joined the staff at the Central and succeeded Rooke as Head of Book Production in 1950. Morris Kestelman, a former student of Fitton's, was a colleague and became head of Fine Art in 1951. Under Collins the School of Book Production gradually adopted a more specialised and technocratic discipline demanded by the commercial clients of the 1950s. It was eventually renamed the School of Graphic Design in 1966.[10]

The picture making of the AIA was a reflection of a popular desire for political and social change. The changes in printing technology enabled artists to extend the visual language of commercial art into the political arena. The first artists' images were the Contemporary Lithographs of 1937 and 1939.[11] Published by The Zwemmer Gallery in association with John Piper they were aimed at the educational market. The advent of war increased the requirement for these propagandising images of national life, and several different series were published.

Clarke Hutton drew a set of educational prints for circulation by the Oxford University Press.[13] Hartrick made a set of images for the Ministry of Information. The National Gallery and the War Artists' Advisory Committee published a set of poster prints as an exhibition package that included images by Paul Nash, Barnett Freedman and Edward Ardizzone.[12] These were to be displayed in the public spaces of the war economy and its administration.

The Council for the Encouragement of Music and Art, later renamed the Arts Council, produced a set of poster prints as one of its first interventions in the arts.

10 Pearl Binder, *Mischa learns English*, written and illustrated by Pearl Binder, Puffin Picture Book no 25, 1942. Private collection.

11 Kathleen Hale, *Orlando's home life*, written and illustrated by Kathleen Hale, Puffin Picture Book no 26, 1942. Private collection.

After the war Lyons teashops commissioned three sets of artists' prints. Brenda Rawnsley published the first of her School Prints series in 1946.[14] These were originally produced so that primary schools which had no art of any kind could see original modern pictures at a very reasonable price.

Clarke Hutton had been a student of Hartrick in 1927 and under his encouragement began to make lithographic prints. Hutton joined the teaching staff at the Central in 1930 and immediately began to use the autolitho technique for his book illustrations.[12]

The interest in colour lithography as a means of producing inexpensive and original children's books had grown as a consequence of changes in the processes of lithography. Colour separation could now be drawn on acetate sheets in the studio and transferred photo-mechanically to the metal plates used in offset litho. These changes made the make-ready of lithography less dependent on artisan craftsmen and made for a speedier turnaround at the press. Eventually, printing technologies would enable inexpensive and short-run colour printing to be possible.

The inspiration for producing inexpensive colour-illustrated children's books has come from titles published in France and in Russia. It was not entirely surprising that Allen Lane, founder of Penguin Books, should see the potential in this and should ask Noel Carrington, of Country Life, to edit a series of artist illustrated books for Penguin. Carrington had been producing children's books for Country Life, had worked with Kathleen Hale on the first of the Orlando titles, and had seemed like a natural choice for Lane.[11] The Picture Puffins were a chance for Carrington to work with much larger editions and to reach a wider audience.

The Carrington project covered a series of subjects that promoted English values and provided an alternative political projection from that favoured by the radicals Fitton and Holland. The card-carrying activism of Fitton was characteristic of an important strand in British cultural activity at the end of the 1930s but it was by no means the only avenue available. After the Second World War, Fitton and Boswell worked for the popular illustrated magazine *Lilliput*.

Many artists, whilst supportive of the progressive politics of the Left, worked within the more consensual framework epitomised by Carrington. John Farleigh and John Skeaping provided support for this approach within the Central School. Several Central staff including S.R.Badmin and Clarke Hutton contributed to the series.

During the Second World War this tendency supported the *Recording Britain* project that sent artists out into the

12 Edward Ardizzone, Untitled, one of the Contemporary Lithographs Series, 1937, devised by the Zwemmer Gallery, London, for use in schools. Courtesy Paul & Karen Rennie.

13 Clarke Hutton, 'A Victorian railway station', Oxford University Press Wall Pictures Series, 1950s. Central Saint Martins Museum Collection.

14 James Boswell, 'The winning ride', a School Print, 1951. Courtesy Paul & Karen Rennie.

English countryside to record the distinctive architectures and landscapes of Britain. Noel Carrington was later appointed a Governor of the Central School.

Recording Britain, published in four volumes by OUP, offered an opportunity for artists to contribute to the war effort beyond the normal channels of Ministry and propaganda. Central and St Martin's students and staff were associated with the scheme, including A.S. Hartrick, S.R.Badmin, Phyllis Ginger and Mona Moore.[15, 16] Ginger had been taught by Badmin before winning a scholarship to the Central where she was taught by John Farleigh and Clarke Hutton.

The educational propagandising in books and prints was an early manifestation of a political movement that, radicalised by the social experience of war, voted for reform in 1946. The integration of art, architecture and design into a coherent template for the reconstruction of Britain was exemplified by the visual style of the Festival of Britain in 1951.

The relaxed atmosphere and co-educational environments pioneered by the Schools made classes there

15 A. S. Hartrick, 'Chiswick House: the cedars and sphinx', from *Recording Britain*, Oxford University Press and the Pilgrim Trust, 1948. Courtesy Paul & Karen Rennie.

16 Phyllis Ginger, 'The Promenade, Cheltenham', from *Recording Britain*, Oxford University Press and the Pilgrim Trust, 1948. Courtesy Paul & Karen Rennie.

attractive to female students. The commercial art environment of the 1930s was remarkable in the opportunities it offered women artists for economic independence. Margaret Calkin James and Enid Marx were amongst the vanguard of female designers between the wars.[13] The textile designer Dora Batty was able to combine her work as teacher with designing some 27 posters for London Transport.[17] Heather 'Herry' Perry produced some 13 designs and Freda Lingstrom some 12. In contrast Enid Marx produced only 3 posters but worked in a wide variety of media and emerged as probably the most talented all-rounder of her generation.

After 1945

The war changed everything in Britain, including the printing industry. The demands of war propaganda had greatly increased the requirement for speed in printing and especially in relation to the make-ready processes prior to presswork. In fact, the war had simply accelerated a process that had begun after the First World War and had been resisted, more or less effectively, by a combination of craft self-interest and industrial complacency.

The urgency of print requirements during war had required an engagement, on behalf of printers and designers, with new systems of graphic reproduction. The processes of mechanical reproduction, photolithography and offset litho were adopted and used to serve the propaganda requirements of the various war departments. After the war, the creation of the Welfare State required its own forms of print communications and propaganda. This post-war period of State purchasing offered a lifeline to printers and advertising executives whose commercial clients were still weakened by the ravages of the war economy and the need to export goods and services.

These changes were reflected in the scope of *Illustration and reproduction* by John Biggs published by the Blandford Press in 1950 where he distinguished between autographic and reprographic processes.

The Festival Style promoted as a template for post-war reconstruction was defined in relation to architecture and manufacturing by reference to technology, science and manufacturing. The social relations defined by the template were meritocratic, relaxed egalitarian (at least more so than before the Second World War). The visual style conjured up to project these values drew on a mystical symbolism and strange beauty sometimes associated with the popular arts of Staffordshire figures and canal boats as well as the more straightforward molecular imagery of atomic Britain. The tensions between the utopian social values of the project and the ancient class

17 Dora Batty, 'Spring is here', an advertisement for London's Underground 1930s. © London's Transport Museum.

18 Betty Swanwick, 'The Woolwich Ferry', poster for London Transport, 1949. © London's Transport Museum.

distinctions of British society were played out through the Ealing film comedies.[14] Many staff and students from both colleges produced illustrative work for the Festival including James Fitton's comic frieze for the seaside section and Hans Tisdall's murals for the fun fair at Battersea. Tisdall was a prolific illustrator and a very versatile artist. He designed textiles, book jackets and murals, and taught at the Central School from 1947 to 1962.[19]

Betty Swanwick was able to give a powerful visual expression to the poetic potential implicit in her posters.[18] Swanwick had studied at Central and later taught at the Royal Academy schools, the Royal College and Goldsmiths. She illustrated several books during the 1940s, was commissioned to design posters for London Transport in 1950 and painted a mural at the Festival's South Bank site in 1951. Her career in teaching and illustration continued until the late 1970s.

Another artist who flourished in the post-war period was Paul Hogarth.[20] Hogarth had studied at St Martin's at the end of the 1930s where he had been assistant to James Boswell. He later joined the art department at Shell and worked on the promotional and educational publications of the oil giant. He returned to teaching, joining the staff at Central in 1951 where he taught illustration and forged a style based on an idea of graphic reportage. He pioneered the creation of informal travel journalism that perfectly matched the popular explosion of interest in travel. Hogarth was elected RDI for illustration in 1979 and RA in 1984. Another manifestation of this taste for the 'Continental' was the success of Elizabeth David's cookery books illustrated by John Minton.

The Festival marked a kind of climax for public art in Britain. As commercial values re-asserted themselves many of the projects which had started after the Second World War lost momentum and were replaced by straightforward art-market ventures. The educational print market lapsed and was re-cast as the limited edition print market. Murals and decorations for public building were undone by cost considerations. Fortunately, the revival of market forces in the late 1950s brought with it many more opportunities in commercial art. Magazine publishing expanded and illustrators found a niche promoting popular fashions to the mass market.

The technological foundations of the post-war project implied the idea of specialisation as linked to technical skill. In consequence it was not surprising that the 'allrounder' began to make way for the specialist and that specialists should begin to work together in teams.

From 1947, and at two yearly intervals, the Society of Industrial Artists published a survey of its members' work.

19 Hans Tisdall, mural decoration thought to be one of the designs for SS Queen Elizabeth undertaken in 1939. They were not completed as the ship converted to a troop carrier. Signed Aufseeser. Central Saint Martins Museum Collection.

20 Paul Hogarth, book jacket for *Lord of the Flies* by William Golding, a Pentagram design for Faber & Faber, mid 1980s. Courtesy of Faber & Faber.

The survey is organised by specialist categories and includes selections of poster design, packaging, press advertising, illustration, publishing and typography. Clarke Hutton, Barnett Freedman, S. R. Badmin, James Fitton, James Boswell and Edward Ardizzone all appear in 1947. Lynton Lamb, Pearl Falconer and Edward Wright feature in 1951.

Pearl Falconer had studied at St Martin's and began her career in fashion illustration and press advertising.[21] Her work was included in three pavilions at the Festival of Britain. The precarious nature of the freelance career was evident when, after these successes, the fashion and magazine industries adopted the widespread use of photographic reporting.

Another system of collective representation emerged in the middle 1950s. This was the creative agency and was derived from the model of agency structure found in the advertising industry. Artist Partners was formed in 1954 and published an illustrated prospectus to launch its business. Susan Einzig was a member of both Artist Partners and the Society of Industrial Artists.[22] Einzig had arrived in Britain from Germany in 1939 and had studied at Central. After the war she began teaching and was a colleague of John Minton and Keith Vaughan at Camberwell.

The development of a mass market magazine culture as a support for the developing consumer society of post-war Britain offered an opportunity for younger designers to break free from the relatively conservative environments of literary publishing. The 1930s had offered an opportunity for artists at Central to redefine the idea of bohemian London around a series of communities in London's East End. The mid 1950s offered a similar opportunity to recast bohemian London. The first artists to do so were a group of illustration students at St Martin's.[15]

The progressive fashion course at St Martin's run by Muriel Pemberton set the tone at St Martin's with an emphasis on popular styles from Italy and America as well as France. The fashion course was aimed at developing a popular fashion system for a wider audience than the *Vogue* 'couturier and debutante' styles promoted as 'good taste'. The illustrators adopted the jazz music and clothes fetishism of Soho and integrated it into their own work and projected a gangster style chic beyond the immediate surroundings of St Martin's. The school was certainly well served by its location on the edge of Soho as the cultural centre of gravity shifted from Mayfair eastwards.

The satirical magazine *Private Eye* gave expression to the anti-establishment tendency. Gerald Scarfe was closely associated with the magazine from its beginnings in 1962.

21 Pearl Falconer, Advertisement for Everett's Corsets Ltd. As shown in *Designers in Britain*, 1946. Courtesy Paul & Karen Rennie.

22 Susan Einzig, Advertisement for Electrolux, Artist Partners, 1958. Courtesy Paul & Karen Rennie.

23 Len Deighton, 'London's Country Village Life', poster for London Transport, 1957. © London's Transport Museum.

Scarfe had been at St Martin's and was a contemporary of Ralph Steadman. They both attended evening classes at the London College of Printing. Both Scarfe and Steadman became regulars at *The Sunday Times*.

The 1960s satire was less party political than the social-realist images produced under the auspices of the AIA during the 1930s. Instead, it questioned the idea of progress in an increasingly materialist society and poked fun at the hypocrisy of the political and business classes.

Len Deighton was an illustration student at St Martin's in the early 1950s and was a pioneer of a studiously nonchalant appreciation of American popular culture, jazz and fashion. Deighton often wore an American flying jacket and used this to distinguish himself from the 'duffle' tendency amongst his peers. The School's location and the international fashion styling of its students provided a metropolitan and sophisticated atmosphere in which study and performance were combined. The St Martin's crowd were focused on the lucrative activities of advertising art direction as a career. Deighton's name was added to the roster at Artist Partners when he left the RCA.

An alternative business model to Artist Partners was the creation of a multidisciplinary design practice. Alan Fletcher (ex Central School) was amongst the first to try this model of partnership, first with Colin Forbes and Bob Gill, subsequently with the addition of Theo Cosby and Kenneth Grange. The larger partnership was renamed Pentagram. Fletcher's own contribution was to develop a form of graphic wit expressed through clever visual puns. Fletcher was cleverly able to combine small jobs with larger corporate business so as to offer big ideas in a format that suited his clients. All the designers involved would have received training in illustration.[16]

Deighton became a prominent member of the Pop Art group at the Royal College of Art after his time at St Martin's and helped project an anti-establishment posture into the heart of the establishment. The parameters of the developing youth market were drawn out accordingly. Deighton designed a poster for London Transport in 1957 before illustrating a series of cookery strips, published as Len Deighton's *Cookstrip cookbook* (Bernard Geis 1966), and embarking on a career as a thriller writer.[23] In 1964 Deighton published his own guide to London's 'scene'. *The London Dossier* was subsequently published as a mass-market paperback by Penguin in 1967,

The publication of Deighton's guide marked the beginning of an explosion of visual culture in Britain. In part this was driven by the emergence of television, in both its BBC and commercial forms, as a powerful and populist

24 Michael Foreman, illustration for 'A saga of good yeoman stock' by Robert Schofield, *The Sunday Times* magazine, June 1967. Central Saint Martins Library. © *The Sunday Times*.

medium. Music and books also created whole new areas of activity for commercial artists, illustrators and designers.[17]

The explosion in student numbers, a long-awaited consequence of reforms laid down a decade earlier, fuelled a boom in university cities all over Britain. The boom was expressed through new shops and boutiques selling a version of the King's Road in every High Street in Britain. At a more suburban level, Terence Conran launched the Habitat business with a mail order catalogue. Conran was a textile design student at the Central School in the late 1940s.

By the 1960s the advertising industry had embraced photography and offset litho as the best means of printing large posters. Illustration and publicity were realigned so that illustration became an editorial component of the new magazines.

The expanding magazine publishing environment was driven by new consumer demand and by advertising linked to television. The new style of art-direction created to reflect this dynamic consumer society merged realistic photography, illustration and graphic design. *Queen* epitomised the new type of fashion and life style magazine. The publication of *The Sunday Times* magazine created a populist news, fashion and lifestyle platform for a generation of artists, graphic designers, illustrators and photographers. Brian Duffy, who had moved from painting to fashion at St Martin's, was a constant presence at the magazine and was able to introduce his illustrator, music and fashion friends to the magazine.

Michael Foreman was one such who had been a student at St Martin's in 1958 and 1959. He was ideally placed to benefit from the explosion of magazine and book publishing activity in the 1960s and did so [24]. He worked successfully for *Nova* and for the colour supplements before becoming an illustrator of children's books. He was elected RDI for travel illustration in 1985.

Another axis of influence connected the counter-cultural and satirical world of *Private Eye* with *The Sunday Times*. *The Times* allowed the metropolitan values of the satirists to project nationally. The projection of personality was further advanced by the relatively new medium of television. It was no surprise that the visual invention of Roger Law and Terry Gilliam should eventually find a platform on television.

Early issues of *The Sunday Times* magazine from 1963 show a magazine driven by the news values of photography. The model for the magazine was the weekly photo magazine *Picture Post* that had ceased publication in 1957. *Picture Post* had been driven as much by political idealism as by journalistic values and had been part of the utopian social democratic project that configured the Festival in 1951. *The Sunday Times* magazine was conceived as a life-style supplement funded by advertiser's revenue. The journalism within the magazine reflected these changed priorities.

In the beginning the magazine held on to the idea of black and white photography as properly journalistic. Gradually, the art direction of Michael Rand, from 1964 onwards, began to reflect some of the visual excitement pioneered by the art school students at St Martin's and the RCA.

The magazine began to combine colour photography with black and white. There was room for illustration and graphic design too. The weekly schedule of production drove a relentless need for new stories and new ideas. By the end of the 1960s London was swinging.

Conclusion

The development of commercial art and illustration has played a crucial role in the development of an identifiably British visual culture. In the 1920s and 1930s that visual culture was characterised by craft sensibilities and a low-key politics that promoted the emancipation of ordinary people rather than class war. After the war, the planned economy gave way to the consumer society and set off an explosion of popular visual culture. The role of the Central School and St Martin's has been crucial in providing the talent and energy for this development at every stage of the story.

These brief notes have, hopefully, placed the schools in the contexts of the developing technologies and social trends that have determined this story. The students and staff of the schools have supplied the creative energy and work to drive the project forward.

The evolution of commercial art into graphic design, and the status of illustration within those disciplines, describes an emancipatory trajectory of ideas in the twentieth century. The resulting work is both practical and philosophical.

Notes

1   See Dawn Ades, *The 20th century poster: design of the avant-garde*, Abbeville Press, 1984, pp.22–70, for the standard account of the development of modernist poster design.

2   The most useful documents for tracing the evolution of personnel at both Schools are the annual prospectuses. Copies of these are held in the Central Saint Martins Museum Collection.

3   The technical determinants of poster design are itemised in Margaret Timmers, *The power of the poster*, Victoria and Albert Museum, 1998, p.7.

4   The early history of the Central School is told in Sylvia Backemeyer (ed.), *Making their mark: art, craft and design at the Central School 1896–1966*, Herbert Press, 2000.

5   See Oliver Green, *Underground art*, Studio Vista 1990, for an account of Pick's contribution to the development of advertising art.

6   See Pat Gilmour, *Artists at Curwen*, Tate Gallery, 1977, for a detailed account of Harold Curwen's life and the revival of printing arts during the 1920s. The earlier contribution of Meynell to this project is included in Justin Howes' account of the Johnston lettering class at Central included in Sylvia Backemeyer (ed.), *Object lessons: Central Saint Martins Design Archive*, Lund Humphries, 1996. pp.33-7.

7   A brief account of Pryse's career is included in Frances Spalding, *20th century painters and sculptors*, The Antique Collectors' Club, 1990, p.367.

8   See Barnett Freedman, 'Autolithography or substitute works of art', and Noel Carrington, 'Autolithography of plastic plates', in R.B.Fishenden, *Penrose Annual* 44, Lund Humphries, 1950, pp.62 and 64.

9   See Morris and Radford, *The story of the Artists International Association, the Museum of Modern Art*, Oxford, 1983, for the story of the events and personalities of the AIA.

10 The contribution of Jesse Collins to the teaching at Central is recalled by Anthony Froshaug and quoted in Robin Kinross, *Anthony Froshaug: documents of a life*, Hyphen Press, 2000, pp.99–103.

11 See Paul Rennie, 'The poster print', in Robin Garton (ed.), *British printmakers 1850–1950*, Scolar Press, 1992, p.273.

12 Enid Marx, 'Autolithography for book illustrators, 1930–1960'. In *Matrix* 10, The Whittington Press, 1990, pp.11–20.

13 A detailed account of the opportunities available to women artists during the inter-war period is included in Betty Miles, *At the Sign of the Rainbow*, Felix Scribo, 1996.

14 The film posters of Ealing are included in D. Wilson, *Projecting Britain*, the British Film Institute, 1982.

15 The emergence of Pop Art and associated phenomena are traced in Alex Seago, *Burning the box of beautiful things*, Oxford University Press, 1995.

16 The development of a specifically British quality of wit in graphic design, illustration and commercial art is identified by McAlhone and Stewart, *A smile in the mind*, Phaidon, 1996, as a defining legacy of 1960s anti-establishmentarianism. A more austerely graphic version of this sensibility is included in Ken Garland, *A word in your eye*, University of Reading Department of Typography, 1996.

17 Alex Seago, *Burning the box of beautiful things*, OUP, 1995. pp.181–2.

All change! A personal view of illustration at Central Saint Martins 1980–2004

Andrew Hall is at present Head of Illustration at Central Saint Martins. Prior to this he worked as a freelance theatre designer working on productions in London, the Midlands and the North of England. His research over the last five years has focussed on illustration in America and Japan culminating in the 'Eastmeetswest' show at the Coningsby Gallery, Fitzrovia in July 2003.

It's

a funny thing, illustration. Honestly it is. One minute it's for kids, and is all light and pink and fluffy, the next it's for adults, and it's all heavy and dark and serious. Not to mention all the areas of corporate greyness in between. So what's going on? How can this subject of commercial image-making be so broad in its range, and in the light of its wide and varied audience, how can a college such as ours teach it effectively and with precision?

My chapter in this book deals with the history of illustration at Central Saint Martins over the last 24 years. I would like to offer a personal overview of this period, without pretending to accurately represent each year in detail, and see how the educational experience that the college has offered, and continues to offer, has meshed with the commercial world of visual communication, thereby creating some impressive students along the way. Institutions, as we all know, can be buoyant, dynamic structures, but can also be oppressive, leaden systems that, through lack of change, eventually collapse in on themselves. If Central Saint Martins belongs to the former category, which it surely does, how exactly has it continued to stay abreast of the market and maintain its lifeblood and relevance? I have a hunch it's to do with this thing called 'change'.

The uniqueness and character of a college department can be represented by location and environment, as well as by a community of teaching staff and students. The department has its steady rise, its apex, and then, almost imperceptibly, its eventual decline; the departmental philosophy can become unfocused, the teaching systems can remain static and inflexible, whilst the external market transforms itself beyond all recognition. A situation then arises where the creative results of the students can lack relevance. The more rigid the system that is set in place within the institution, and the greater the change outside, the more disastrous the results can be. So, how can an institution such as CSM counteract the phenomenon of threatened stagnation?

It seems that every so often an agent of change, be it a person or thing, has entered through the illustration

1 Aude Van Ryn
'In defense of anywhere', *Adbusters*, June 2001.
Acrylic paint on paper with acetate overlay.
Artist's collection.

department doors, and has swept away the old order. At first this process may seem destructive, a process that by its very nature re-orders and re-invents without sentiment. But, once change is achieved, then, slowly, a new structure is born from the wreckage, with new ways of working and thinking, and a renaissance of sorts begins.

Often that source of change is not connected with a change of staffing or location, but can be a change foisted upon the department, in particular the accelerated march of technology, and its consequent effects on the commercial market. It can occur that a modern version of the Greek Trojan horse enters the institution, and then, for better or worse, nothing is ever quite the same again. In the case of graphic design at Central Saint Martins it was the arrival of the Apple Mac home computer which entered through the doors of Long Acre in 1986. Packaged in unassuming beige boxes this was to have a profound and inestimable effect on the subject of design and illustration that very few, even within the communication industry, could have accurately predicted.

Though we might wish to pretend otherwise, technology has always ridden shotgun with visual communication. The subject is inherently to do with mass communication, so how could it be otherwise?

And just as Ruari McLean stated that Gutenberg's printing press 'changed the world',[1] so too, did the Mac. Shortly after its arrival, it proceeded to devastate a thriving and healthy illustration industry, and tore apart the relationship between designer and illustrator. As Rick Poynor, a leading British illustration and design critic, pointed out 'Illustration's recent problems can be summarised in a single word: technology'.[2] The Mac had the unprecedented power to democratise the production of the image within the communication design industry. Whereas the illustrators had previously wielded exclusive control over their market, they now saw designers in their droves abandoning the hand-authored craft of the illustrator. The designers employed methods that, though perhaps sacrilegious to the illustrator, were already familiar to the designer: tracing and collaging type, arranging 'found' imagery, cutting and pasting, manipulating photography and blurring its origins. Suddenly the territory of illustration was looking largely irrelevant as manipulated type and photographic imagery took their place. Even the *European illustration annual* of 1992, a showcase and cornerstone of the art of illustration, was visually dominated by the work of its designer, ironically a former CSM student, Jonathan Barnbrook. One could argue, perhaps unfairly, that the illustrators had it coming.

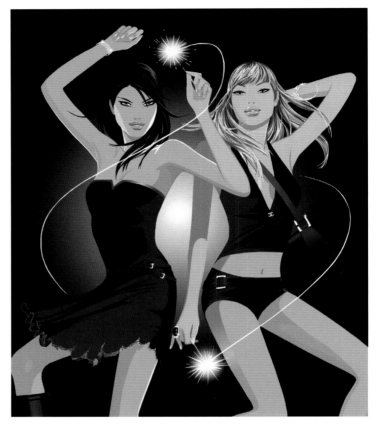

2 Jason Brooks, 'New Year', *Elle* (International Editions) January 2004. Artist's collection.

3 Jason Brooks, 'Valentine 2004', *Elle* (International Editions) February 2004. Artist's collection.

During the 1980s, the illustration industry had enjoyed one of its most successful relationships with the design and advertising industries, and had ignored the fact that it might need to keep abreast of change in order to maintain its financial foothold within these industries. In particular, it largely ignored the newly available computing technology. Consequently, the early nineties were the worst period for freelance illustrators in the last hundred years: many illustration giants of yesterday were now in the commercial bargain bin, or worse still, on the scrapheap. The Mac and its software options swept aside their ownership of the industry, and heralded a broad stylistic change that made many illustrators' work look antiquated and folkish, even whimsical; it seemed that what everyone had wanted yesterday, no-one wanted today.

And what could be done about all this? Would the subject of illustration even survive? In the article for *Frieze* magazine, Rick Poynor wrote:

> Not long ago, one talented British illustrator told me that illustration was in such a perilous state that it would have to die before it could be re-born.[3]

It would take perhaps more than a decade to achieve a new footing for illustration within the communication industry, an industry that had chosen to all but abandon it. As the new technology swept in (and as all that pre-dated it was declared irrelevant and backward), a schism occurred between traditional image-making methods and the new, clean, digital technologies. And it was not until the turn of the new century that these two factors were publicly re-united, in the shape of the Pentagram designer Angus Hyland and Roanne Bell's illustration publication *Hand to eye*.[4] So, how did these dramatic commercial and technological changes affect illustration at Central Saint Martins?

Framework one: 1980–1993.
Location: Long Acre, London.
Personnel: Wendy Coates-Smith with Robert Mason, Anne Howeson, Chris Brown, Janet Woolley, Robin Harris, Matilda Harrison and Ian Ribbons.

As has already been mentioned, the 1980s were a hey-day for illustration. The political illustrators, the so-called 'Radical Illustrators', had brought some much-needed commentary and political dialogue to commercial image-making, and had encouraged other young illustrators to infuse the subject with opinion and content derived from the traditions of fine art. As Robert Mason, a leading member of this movement, stated in his editorial to their manifesto publication *Radical illustrators*, they were a group,

whose work exists, or once existed, on the fringes of mainstream illustration; whose work makes use of a range of
media, techniques and thought not often associated with
illustration until perhaps ten years ago; whose work is as
often found hanging on gallery walls, or seen flickering on a
screen, as it is discovered on the printed page.[5]

Margaret Thatcher had risen to power in 1979 and had
promptly begun to deconstruct the machinery of government – in particular, its control over commerce – and was
intent on letting the markets breathe and grow with little
or no government intervention. Even St Martin's School of
Art felt the full force of government policy. In 1985 suited
ministers were dispatched to the college to explain the
rationale for merging with the Central School of Art &
Design, to become 'Central Saint Martins' under the overall administrative umbrella of The London Institute. The
air was full of a heady, euphoric optimism, as the spirit of
the entrepreneur was re-awakened in all strata of society,
and everyone believed that one day, and soon, they too
could own a Porsche. It would take three ministerial terms
before this particular Conservative Party's vision
descended into a parody of xenophobia and greed.

For the illustrator, too, it was a flourishing market. The
graphic design and advertising industries, as well as the
publishing industries, were keen to commission illustrators for high-profile jobs. the *New Scientist*, the *Radio
Times*, and the *Listener* magazines all championed the
hand-authored work of the illustrator. A rash of re-brand-
ing exercises by high street giants (Tesco, Boots, Safeway,
and a plethora of large banks and building societies)
offered the jobbing illustrator some of the most lucrative
work they had ever been commissioned for; even the
modest 'company report' was dominated by the illustrator.
As the illustrator Debbie Cook explained to me in a recent
conversation: 'if a designer had a visual problem, then the
choice of a particular illustrator would be the solution to
that problem'.[6]

There was also a proliferation of illustration agencies in
London, including fledgling ones such as CIA and Sharp
Practice, alongside a host of more established agencies
that included Folio, Debut Art and Advocate. Everything
within the business of illustration seemed rosy.

During this buoyant period, the illustration department
had the most glamorous of locations in Covent Garden, an
area whose character was defined until the 1970s by
London's main fruit and vegetable market. It was run
exclusively by jobbing, freelance illustrators. The department itself was headed by Wendy Coates-Smith, whose
own working industry background had been in illustrating
for television.

She describes how the illustration department of that period was created.

The Illustration Option, as it used to be called, began in 1982. When I joined St Martin's School of Art in 1980 Gordon Ramsay was the Head of Department. On his retirement, Cal Swann was appointed. He came with a desire to update the programme of study and decided that greater clarity and coherence would result from a restructuring of the course as a whole. The idea was to focus groups of staff to teach specialisms, still broadly based, but defined by professional parameters, over years two and three. The first year was taught with a view to introducing all students to the main issues connected with communications design, but also allow students to identify, and work towards a specific area. Information design, advertising design, typography and illustration became the main specialisms. Over time these were re-aligned, and a small but fiercely independent group of animators emerged. I was asked by Cal to develop the illustration option. There was a rich tradition of illustration in the department, but it had been weakened by a decision to staff illustration only in year three. The teaching staff had been extensive, with Fritz Wegner, Ivan Lapper, Ian Ribbons and Carol Barker among the regular teaching staff, while others such as Michael Foreman, Ann Morrow and many others had joined to teach one day a week on leaving the RCA. The curtailment of illustration in year two had been the result of an unfavourable NCDAD (National Council for the Development of Art and Design) report, which identified illustration as the prevailing dominant subject, at the expense of design. Once the re-structuring had taken place, and the options were officially recognised as the means to study a specialism, each specialism began to develop strongly and establish its own identity. The staff were optimistic that this clarification would allow a greater understanding of each discipline and lead to increased experimentation and cross-fertilisation. That proved to be the case.[7]

After a brief period of flux that saw Robert Mason and Ian Pollock (also allied to the 'Radical Illustrator' group) teaching within the department, a core group of illustration staff eventually emerged. These were: Chris Brown, an editorial illustrator whose influences lay in theatre and French literature; Janet Woolley, whose work lay in editorial and publishing (she was to become Visiting Professor at the London Institute in 1996); Ann Howeson (who later left to teach at Chelsea and Camberwell, as well as at the RCA), whose work was based in editorial and publishing with a slant towards social commentary; and Robin Harris, whose work in editorial and publishing had a strong element of social and political commentary. Later Matilda Harrison joined the teaching staff from the CSM, MA programme, again an illustrator connected with editorial and publishing, who unofficially headed the department during Wendy Coates-Smith's time as Dean of Graphic & Industrial Design.

All of these instructors knew how to operate successfully within the commercial market, and a traditional approach to illustration, based firmly within the disciplines of drawing and painting, was the applied norm. In terms of the commercial territory at this time, whereas photography had regained unofficial ownership of the depiction of the external world, illustration still had a firm hold on the internal world, the human world of thought and feeling. Elements of surrealism, of expressionism, and of magical surrealism, were all present within the mainstream of illustration.

One can surmise from this group that the illustrator's gaze was firmly fixed on the fine artist for inspiration; the influences of Magritte, Matisse, Chagall, Hockney, Picasso and Grosz could easily be traced within the work of successful practitioners. Commercial illustrators were adept at taking a visual vernacular that the public were familiar with and then personalising and refining that vernacular towards the answering of a commercial brief. The client would receive a 'picture', a unit of visual dialogue that was akin to 'art'. This was what the market demanded at that time and the students at Long Acre were trained to meet that need.

Literature was a key component of the work produced within the Long Acre illustration studio; serious, well-respected writing was used by the CSM illustration staff and students to develop their intellectual and visual themes, elucidate the content of a text, and piece together a portfolio that would locate their work within a literary and editorial tradition. Robin Harris and Anne Howeson were important in encouraging the students to develop a critique centred around global politics, and to this end in 1986 Robin Harris produced a series of images for Amnesty International's Campaign for Human Rights.[8]

There were many successful graduates from this era. Nick Sharratt who whilst at college produced a powerful body of work drawn from the themes of ballroom dancing. His imagery is now computer-based, and he is writing and illustrating his own books, as well as working with Jacqueline Wilson on her phenomenally successful books for children [4]. Ann Magill who whilst at college sought direct involvement with her subject matter, including a series of drawings based on boxers. She even lived for a short while with the nuclear protesters at Greenham

4 Nick Sharratt, book cover for *Best friends* by Jacqueline Wilson, Doubleday, 2004. Artist's collection.

Common and recorded these women's activities in a large series of charcoal drawings. Her work [5–7] has been used extensively by magazines and corporate clients such as the Body Shop, and she now works as a fine artist and is represented by The Medici Gallery, Mayfair. Ashley Potter whose colourful, painterly work [8] seemed to be everywhere for a while, be it on stamps or book covers, now, among many projects, works with Mario Cavalli at Colony Media for BBC Wales in the field of animation, as well as heading the illustration course at Exeter. Lucinda Rogers whose graphic, documentary drawings [9] have been used by British Airways, Habitat and Penguin, and more recently were featured in the Laurence King publication *Hand to eye*. Of her time at CSM she says:

> It was very important that we were being taught by people who were actually involved in the industry. I remember them [the teaching staff] coming in tired after working all night, because it was the eighties boom, and I remember that it was good to see so much staff work in contemporary publications.[9]

And then, just as everything seemed to be going so well, the wind changed direction.

The financial markets, that the conservatives had successfully re-generated, inexplicably began to crash; interest rates rose so sharply that house 'repossession' became a sign of the times, and the Apple Mac, arriving in Long Acre around 1986, gathered momentum in wreaking havoc on the traditional illustration business. The cold wind of modernism was blowing hard through the corridors and studios of Long Acre and would leave a sea of wreckage in its wake. What had been a fertile relationship between artistic expression and the communication industry, would now be fractured and torn apart through the process of modernisation, and divorce seemed imminent. So what exactly happened within this era of forced modernisation?

It seemed that the large corporate clients no longer wanted to be branded exclusively by the illustrator (much of whose work now appeared over-personal and over-authored) and were in search of a more impersonal, ambient identity that would imply new and aspirational messages to a wider audience. Photography stepped confidently into the territory that had been exclusive to the illustrator in the 1980s. Ambient, blurred photographic imagery was now the designer's (and thus the corporate client's) best friend. Alongside this was a re-invention of the manipulation of 'type as image', championed in the book *The end of print* by Californian designer David Carson and writer Lewis Blackwell,[10] as well as by such British

5 Ann Magill,
book cover for *Hear us
O Lord From Heaven thy
dwelling place* by
Malcolm Lowry,
Picador Classics, 1985

6 Ann Magill,
book cover for *Airships;
Ray*, by Barry Hannah,
Vintage, 1991.
Acrylic on board.

7 Ann Magill,
illustration for
Waterstones Journal,
mid-1980s.

All from the artist's collection.

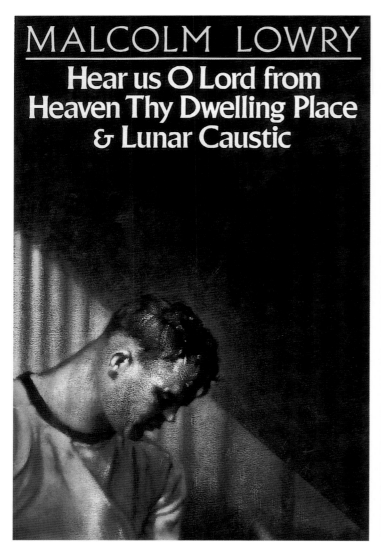

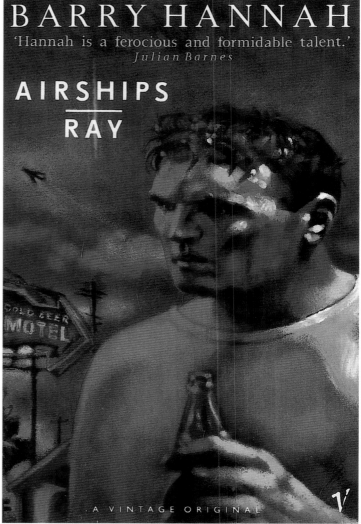

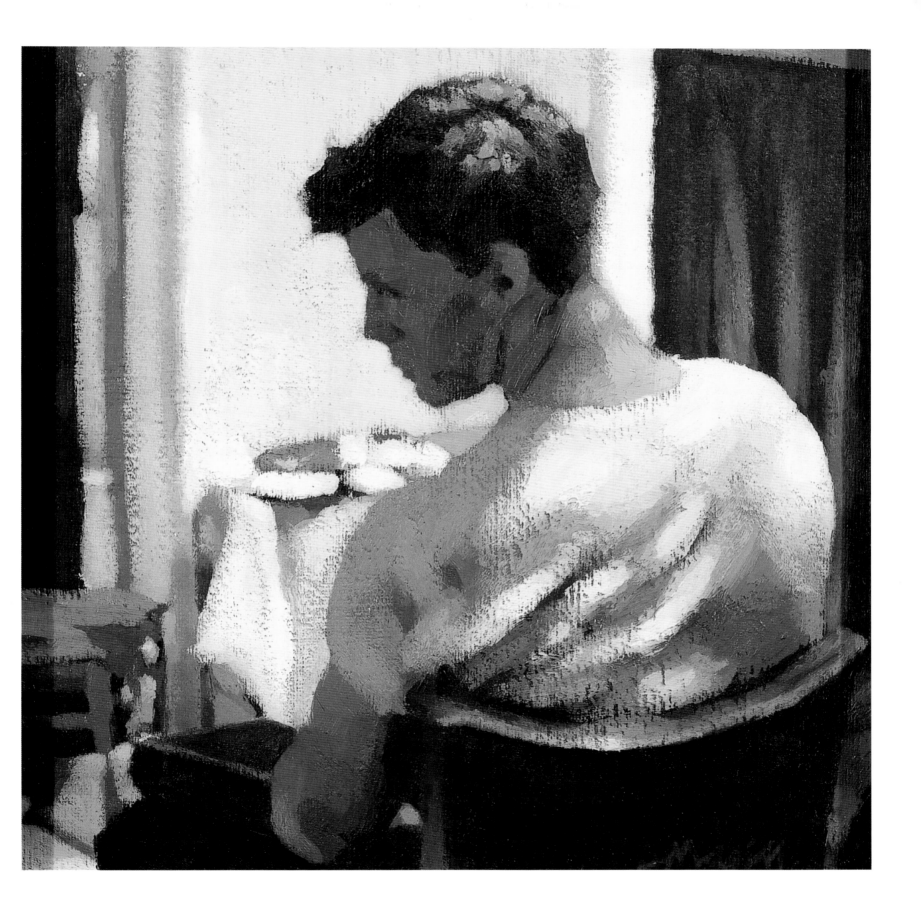

companies as Why Not Associates and Tomato, both comprising former Central Saint Martins students. At *The Face* magazine (the 1980s market leader in fashion and lifestyle editorial), the art director Neville Brody even made the decision that no illustration would be used. Type and photography were to be used exclusively by the magazine in a re-invention of Russian constructivism. The 'brave new era' had clearly arrived (even though the irony had not escaped some that Brody's background lay in commercial illustration).

How could an illustration industry that had enjoyed unparalleled success, though in the process had perhaps allowed itself to stagnate, extricate itself from a situation that it had failed to anticipate, and reclaim a central role for itself? How could it re-focus a public that was in love with the vacuous, ambient image of itself in the mirror – a task that in retrospect would take over a decade to achieve? And above all, how could an educational establishment such as Central Saint Martins, with limited funding, react in time to these changes?

Framework two 1993–98.
Location Long Acre, London.
Personnel Chris Corr with Elisabeth Harbour, Nick Oates, Douglas Bevans, Trilokesh Mukherjee, Susan Curtis, Sara Safullah and Susannah Edwards.

In 1992, and still experiencing the hangover from the 1980s' party, CSM Illustration, under the overall course directorship of Andrew Whittle, had an influx of fresh instructors, and in so doing brought some new answers to the question of teaching an illustration course amidst dramatic technological and market changes.

Into this early nineties wasteland – where illustration had been severely marginalised by the design and photographic industries and therefore looked towards a very uncertain future – stepped Chris Corr. Corr's commercial work was based firmly within the established traditions of drawing and painting, but he also recognised that illustration needed to start looking outwards. The notion of travel (crucial to his own work for clients such as the Royal Mail and Qantas, in Russia, China and India), and the choice of the 'real world' as a starting point for the illustration student, became central to the new departmental ethos. He re-sowed the seeds of artistic integrity within the illustration department and took the inspired decision to look towards the hand-made and craft-oriented as a specific means by which to regenerate the subject. Chris Corr himself describes his (then) new ideas for the department as follows.[11]

8 Ashley Potter 'Soho', 1990, oil and acrylic on canvas. Artist's collection.

9 Lucinda Rogers, 'Chef Shaun Hill in the kitchen at Gidea Park Hotel' for the series Britains New Wave Chefs, published in the *Independent on Sunday Review*, 1992. Pen and ink with watercolour. Artist's collection.

The general idea was to equip the students with a good practical skills base, a kind of image-making foundation to begin with. For students to build a confidence in their powers of expression, through developing their graphic abilities in as broad a way as possible – through model-making, printing (all types), letterpress, photography, all kinds of drawing, bookmaking, film … it was really about developing your own visual language and not putting on the house style.

In terms of the teaching staff, he chose

visiting tutors from all forms of image-making. They were professionals who could share their experiences and show that all art forms were employable. We embraced graphics too, in all its forms, and computer skills were an essential part of the course.[12]

To this end, he appointed teaching staff who had specialisms within these fields: Elisabeth Harbour, a drawing-based editorial illustrator; Douglas Bevans from San Francisco, whose playful illustration work was focused within the media of print; Trilokesh Mukherjee from a design background; Spencer Thursfield, who specialised in 'the automaton' and three-dimensional illustration work; Susan Curtis, whose work focused on the conceptual and the sculptural; Nick Oates, an all-round designer and commercials set-designer; Sara Safullah, whose work was used by the famous Harvey Nichols window on various occasions; and Susanna Edwards, a student and then later a teacher of this era, who worked within the tradition of letterpress, and was further investigating the use of 'type as image'. Even pottery classes were offered, including the facility of a small kiln, and several industrial sewing machines began to be visible within the top floor Long Acre illustration studio.

A process of re-invention was now actively being engaged in. And, as these older, traditional technologies were being re-explored and re-evaluated, the illustration students would also begin to make forays into the new computer room to see how they, as well as the designers, could use the new digital technology. As the commercial illustration industry had suffered so much in the late 1980s and early 1990s, in a way it could only start to rise again.

The challenge within the department was to react to this situation and to re-evaluate the skills needed to become a visual communicator. As Susannah Edwards says of this time: 'It was no longer about having a particular visual style, but more about finding your "voice"'.[13]

This autobiographical 'voice', inspired by the more accessible life-style of the teachers, could then be expressed using drawing, type and photography. Even moving image and animation were becoming far easier to

achieve using the new technologies, and started to creep into the illustrator's graduation portfolio. The illustration department also began to look outwards within the Graphic Design department itself. An innovative contextual studies programme was peculiar to an educational establishment in linking theory and practice more closely together, and 'context' became highly evident within the studio; the typography department, run by Phil Baines, was helping illustrators in setting up a typographic discourse with their work; and in general, type-based and image-based communication were not so separate as they had once been.

Illustration within CSM education had managed to change its outlook in relation to the demands of the industry. It no longer sought solely to represent a sensation-based, painterly inner world; it had shown that it could look outwards, towards the world, and engage with that subject matter. In the same way as Marshall Arisman's ethos influenced the programme of the School of Visual Art's Masters Illustration Programme in New York City, so the idea of the 'visual journalist' became re-invented with vigour within the CSM programme. Key staff members were well-versed in this area and, like all good teachers and teaching, the ideas spread rapidly to the students; and it was during this time that the idea of the 'illustration department trip' was re-born.

Seminal visits to Russia (Leningrad in wintertime!), and to Cuba and New York, offered the illustration students new ways of making their work relevant and showing that their discipline could compete within a global communication design discourse. It was also a time when the illustration students began to use the camera in earnest, whether as an end in itself or as an aid to further drawing.

Out of this era came a new crop of talented visual communicators. Aude Van Ryn, whose work has an air of existential unease that seemed entirely appropriate for the late nineties, now works globally within the field of editorial illustration [**1, 10**]. Her work has also been featured in *Hand to eye*.[14] Of her time at CSM, she remembers the illustration staff that influenced her:

> Douglas Bevans, and his beautiful hand-written type [sic] and his positivism. Chris Corr, by the way he was so prolific and enthusiastic about many things.

In general, she says that

> the course gave me so much space, and directions only when it was necessary. I felt completely free to experiment.

Jason Brooks' work was influenced by Japanese Manga comics and after studying at the RCA with Graham

10 Aude Van Ryn, 'The candida controversy' for the *Holland and Barrett Magazine*, November 2002. Acrylic paint on paper and computer. Artist's collection.

11 Lizzie Finn, stitched fabric poster made especially for inclusion in book *Where is Silas?*, Lawrence King, 2003. Exhibited in 'Where is Silas?' exhibition, Parco Gallery, Tokyo, 2003. Artist's collection.

Rounthwaite in spectacular fashion he almost single-hand-edly re-invented the honoured tradition of fashion illustration.[2–3] His work appeared in the influential publication *Fashion illustration now*.[15] He won the Vogue-Sothebys Award for fashion illustration whilst still at the Royal College, and has always cited the illustration visit to Cuba as a major influence on his work. Lizzie Finn who graduated within the design department, has now combined the sewing machine with the Mac, and works for such publications as *Dazed and Confused*, *Vogue*, and the British rock band Oasis; her work has also been featured in *Hand to eye* [11].

At first glance this new batch of nineties illustration work did not look that dissimilar from the abundance of line-drawn eye-candy that began flooding into the illustration market in the mid-to-late nineties, but there were crucial differences. Though the images had been assembled in a computer, and outputted through a printer, all the work reflected a high level of observational drawing skill and intelligence. They were fiercely individual, they had content, character and atmosphere, and yet they sat centrally within the commercial world's chosen visual vernacular; they had hit centre-target.

As all this was happening, the field of fine art – led by Goldsmiths' College's Michael Craig-Martin – wandered off into a forest of dissected cows, dirty bed-linen and typographic sloganeering, and it had a profound effect on the discipline of illustration. As well as allowing illustration to reclaim areas of figurative visuality that we had last seen in the seventies, it also heralded in a rigorously conceptual approach to image-led communication that perhaps was much needed since the demise of the previous figurative, fine art tradition.

Illustration could again represent the aspirations of a generation, and a younger generation at that. Just around the corner was also the re-birth of the design co-operative: designers, illustrators, animators and film-makers, such as the design collective Abake, were working with each other on the same job and in the same space. Drawing, albeit in rather impersonal and 'instructional' forms, was creeping back into the design agenda through the possibilities offered by the new technologies, and as yet lacked any central illustrative ownership. With the boundaries becoming so blurred, was the subject of illustration in danger of being subsumed by design? And could it compete within a market drunk on the potential power of the web? Could illustration hold on to what it was good at, and at the same time continue to be commissioned and command reasonable fees within the fields of graphic design and advertising? And with the studios at Long Acre looking more and

more ragged, neglected and under-used, and surrounded by the blandness of Covent Garden's new sanitised, branded look, was it time to head off and re-locate to a new area of London?

Framework three: 1998 onwards.
Location: Long Acre, Southampton Row from 2000
Personnel: Andrew Hall with David Blamey, Debbie Cook, Susannah Edwards, Nick Oates, Chris Jones, Alex Reuben, Sion Ap-Tomos, Ann Course and Howard Read.

By 1998, Labour had finally constructed a credible alternative to a now sleaze-ridden Conservative Party. The dotcom bubble was expanding at an alarming rate (without a pin prick in sight) and on the whole the impact of the new technologies seemed positive. Emails were the newest communication tool, and unprecedented quantities of information could be transmitted globally with relative ease and minimal expense. The dark and amoral world of Brett Easton-Ellis' writing (*Less than zero* and *The informers*) had splintered into the mainstream; ecstasy was still the contemporary 'peace and love' drug of the time; and it was so hip not to care.

Around this time, too, things were looking up for the illustrator. As Rick Poynor pointed out:

> After the sound and fury of the first half of the 1990s, graphic design is in a lull … illustration's territory is the image, and it was presumptuous of designers to imagine that Freehand and Photoshop were enough. The standard of intelligent image-making has declined in the typographic-led 1990s, even as the bombardment of digital and photographic imagery grew even more relentless.[16]

Large companies such as Levi's and Virgin were abandoning the use of photography for their ad campaigns in favour of the 'new illustration'. Animation started to re-emerge into the mainstream (though with a nostalgic visual language that borrowed heavily from 1970s instructional drawing) with a series of prominent ad campaigns for NatWest Bank; and hand-authored editorial illustration started to re-appear in magazines like *Wallpaper*, *The Face* and *The Independent Magazine*. The 'painterly' style of illustration, so successful in the 1980s, had largely disappeared by now, and was replaced by a cool, impersonal way of working that seemed right for the age.

Within graphic design too, the divisions between design and illustration continued to blur. The illustrator's demonisation and resentment of graphic designers, prevalent in the early nineties, had somewhat evaporated by now, and the illustrator could see the potential that the new market offered. Just as the designers had stepped into the

12 Per José Karlan, 'We are all unique' image used in children's book and interactive CD-ROM which will be published by www.raben.se The art work has won several awards including the Quentin Blake Narrative Illustration Award, 2002, Thames and Hudson and the RCA Society Art Book Prize, 2002 Artist's collection.

territory traditionally given to illustration, so too did the illustrator begin to eye up the territory of design.

Again, at Long Acre, a major change of personnel occurred. Andrew Hall, who had worked nationally within the UK as a theatre designer, was invited by Andrew Whittle to head the illustration department. A fresh group of instructors also joined the department. David Blamey, whose personal practice was based in fine art and curation; Debbie Cook, an illustrator working across many areas of visual communication; Susannah Edwards, who continued to teach a typographic and design element within illustration and fearlessly began to set up projects with organisations outside the college; Howard Read, a specialist in editorial illustration; Ann Course, a fine art animator and sculptor, whose work was recently exhibited at Tate Britain; Alex Reuben, whose specialism lay in sound and moving image with a focus on dance; Chris Jones, a web designer, who started to teach the illustration students the basics of web design and web self-promotion; and Sion Ap-Tomos, who joined the department after graduating, to start building a new illustration drawing programme. Nick Oates also continued to teach within the department for three years.

As this new department took shape, a more acerbic and confrontational form of teaching was established, in particular with the employment of David Blamey. Though the students primarily continued to derive their work from an autobiographical source, cumbersome modes of visual delivery were abandoned: instead the work was light, quirky, conceptual and controlled. It was all in the edit, and the students were taught to use the right language for the right idea.

With diverse influences from contemporary American literature, narrative and story-telling became the new driving forces of the department. The illustration student now began to enjoy all of the technological advances of the previous decade and the department also began catering for the maverick designer and film-maker, as well as the 'traditional' illustrator. The theme of the 'visual journalist' continued, and the department sought to re-focus its relationship with various traditional and newer employment options for the students. To this end some large clients (such as the London Philharmonic Orchestra) came into the college to commission work. A 'Cross Pollination' seminar was also set up in conjunction with the Association of Illustrators, to explore the impact of new technology on the business of illustration.

The 'Work In Progress' show, absent for the previous few years, was also re-instated. Traditionally timetabled in March, it showcased the emerging CSM Third Year

illustrators' work outside college in a professionally-managed commercial gallery. At first at the Colville Place Gallery in Fitzrovia, the yearly show then moved, with curator and gallery manager Keith Watson, to the Deluxe Gallery in Hoxton Square. From its large end window, one could see Jay Joplin's White Cube Gallery, perhaps a reflection of illustration's continued relationship with the world of fine art.

Also, importantly, in 2000, the CSM graphic design course moved from Covent Garden to Southampton Row in Holborn. The course took over the floor that had formerly been used by fine art printmaking, and in so doing allowed a re-unification of craft and technology to take place. There was a horizontal layout (as opposed to a vertical one at Long Acre), with a host of traditional printing facilities, coupled with a brand new two-storey digital studio at its focus, and a series of main study and secondary-study satellite briefing rooms and workshop areas surrounding it. In general the illustration course continued to look outwards towards the world, and also to look for artistic influences beyond the grey, rainy shores of Britain.

Illustration trips were organised, and road trips at that. In 1999, California was visited, with students arriving in San Francisco, driving down the wild coastline of Route 1 to Los Angeles, and seeing design agencies in both cities. There were also two visits to the Kingdom of Morocco in 2001 and 2003 that saw the CSM illustration students riding camels and camping out in the Sahara Desert near the border with Algeria. And more recently, a post-'September 11' New York was visited by the second years for a week in 2004.

From this period some new illustrators are beginning to emerge. Per Karlan [12] left Central Saint Martins for the RCA and now works for such clients as IBM and *The Independent Magazine*; Kerrie Stritton, a member of the Californian illustration party, while at the RCA won the Folio Society prize for images depicting the mid-west of America [13–15]; Yuko Kondo left CSM for the RCA and has a client list including the fashion designer Bella Freud [16].

As the illustration option continues to grow in popularity, with over a hundred students in its ranks, one wonders where our own future departmental blind spots will be. Perhaps we will suffer from a reluctance to teach the more practical skills connected with image making. Perhaps the weight of criticism and discussion that the department places on the image will eventually kill the simple pleasure of creating that image.

But that is quite a different story, and an inappropriate one for me to tell. That task will fall to our successors.

13 Kerrie Stritton, *Back alley*, 2004, mixed media. Artist's collection.

14 Kerrie Stritton, *The Factory*, 2003, mixed media. Artist's collection.

15 Kerrie Stritton, *The funfair*, 2004, mixed media. Artist's collection.

In conclusion

It has been a bumpy ride for CSM illustration and its students over the last 24 years. We have seen talented and inspirational tutors come and go, and not always in the best of circumstances; we have lost the old Long Acre building; and we have seen a technological revolution in society that caused the illustration industry to falter and nearly fall.

But, having said that, in all three of the frameworks outlined above, CSM illustration has somehow managed to hold on to its philosophical focus against great adversity. At Central Saint Martins we will always celebrate the individual, the exception, the 'freakish' point of view and the crazy idea, ignoring the mainstream and trying (and failing sometimes) to find new ways forward and new languages for our messages. In the nick of time, we have managed to recognise when and where change is needed, and have steered the boat in entirely new directions.

Perhaps it is ironic that I should chose to end this discussion on illustration with a quote by a graphic designer, but then illustrators have always relied upon a healthy dynamic with the design community, and it is a quote regarding this strange thing called 'communication' that constantly intrigues me. It was spoken by Peter Saville, a fine designer, whose seminal album cover work for Joy Division, New Order and Suede, as well as innovative publicity for the fashion designer Yohji Yamamoto, recently featured in a major retrospective of his work at the Design Museum, London. He is also a designer who has often used the image, and with great power, in his work.

In recent conversation with an interviewer, Peter Saville was asked the following:

> 'Do you think design is ...'
> 'No.'
> 'What?'
> 'No.'
> 'Do you think design is ...'
> 'No. No, I don't.'[17]

One can only guess at what he meant by this, but one suspects that his seemingly bemusing response may have something to do with a refusal to have his subject pigeon-holed.

I hope that we can apply the same lateral thinking to new pathways and investigations within illustration, that we be wary, like Peter Saville, of easy, prescriptive definitions of our subject, and, as the wind of change rattles hard on our windows at Southampton Row, that we get down to the real business at hand – the work.

16 Yuko Kondo
Image for poster and flyer for AGEHA, Japan.
August 2004.
Artist's collection.

Copyright © Andrew Hall 2005

Notes
1 Ruari McLean, *The Thames & Hudson manual of typography*, Thames & Hudson, 1980.
2 Rick Poynor, 'Illustrate this', *Frieze* 49, Nov/Dec 1999.
3 *Ibid*.
4 Angus Hyland and Roanne Bell, eds, *Hand to eye: contemporary illustration*, Laurence King, 2003.
5 *Radical Illustrators* 38, Autumn 1981.
6 Verbal discussion with Debbie Cook, May 2004.
7 Email discussion with Wendy Coates-Smith, May 2004.
8 Robin Harris; eight images for Amnesty International, 1986.
9 Telephone discussion with Lucinda Rogers, May 2004.
10 Lewis Blackwell, *The end of print: the graphic design of David Carson*, Laurence King, 1995.
11 Email discussion with Chris Corr, May 2004.
12 *Ibid*.
13 Email discussion with Susanna Edwards, May 2004.
14 Email discussion with Aude van Ryn, May 2004.
15 Laird Borrelli, *Fashion illustration now*, Thames & Hudson, 2000.
16 Rick Poynor, 'Illustration's last stand', *Found Image*, August 1999.
17 Interview by Christopher Wilson in 'Designed by Peter Saville', *Frieze*, 2003, p.192.

Further reading / Brief biographies / Index / Acknowledgements & picture credits

Further reading

Sylvia Backemeyer, ed., *Object lessons: Central Saint Martins Art & Design Archive*, Lund Humphries, in association with the Lethaby Press, 1996.

Sylvia Backemeyer, ed., *Making their mark: art, craft and design at the Central School 1896–1966*, Herbert Press, 2000.

S.R.Badmin and Chris Beetles, *S.R.Badmin and the English landscape*, Collins, 1985.

Martin Baker, *Artists of the Radio Times: a golden age of British illustration*, Oxford: Ashmolean Museum, 2002.

Colin Barnes, *Fashion illustration: the techniques of fashion drawing* (introduction by Elizabeth Suter), Macdonald Orbis, 1988.

Chris Beetles, *Mabel Lucie Attwell*, Pavilion, 1988.

Chris Beetles, *S.R.Badmin and the English landscape*, Collins, 1985.

John Biggs, *Illustration and reproduction*, Blandford Press, 1950.

Caroline Bott, *The life and works of Alfred Bestall, illustrator of Rupert Bear*, Bloomsbury, 2003.

Simon Brett, *Engravers: a handbook for the nineties, compiled for the Society of Wood Engravers*, Silent Books, 1987.

Mark Bryant, *Dictionary of twentieth century British cartoonists and caricaturists*, Ashgate, 2000.

Mel Calman, 'The gentleman touch', *Penrose Annual*, 69, 1976, pp.157–68.

Brian Cook, *The Britain of Brian Cook*, Batsford, 1987.

David Driver, *The art of the Radio Times: the first sixty years*, BBC, 1981.

Frank Eyre, *British children's books in the 20th century*, Longman, 1971.

William Feaver, *When we were young: two centuries of children's book illustration*, Thames & Hudson, 1977.

Folio 50: a bibliography of the first fifty years of the Folio Society, 1947–1997, Folio Press, 1997.

Barnett Freedman, 1901–1958: catalogue of an exhibition of paintings, drawings and graphic art, Arts Council, 1958.

Robin Garton, ed., *British printmakers 1855–1955: a century of printmaking from the etching revival to St Ives*, Scolar Press, 1992.

Pat Gilmour, *Artists at Curwen: a celebration of the gift of artists' prints from the Curwen studio*, Tate Gallery, 1977.

Ann Gould, ed., *Masters of caricature: from Hogarth and Gillray to Scarfe and Levine*, with introduction and commentary by William Feaver, Weidenfeld & Nicolson, 1981.

Oliver Green, *Underground art: London Transport posters, 1908 to the present*, Studio Vista, 1990.

Mary and Pete Gross, eds., *Anthony Gross*, Scolar Press, 1992.

A.S.Hartrick, *Lithography as a fine art*, Oxford University Press, 1932.

Paul Hogarth, *Creative ink drawing*, Watson-Guptill, 1974.

Alan Horne, ed., *The dictionary of 20th century British book illustrators*, Antique Collectors' Club, 1994.

Sue Hoskins and Ian Rogerson, *Barnett Freedman: painter, draughtsman, lithographer: the prints, book illustrations, dust-wrappers, postage stamp designs, packaging, advertising and correspondence in the Freedman Archive in the Polytechnic Library*, catalogue, Manchester Polytechnic Library, 1990.

Penelope Hughes-Stanton, *The book illustrations of Blair Hughes-Stanton*, Private Libraries Association, 1991.

Angus Hyland & Roanne Bell, eds, *Hand to eye: contemporary illustration*, Laurence King, 2003.

John Lewis, 'Book illustrations of John Minton', *Image* 1, Summer 1949, pp.51–62.

John Lewis, *The 20th century book: its illustration and design*, Herbert Press, 1984.

George Mackie, *Lynton Lamb, illustrator: a selection of his work*, Scolar Press, 1978.

The magic pencil: children's book illustration today, The British Council & The British Library, 2002.

Douglas Martin, *The telling line: essays on fifteen contemporary book illustrators*, MacRae, 1989.

Michael Middleton, 'The drawings of Leonard Rosoman', *Image* 3, 1949-50, pp.3-22.

William Packer, *Fashion drawing in Vogue*, Thames & Hudson, 1983.

Gladys Perint Palmer, *Fashion people*, Assouline, 2003.

Mervyn Peake, *The craft of the lead pencil*, A.Wingate, 1946.

Monica Poole, *The wood engravings of John Farleigh*, Gresham, 1985.

Alan Powers, *Children's book covers*, Mitchell Beazley, 2003.

Alan Powers, *Front cover: great book jacket and cover design*, Mitchell Beazley, 2001.

Ian Rogerson, *Noel Carrington and his Puffin Picture Books: an exhibition catalogue*, Manchester Polytechnic Library, 1992. (It contains a complete list of Puffin Books.)

Judith Russell & Simon Brett, eds., *The wood-engravings of Gertrude Hermes*, Scolar Press, 1993.

Roger Sabin, *Comics, comix and graphic novels: a history of comic art*, Phaidon, 1996.

Gerald Scarfe, *Gerald Scarfe*, Thames & Hudson, 1982.

Joanna Selborne, *British wood engraved book illustrations, 1904–1940: a break with tradition*, Clarendon Press, 1998.

Hilary Spurling, *The drawings of Mervyn Peake*, David-Poynter, 1974.

John Russell Taylor, *Muriel Pemberton: art and fashion*, Chris Beetles, 1993.

Margaret Timmers, ed., *The power of the poster*, Victoria & Albert Museum, 1998.

Henry Trivick, *Autolithography: the technique*, Faber & Faber, 1960.

Norah Waugh, *The cut of men's clothes 1600–1900*, Faber & Faber, 1964.

Norah Waugh, *The cut of women's clothes 1600–1930*, (with line diagrams by Margaret Woodward), Faber & Faber, 1968.

Joyce Whalley and Tessa Chester, *A history of children's book illustration*, Murray, 1988.

David Wootton, *The illustrators: the British art of illustration*. A series of illustrated catalogues published from 1984 by Chris Beetles Ltd.

Brief biographies *of some of the illustrators in this book*

Mabel Lucie Attwell 1879–1964
Illustrator, author. She was born and educated in East London and attended Heatherley's and St Martin's (1895–1900). She undertook a wide range of commissions including posters for London Transport and posters and greeting cards for Valentines. Her first 'gift book' was produced by Raphael Tuck in 1910. She is best remembered for her pictures of chubby, winsome children which appeared on cards, bathroom plaques and other ephemera as well as in her popular annuals. She also illustrated a wide range of other books for children including classics such as *Peter Pan and Wendy*, *Grimm's Fairy Tales*, and *Alice in Wonderland*.

Colin Barnes 1934–1994
Fashion illustrator, author. Evacuated from Singapore as a child he trained initially as an actor at RADA. While he was working in Heals, the designer Clare Wallis recommended he speak to Margaret Woodward at the Central School who sent him to Muriel Pemberton. He studied fashion drawing at St Martin's under Elizabeth Suter, who became a lifelong friend. He worked for many major companies and magazines including *Harrods* and *GAP*, *Cosmopolitan*, *Vogue* and *Vogue Homme* and *Elle* in Paris. At the time of his sudden death he had studios in London and Paris. In the 1980s he wrote several books on fashion including *Fashion illustration: the techniques of fashion drawing* (Macdonald Orbis 1988).

Alfred Bestall 1892–1986
Cartoonist, comics artist, author. He was born in Mandalay, Burma. Following service in the First World War, he studied illustration at Central (1919–22). He contributed to *Blighty*, *The Bystander*, *Eve*, *Gaiety*, *London Opinion*, *Passing Show*, *Piccadilly*, *Punch* and *Tatler*. In 1935 he took over the 'Rupert Bear' strip in the *Daily Express* and wrote and illustrated over three hundred stories between 1935 and 1965. He was contributing to the 'Rupert' annuals up to his 90th year. He was awarded an MBE in 1985.

Brian Bolland 1951–
Comics artist, author. He studied graphics at Central (1973–4). He self-published his first comic, and had strips published in British underground publications including *Oz*, *Cozmic Comics* and *Frendz*. He was hired by adventure comic *2000AD* and became famous for his rendition of future lawman 'Judge Dredd'. His first major work for an American publisher, DC's *Camelot 3000*, proved that the industry was ready for a direct-market-only 'maxiseries'. When the next wave of the 1980s 'British invasion' struck, he provided cover art for Grant Morrison's metatextual *Animal man*,

and art for the Alan Moore-scripted *Batman: the killing joke*. Today, he mostly produces covers for the super-heroes of his youth (*Wonder Woman*, *Superman*, etc.). He also ventures into offbeat fare including 'The actress and the bishop', 'Mr Mamoulian', and, more recently, short stories written and drawn for DC/Vertigo's genre-oriented revivals of such classic Silver Age titles as *Strange adventures*.

Simon Brett 1943–
Wood engraver, author, teacher. He was educated at Ampleforth College before attending St Martin's (1960–4). He studied under Frederic Gore and Peter de Francia in the Painting School and was taught wood engraving by Clifford Webb, who influenced him greatly. He won a travel grant to study in New Mexico (1965–7) and travelled as a painter in Denmark and Provence. He taught at Marlborough College (1971–89). He won the Francis Williams Illustration Award for *The animals of Saint Gregory* (1981) which was published under his own Paulinus Press imprint. Since the 1980s he has worked primarily as a wood engraver for private presses, and has illustrated 14 books for the Folio Society. He is Chairman of the Society of Wood Engravers and has published a handbook for engravers: *Engravers: a handbook for the nineties* (Silent Books) (1987).

Jo Brocklehurst
Fashion illustrator, artist. She was born in London and when only 14 became a student at St Martin's where she was taught by Freddie Gore and John Minton. After a year at Woolwich Polytechnic she returned to St Martin's for a further two years under Muriel Pemberton and Elizabeth Suter. In 1979 she had a one-person show in Amsterdam and in 1980 contributed to 'Women's images of men' at the ICA. In 1981 she had her first solo exhibition in London at the Kyle Gallery and a second in 1982. The V&A purchased her work for their Permanent Collection in 1982 and 1994 and it was shown in their exhibiton 'Street style' in 1994. Her work has also been shown in New York, Connecticut, Berlin and Glissen in Germany, and Poland. In 2004 she showed her 'Brocklehurst Through the Looking Glass' drawings in a studio installation, literally a 'drawing room'.

Peter Brookes 1943–
Political cartoonist, illustrator, teacher. Born in Liverpool, he was a cousin by marriage of Matthew 'Matt' Pritchett. He studied Graphics at Central (1966–9) and was a tutor there (1976–8). In the 1960s and 1970s he freelanced for magazines both overground (eg *New*

Society) and underground (e.g. *Oz*, *Frendz*, *Time Out*). He became a political cartoonist and illustrator for *The Times* in 1982, and was cover artist (with Nicholas Garland) of *The Spectator* from 1986 to 1998. He has also contributed to *Time*, *Radio Times*, *New Statesman*, *Marie Claire*, *Cosmopolitan* and others, and has designed stamps, book covers, adverts, etc. He has received many awards, including the Macallan Best Political Cartoon Award in 1997.

John Burningham 1936–
Children's book illustrator, author, teacher. After attending Summerhill he completed alternative National Service. Uncertain about a career, a friend recommended the combined Graphics and Illustration course at Central. From 1956 to 1959 he was taught there by Laurence Scarfe, Bernard Neville, William Roberts, Clarke Hutton and Keith Vaughan. He taught part-time at the Central School in the 1960s and did advertising work including posters for London Transport. Success came with *Borka*, t*he adventures of a goose without feathers*, (Cape 1963), which won the Kate Greenaway Medal. His distinctive style developed with *Mr Gumpy's outing* (Cape 1970), and for this he won both the Kate Greenaway Medal and the *Boston Globe* Horn Book award for illustration. He has been illustrating his own books for over 40 years and illustrated Kenneth Grahame's *The wind in the willows* in 1983. His book *Granpa* (1984) was turned into an award-winning animated film for UNICEF (Prix Jeunesse 1990).

Mel Calman 1931–1994
Cartoonist, pocket cartoonist, illustrator, author. Born in London, he studied at St Martin's (1951–3). He was a cartoonist on the *Daily Express* (1957–63), *Sunday Telegraph* (1964–5), *Observer* (1965–6), *The Sunday Times* (1969–84), and most famously *The Times* (1979–94). He also contributed to magazines (e.g. *Cosmopolitan*, *House and Garden*), wrote plays for BBC Radio, and made an animated cartoon, *The arrow*. He was a regular exhibitor at the Royal Academy Summer Exhibition, and was founder of The Cartoon Gallery, and co-founder of the Cartoon Art Trust.

Laurence Campbell 1969–
Comics artist, teacher. Born in London, he studied Graphics at Central Saint Martins (1993–6). He spent six years as a 'visualiser' in a design group, attended evening classes at the London Cartoon Centre and produced art for the Paul Carstairs-scripted *Something inside* (Caliber Comics), followed by strips for the Caliber anthology *Negative burn*, and *The Disciples* (2001) for Image. He produced

various strips for *2000AD* and its sister publication *The Megazine* (Fleetway/Rebellion), including 'Judge Dredd', 'Bison' and 'Synnamon'. He has been a part-time tutor at CSM since 1996.

Len Deighton 1929–
Illustrator, author. Born in London he studied at St Martin's and the RCA and produced a variety of commercial art work including a poster for London Transport and a cookery strip for the *Observer* and a number of book jackets as well as undertaking a range of jobs, e.g. flight attendant for BOAC, pastry cook and waiter. With the success of *The Ipcress file* (1962) he turned to writing, mainly thrillers.

Andrew Dodds 1927–
Illustrator and teacher. Dodds attended Colchester School of Art (1942–4) and after serving in the Royal Navy during the Second World War he studied at the Central School of Arts & Crafts from 1947 to 1950. After graduating he worked as a freelance artist for *Lilliput*, *Readers Digest*, *Homes and Gardens*, *Farmers Weekly* and *Radio Times* (he drew the characters for The Archers) and many companies and publishers. Alongside his freelance work he worked as a part-time teacher of illustration from 1953 to 1972. He worked full-time at Suffolk College from 1972 until his retirement from teaching in 1989. He has produced a number of collections of his sketches and watercolours: *East Anglia drawn* (1987), *London then* (1994), *East Anglian sketchbook* (1999) and *Here and there* (2003). All are published by the Jardine Press.

Susan Einzig 1922–
Illustrator, teacher. She came to England as a refugee aged 16 in 1939. She studied at the Central School under John Farleigh, Noel Rooke, Bernard Meninsky and William Roberts, and was evacuated to Northampton with some of the other London art schools. She was also taught by Jeannetta Cochrane and Bernard Adeney. After the war she taught at Camberwell (1946–51), St Martin's (1948–51), Chelsea (1959–65) and was closely associated with John Minton and the neo-romantics, Keith Vaughan and John Craxton. She worked for *Lilliput*, *Radio Times*, *House and Garden*, *Picture Post*, and the *Saturday Book*. A prolific book illustrator her work includes Philippa Pearce's *Tom's midnight garden* (OUP 1958) which won a Carnegie medal in 1958, Elizabeth Poston's *Children's song book* (Bodley Head 1961) and Edith Nesbit's *The Bastables* (Nonesuch Press 1965).

Michael Foreman 1938–
Illustrator, author, teacher. Studied at Lowestoft School of Art (1954–8), St Martin's School of Art (1958–9) and the RCA (1960–3) where he studied under Edward Bawden. He won a silver medal and travelling fellowship to the USA. He has taught at St Martin's (1963–8), LCP (1966–8), RCA (1968–70) and Central School (1972). He has worked as a

freelance illustrator since 1961. His first illustrated book was *The General* (Routledge 1961). He has illustrated over 190 books, some of which were also written him. He has won several awards for illustration including The Francis Williams Book Illustration Award in 1972, the Emil/Kurt Maschler Award in 1982, and the Kate Greenaway Medal in 1982 and 1989.

Peggy Fortnum 1919–
Illustrator for books and TV. Born in Harrow, Middlesex, she studied at Tunbridge Wells School of Arts and Crafts (1936–9) and then served as a signals operator in the ATS during the Second World War. From 1944 she studied at the Central School under John Farleigh. She illustrated some 80 books for children for many publishers (including OUP, Dent, Collins and Bodley Head). She has also done illustrations for children's TV: *Play School* and *Jackanory*. She is best know for her illustrations of Paddington Bear for Michael Bond's successful series.

Barnett Freedman 1901–1958
Illustrator, teacher. The son of poor Jewish immigrants he was born in Stepney, East London. He worked from 1916 as a draughtsman for a firm of monumental masons and took evening classes for five years at St Martin's. He studied at the RCA from 1922 to 1925. He later taught still life drawing there and also taught at the Ruskin School, Oxford. He is best known for his illustrations in colour in the medium of autolithography, drawing directly on to the stone or plate. He worked at the Curwen Press and Chromoworks but is probably best known for his connection with Thomas Griffits of the Baynard Press, considered to be the most influential lithographer of his time. He did a lot of work for Faber and Faber including *Memoirs of an infantry officer* (1930) and many other book jackets. Other work includes *War and peace* and *Anna Karenina* for the Limited Editions Club and work for the Folio Society. He was awarded a CBE in 1946 and elected RDI in 1949.

Kathleen Hale 1898–2000
Ilustrator, writer, painter. Born in Broughton, in Lanarkshire, Scotland, she was brought up and educated in Manchester where she attended life classes each week at the Manchester School of Art. She studied at the Art Department, Reading University (1915–17) and then, after her marriage, studied under Bernard Meninsky at the Central School of Arts and Crafts (1928–30). The adventures of Orlando the Marmalade Cat, her famous series of books for children, started as bedtime stories for her sons. The first two were published by the Country Life Press by the process of autolithography pioneered in this country by Noel Carrington. Hale continued to work as a painter all her life. She was awarded an OBE for her work as an illustrator in 1976.

Glynn Boyd Harte 1948–2003
Illustrator, poster designer, painter, composer, writer. His father was a commercial artist and his grandfather worked in a printing firm. Born in Rochdale, he attended Rochdale School of Art before transferring to St Martin's where he was particularly influenced by his teacher Fritz Wegner, as well as fellow students such as Nicola Bayley. They both transferred to the RCA. At his final show in 1973 he sold all his work. He mixed the careers of illustrator, poster designer and painter. During the 1970s he drew a series of striking portraits of writers and artists. He also worked as a composer and writer. He was artist in residence at the Royal Opera House during the rebuilding period creating a series of paintings on the work in progress. His tragic early death from leukaemia in 2003 meant the loss of one of our most talented artists.

Gertrude Hermes 1901–1983
Wood engraver, teacher. She studied art at Beckenham School of Art and the Underwood School of Painting and Sculpture where she met Blair Hughes-Stanton who was a great influence on her work and to whom she was married from 1926 to 1931. She won the Prix de Rome for engraving in 1925. She taught wood engraving part-time at Westminster School of Art, Camberwell School of Art, St Martin's and the Central School in the period 1939 to 1966. She also taught life drawing. Hermes is regarded as one of the most versatile and accomplished 20th-century wood engravers. She was a member of the Society of Wood Engravers (1932) and the London Group (1935). She was appointed RA and awarded an OBE in 1971.

Rachael House 1961–
Comics artist. Born in Kent, she studied Fine Art at Central Saint Martins (2001–4). She started drawing comic strips in 1990, when she was in a hospital bed having broken her leg on a wet dance floor. Her autobiographical *Red hanky panky* was self-published from 1991 to 2001, during which time there was a surge of queer zines and comics being produced in the UK and USA. Other publications include: *Bumper summer fun!* self published comic book (2003), *Ladyfest London*, programme illustrations (2002); and *Art students stole my vibrator*, self published fanzine (2001). House has also organised live art events including a fancy dress picnic for dogs, 'Peckham Pet-Tastic'.

Faith Jaques 1923–1987
Illustrator and writer. She was born in Leicester and attended Leicester College of Art (1941–2). After war service based in the New Bodleian library in Oxford where she attended evening classes in life drawing under William Roberts and Bernard Meninsky at the Oxford School of Art, she continued her training at the Central School (1946–8). She worked as a part-time tutor of illustration at Guildford

School of Art (1948–53) and Hornsey School of Art (1960–8) as well as working freelance for most of the leading magazines of the day including *Radio Times* (1948–73). She has produced a huge number of book illustrations both for her own and other people's books. She wrote and illustrated *Tilly's house* (Heinemann 1979). Her last book *The Orchard book of nursery rhymes* was published after her death in 1990.

Judith Kerr b.1923

Illustrator, author. Born in Berlin, she escaped with her family from Nazi Germany in 1933 living in Switzerland and Paris before settling in London in 1936. She studied art as an evening student at the Central School and St Martin's during the war and won a scholarship to study at the Central School under John Farleigh (1945–8) where she specialised in life drawing and painting. She has worked as a television scriptwriter and writer as well as an illustrator of children's books. She is known for her autobiographical trilogy *Out of the Hitler time* (Collins 1971). She has written and illustrated a number of picture books for young children including *The Tiger who came to tea* (Collins 1968) and a series of books about 'Mog the cat'.

John Lawrence 1933–

Wood engraver, teacher. Studied at Hastings School of Art (1951–3) and after National Service (1953–4) at the Central School of Arts and Crafts (1955–7) where he studied wood engraving under Gertrude Hermes, and illustration with Keith Vaughan and Laurence Scarfe. Lawrence has had a career as a very prolific book illustrator using many media, including wood engraving, lino and vinyl cuts, pen and ink and pen and wash. He has worked for many publishers including the Folio Society. He recently produced a series of wood engravings for *Lyra's Oxford* which accompanies the Philip Pullman trilogy *His dark materials*. He has taught part-time at Maidstone School of Art, Brighton College of Art and Camberwell School of Art.

John Vernon Lord 1939–

Illustrator, administrator, teacher. Born in Glossop, Derbyshire, he studied at Salford School of Art (1956–60) and at the Central School (1960–1). He has worked in education as Head of Department of Visual Communication at Brighton Polytechnic (1974–81) and was made Professor of Illustration at Brighton in 1986. He was chairman of the Graphic Design Board of the CNAA (1978–81). He has worked as a freelance illustrator since 1970 creating hundreds of black-and-white pen-and-ink illustrations both for his own and other people's books, including *Aesop's Fables*, which won the WH Smith Illustration Award in 1990, and *The nonsense verse of Edward Lear*. His early career included much work for magazines (such as *Radio Times*, *The Listener*, *Punch*), books and advertising.

Helen Oxenbury 1938–

Illustrator, designer, author. She studied at Ipswich School of Art and then Theatre Design at the Central School (1956–8). She left after two years as she found it rather difficult to adapt to the course which at that time was in a state of change after the death of Jeanetta Cochrane. She worked in the theatre and then in Israel with John Burningham whom she later married. She did some work for television on her return and also designed greetings cards for Gallery Five. Her first book was published in 1967 and she won the Kate Greenaway Medal for her version of Lear's *The Quangle Wangle's hat* and Lewis Carroll's *The hunting of the Snark* in 1970. *We're going on a bear hunt* won the Smarties Book Prize in 1989. She writes, and also illustrates her own and other people's books.

Gladys Perint Palmer 1947–

Fashion illustrator, journalist, author, teacher. She was born in Hungary but educated in England. After the general art course at St Martin's she studied in the fashion department under Muriel Pemberton and Elizabeth Suter. She is also a graduate of Parson's School of Design in New York. Early in her career she worked in Hong Kong for the *South China Morning Post*, and taught drawing at the University of Hong Kong. She has also been a visiting lecturer at St Martin's. Her later career has taken her around the world; she is currently Executive Director of Fashion at the Academy of Art University in San Francisco. Still an active freelance illustrator she has worked for the American, British, Italian, Japanese, German, Spanish and Australian editions of *Vogue*; and for the *New York Times*, *San Francisco Examiner* (where she was fashion editor), *Washington Post*, *Los Angeles Times*, *New Yorker*, *Elle* and *The Sunday Times*. She has many advertising clients and appears in *The fashion book* (Phaidon 1998) 'as one of 500 people of influence since 1860'. Her book of satirical drawings with scurrilous comments on haute couture, *Fashion people*, was published in English and French by Assouline in 2003. She has an Honorary Doctorate from the University of San Francisco.

Shari Peacock 1956–1999

Fashion illustrator, teacher. Born in Sofia, Bulgaria, to Iranian immigrant parents, she was educated in the Russian language and at only 15 was admitted to the Institute of Architecture in Sofia where she studied for three years. With relatives' support she studied at the Architectural Association in London and later fashion drawing at a St Martin's evening class, taught initially by Colin Barnes and then by Howard Tangye. She too taught illustration, working at Epsom and Medway colleges and St Martin's. She won *Vogue*'s prestigious Cecil Beaton Award and became a successful illustrator with work in *Vogue*, the *Guardian*, the *Independent*, *Ms London* and elsewhere. In 1989 she designed the cover of

The molecular biology of cancer. Moving from drawing to writing, her semi-autobiographical novel, *English as a foreign language* (1998), was written in English and published in English in Bulgaria. In a final change of direction she decided to retrain in dance and ballet and had just enrolled at the Eurythmie School in Hamburg, first learning German and convincingly giving her date of birth as 1965, when after a very brief illness she died of lung cancer.

Charles Peattie 1958–

Cartoonist, portrait painter, strip cartoonist. He was born in Manchester and studied fine art at St Martin's (1977–80). After a successful period as a portrait painter he became a full-time cartoonist creating 'Ad nauseam' for *Direction* (1986–8), 'Dick' for *Melody Maker* (1985–8) and 'Celeb' (with Mark Warren) about an over-the-hill rock star, for *Private Eye* (since 1987). The latter was made into a TV series starring Harry Enfield. Peattie is perhaps best known as the creator (with Russell Taylor) of the 'Alex' strip about a 20-something City whizz-kid, a satire on yuppie values. The series began in the *London Daily News* (Feb–July 1987), moved to the *Independent* (1987–91) and has been running in the *Daily Telegraph* since 1992. Today it is syndicated in papers all over the world.

Muriel Pemberton 1909–1993

Fashion illustrator, teacher. Born in Stoke-on-Trent, the second daughter of the local photographer (her eldest sister Mrs Phyllis Johnson taught pattern cutting at St Martin's from the war until the 1970s). In 1923 as a young scholarship student she studied at Burslem School of Art. In 1928 she won a scholarship to the RCA where she graduated with the first ever diploma in fashion in 1931. She taught at St Martin's for over 40 years from 1931, creating and running the fashion department, and also working freelance for Liberty and Emcar among others, and as an illustrator for many publications, notably covering Christian Dior's New Look in 1947 for the *News Chronicle*. In 1941 she married John Hadley-Rowe, Head of Commercial Art and later Vice-Principal at St Martin's. She painted and exhibited regularly throughout her life and was elected Fellow of the Watercolour Society in 1974. She became a Senior Fellow of the RCA in 1985 and had a major retrospective exhibition: 'Muriel Pemberton: painter and teacher of fashion' at the Chris Beetles Gallery in June 1993. Her niece, Liz Griffiths, also a CSM graduate, designs for Missoni.

Matthew Pritchett ('Matt') 1964–

Cartoonist, pocket cartoonist. The son of journalist Oliver Pritchett, and grandson of novelist Sir Victor (V S) Pritchett he studied Graphics at St Martin's (1983–7). He failed to get a job as a film cameraman and became a waiter in a pizzeria instead, drawing cartoons in his spare time, which were published in the

New Statesman, *Punch*, the *Spectator*, and *Sunday Telegraph*. He became a pocket cartoonist at the *Daily Telegraph* in 1988. He won Granada TV's 'What the Papers Say' Cartoonist of the Year Award, 1992, and was awarded an MBE in 2002.

Fitzgerald Spencer Pryse 1881–1956

Lithographer, teacher. He was born in France and educated at Eton. He served with distinction during the First World War and was awarded the Military Cross and the Croix de Guerre. He was appointed a war artist and produced energetic drawings directly onto the litho stone while in the trenches. He taught lithography with A.S. Hartrick at the Central School (1922–32). He worked as a lithographic artist and poster designer for London Transport and for the Labour Party. He designed posters for the Empire Exhibition at Wembley in 1924 and produced the illustrated guide to the Pageant of Empire Souvenir. He also designed posters for the Empire Marketing Board, London Midland & Scottish Railway and for London & North Eastern Railway.

Gerald Scarfe 1936–

Cartoonist, illustrator, set and costume designer, film director. He was born in London and studied life drawing at St Martin's in the early 1960s. After a brief period at the RCA he established himself as a satirical cartoonist, working for *Punch* and *Private Eye*. He has had many exhibitions worldwide and 50 one-man shows. He has designed the sets and costumes for plays, operas and musicals in London, Houston, Los Angeles and Detroit. His film work includes designing and directing the animation for Pink Floyd's *The Wall*. Scarfe has written and directed many live action and documentary films for BBC and Channel 4 and has published many books of his work, the most recent being *Heroes and villains: Scarfe at the National Portrait Gallery* (2003). Gerald Scarfe has been a political cartoonist for *The Sunday Times* for 36 years, and has worked for the *New Yorker* for 10 years.

Posy Simmonds 1945–

Cartoonist, comics artist, illustrator, author. Born in Berkshire she studied at the Sorbonne, Paris, and Graphics at Central (1964–8). Her first appearance in print was on the woman's page of *The Times* in 1968. She then worked briefly on a strip for the *Sun* and illustrations for *Cosmopolitan*. In 1977 she began her regular Monday strip for the *Guardian*, about sociology lecturer George Weber and family, which ended in 1987. Her children's books include *Fred* (1987), *Lulu and the flying babies* (1988) and *The chocolate wedding* (1990). In the 1990s and 2000s she has become best known for her adult-orientated strip books, including the graphic novel *Gemma Bovery* (1999), a reworking of Flaubert's classic, and *Literary life* (2003), a satire on the pomposity of the literary

circuit. Both were pre-serialised in the *Guardian*. She was awarded an MBE in 2002.

Claire Smalley 1963–2003

Fashion illustrator. She was born in Chesterfield. Her father became a Head of Art in Hertfordshire and she did her foundation studies at St Alban's College of Art. She studied fashion at St Martin's and graduated with a first in 1986. She worked as a freelance illustrator for Galliano the following year. Her working methods relied upon close communication with the designer. Before her premature death in 2003 she worked for *View*, a fashion forecast journal which predicts fashion trends up to three years ahead. Her illustrations for *View* turn abstract concepts about future fashion into visual images, are far removed from traditional fashion drawings, and perhaps suggest the direction her future work might have taken.

Elizabeth Suter 1926–

Fashion illustrator, teacher. She attended Central School towards the end of the Second World War and was taught by Meninsky who suggested fashion drawing as a possible career. After a brief spell in the WRNS at Bletchley she returned to art education at a small private art school in Chelsea and was taught by Sam Rabin, who had trained at the Slade under Tonks. She later attended his private classes and did freelance drawing for Jaeger, Simpsons and Liberty and various publications, notably *The Times*, *Good Housekeeping* and *Country Life*. She taught at St Martin's (1953–78) and throughout this period continued to cover the Paris collections for the British press (although at this time the collections were shrouded in secrecy and drawing was not permitted in the salons). For many years she was the only permanent staff member in the Fashion Department apart from Pemberton and was briefly Acting Head of Department after Pemberton's retirement in 1976. After leaving St Martin's she continued working as an illustrator, for Hardy Amies and for the weddings of both Princess Anne and Prince Charles for *Country Life*.

Betty Swanwick 1915–1989

Illustrator, painter, author. Born in south London she entered Goldsmiths' College in 1930. She was taught by Edward Bawden and Clive Gardiner and started to receive commissions at an early age, including her first London Transport poster at age 19. She attended the Central School and the RCA simultaneously after receiving scholarships from both. She taught at Goldsmiths' (1948–69), the RA Schools, and the RCA. She did a wide range of commercial illustration work and painted murals for the Festival of Britain (1951) and Guy's Hospital (1955). She illustrated several books for children, including some written by herself, and also made a number of visionary paintings. She was elected RA in 1979.

Howard Tangye 1948–

Fashion illustrator and designer, teacher. Born in Townsville, Australia, and brought up in Central Queensland, he came to the UK in 1968. After some time at a private art school he studied at St Martin's as a 'special' student of Muriel Pemberton. Graduating with a first in 1974 he worked for Zandra Rhodes before taking up a postgraduate exchange scholarship at Parson's School of Design in New York. In New York he worked successfully as an illustrator for several years, even after returning to live in London. Back in London he again worked for Zandra Rhodes as a cutter, assistant designer and illustrator. He designed womenswear under his own label and did illustrations for, among others, Bruce Oldfield, also a CSM alumnus. He also did drawings for prints for various clients including Marks and Spencer's Autograph range, exhibited regularly, and taught drawing at various colleges. He is now the Senior Lecturer for Womenswear for the Fashion BA at Central Saint Martins and continues to draw and exhibit.

Julie Verhoeven 1969–

Fashion illustrator, designer, artist. Born in Kent she left school at 16 to go to Medway College of Art & Design. She attended the fashion drawing evening classes taught by Tangye at CSM; she was also taught by Jo Brocklehurst (at the summer school) and Shari Peacock (at evening classes). She is now a visiting lecturer at CSM. She continued her fashion education in Paris where she worked for Martine Sitbon and designed for Louis Vuitton. She did several collections for the Italian company Gibo, featuring her distinctive sexy girls. As well as her illustrations for *Dazed and Confused*, and other avant-garde fashion magazines in the UK and abroad, she has done illustration work for the music industry, not only sleeve artwork and storyboards but also music videos. She exhibits increasingly as a fine artist and regularly publishes books of her drawings. She published *Fat bottomed girls*, in 2003 following her similarly titled exhibition and in March 2004 had a one-woman show of paintings, *Farewell, my lovely* at the Taché-Lévy Gallery in Brussels.

Norah Waugh 1910–1966

Fashion illustrator, pattern cutter, author, teacher. Norah Waugh worked with Jeannetta Cochrane in the theatre department at Central School. In the late 1930s she was also in charge of costume at the London Theatre Studio run by Michel Saint-Denis. After the war when she had worked in the Ministry of Information press office she returned to Central and wrote several books, both scholarly and practical, on historical pattern cutting: *Corsets and crinolines* (1954), and *The cut of men's clothes: 1600–1900* (1964) both for Faber. She was to have written *The cut of women's clothes: 1600–1930* but her untimely death meant that it was written almost entirely from her notes by Margaret Woodward. It was published in 1968 under her name, with a note from Woodward explaining that she had completed the book 'out of a deep personal affection and respect for the work of my colleague the late Miss Norah Waugh, who died suddenly, at Easter 1966'.

Clifford Webb 1894–1972

Lithographer, wood engraver, teacher. Born in the East End of London, he was apprenticed to a lithographer until the outbreak of the First World War, during which he fought in France, India and the Middle East. He then studied at Westminster School of Art and taught at Birmingham School of Art (1923–6), Westminster School of Art (1934–9) and then St Martin's (1945–65) where he taught wood engraving. He was a founder member of the Society of Wood Engravers and illustrated a number of books for the Golden Cockerel Press. He also illustrated a number of books using poster paint, pen and wash and watercolour, including a number for children. He collaborated with Arthur Ransome on the first two *Swallows and Amazons* books. He produced a number of picture books for children on which he worked with his wife Ella Monckton.

Fritz Wegner 1924–

Illustrator, teacher. He was born in Vienna, came to London as a refugee in 1939, and began studying at St Martin's when he was 16. He worked on the land during the Second World War and was then apprenticed to a designer. He taught illustration part-time at St Martin's (1960–84) and nurtured many of our most-talented book illustrators. He has worked as a freelance illustrator for most of his life designing postage stamps, book jackets, and illustrations for magazines including *Radio Times*. He is best known for his book illustrations, using a variety of media. He has a preference for pen and ink and produces finely drawn, detailed, often humorous illustrations. He was short-listed for an Emil award in 1989 for *The wicked tricks of Till Owlyglass*.

Margaret Woodward 1920–1973

Fashion illustrator, author, teacher. Born into a South Yorkshire pit village she went to Barnsley School of Art. She declined a scholarship at the RCA because she wanted to do theatre studies at Central School. After the war she worked alongside Norah Waugh teaching both the history of costume and the practicalities of making authentic replicas. She illustrated all Waugh's books with technically accurate scale drawings and cutting diagrams. After Waugh's death she wrote *The cut of women's clothes: 1600–1930* (Faber, 1968), using Waugh's notes, as a tribute to her friend and colleague.

Index: *principal artists & artworks*

Acknowledgements and picture credits

The publisher would like to recognise the support given by Central Saint Martins College of Art & Design to this project.

The editor would like to thank all the individuals and organisations who have helped make this book possible: Catherine Pound and Lucy Rushin from the Museum Collection; Jenny Crisp who did most of the photography; the essay writers; all those alumni who gave their time to share their experiences of the Central School, St Martin's and Central Saint Martins; Linda Lambert from the publishers; Phil Baines and Catherine Dixon, the designers; and my husband David Brook who spent many hours of his time proof reading and compiling the index.

The editor and publisher have made every effort to trace the copyright holders of works and photographs: Those that are not indicated in the captions are listed below: their names are followed by the page numbers where their work appears. If any individuals or institutions are incorrectly credited or if there are any other omissions, we would be glad to be notified so that the necessary corrections can be made in any reprint.

Jill Barklem p.47; Nicola Bayley p.48; Mitchell-Beazley p.111; Celia Berridge pp.26, 27; Val Biro pp.45, 161; Patrick Benson pp.19, 49; Ruth Boswell p.169; Simon Brett p.10; Dr E. Breuning pp.104, 161; Jason Brookes & Elle International, Germany, p.182; John Burningham pp.22, 50, 52; Sue Buswell (Harper Collins) pp.21, 45, 47; Conville & Walsh Ltd pp.22, 50, 52; Laura Cecil Literary Agency p.138; Paul Clarke Hutton pp.37, 102, 169; Sarah Crowley p.99; Daily Express p.83; J.M. Dent division of the Orion Publishing Group p.99; Andrew Dodds p.18; Egmont Books Ltd p.24; Susan Einzig pp.21, 43, 113, 174; Jennifer Ellis p.18; Penelope & Charlotte Ellis p.100; Faber & Faber pp.96, 173; The Folio Society for providing illustrations nos.1–22 in chapter 6 and for clearing copyright with the individual artists and their executors; Michael Foreman pp.23, 50, 51, 176; Peggy Fortnum pp.14, 44; Vincent Freedman p.97, 164; Gollancz division of the Orion Publishing Group p.51; C. Boyd Harte pp.19, 112; Michael Harvey p.108; Harper Collins p.108; Heinemann pp.24, 44; David Higham Associates pp.17, 109; Sheila Jackson p.25; Barbara Kane p.14; Judith Kerr pp.21, 45; Gillian Lamb pp.10, 105, 164; John Lawrence pp.16, 112; Angela Letts pp.24, 44; John Vernon Lord p.17; Macmillan Publishers p.108; G.M. Masters p.103; Sara Midda p.47; Mrs.O'Connor p.9; Helen Oxenbury pp.26, 52; Oxford University Press pp.38, 102, 104, 106, 107, 112; Pavillion Books p.50; Penguin Books pp.18, 25, 37, 102, 114, 168, 188; Linda Pooley pp.14, 31, 44; Radio Times for the illustrations in chapter 7: these appear by permission of the artists and of the BBC; Random House Group Ltd pp.22, 49, 52, 90, 186; Judith Russell p.16; Nicolas Scarfe p.47; Isobel Tisdall pp.108, 173; Lou Taylor pp.36, 168, Taylor & Francis p.23; Victoria and Albert Museum/V&A images p.170; Walker Books pp.19, 20, 26, 27, 46, 48, 113; Frederick Warne & Co. pp.42, 101, 168; Fritz Wegner pp.20, 46, 113; Norah West p.10.